ABOUT THIS PUBLICATION

FOR SERVICE ASSISTANCE

Customer Service Department
1.704.898.0770

North Carolina General Statues is published by The Muliti-Media Group of Greater Charlotte in Charlotte, North Carolina. Copyright 2015 by the Multi-Media Group of Greater Charlotte. This book or parts thereof may not be reproduced in any form, stored in a retrieval system, or transmitted in any form by any means—electronic, mechanical, photocopy, recording or otherwise—without prior written permission of the publisher, except as provided by United States of America copyright law.

The records required by U.S. Code 2257(a) through (c) and the pertinent regulations 28 C.F.R. Cli. 1, Part 75 with respect to this publication and all materials associated with such records are maintained by The Multi-Media Group of Greater Charlotte, Publisher and available for review by Attorney General.

www.visionbooks.org

Copyright © 2015 by MMGGC
All rights reserved!

TID: 5037881
ISBN (10) digit: 1502745658
ISBN (13) digit: 978-1502745651

123-4-56789-01239-Paperback
123-4-56789-01239-Hardback

First Edition

090520140547

Printed in the United States of America

2015 EDITION

North Carolina Criminal Law And Procedure-Pamphlet # 26

Printed In conjunction with the Administration of the Courts

North Carolina Criminal Law and Procedure
Pamphlet Reference Guide

Chapters	Pamphlet
Chapter 1 Civil Procedure	1
Chapter 1 Civil Procedure (Continue)	2
Chapter 1A Rules of Civil Procedure	2
Chapter 1B Contribution.	2
Chapter 1C Enforcement of Judgments.	2
Chapter 1D Punitive Damages.	2
Chapter 1E Eastern Band of Cherokee Indians.	2
Chapter 1F North Carolina Uniform Interstate Depositions and Discovery Act.	2
Chapter 2 - Clerk of Superior Court [Repealed and Transferred.]	3
Chapter 3 - Commissioners of Affidavits and Deeds [Repealed.]	3
Chapter 4 - Common Law	3
Chapter 5 - Contempt [Repealed.]	3
Chapter 5A - Contempt	3
Chapter 6 - Liability for Court Costs	3
Chapter 7 - Courts [Repealed and Transferred.]	3
Chapter 7A – Judicial Department	3
Chapter 7A – Continuation (Judicial Department)	4
Chapter 7A – Continuation (Judicial Department)	5
Chapter 7B - Juvenile Code	5
Chapter 8 - Evidence	6
Chapter 8A - Interpreters for Deaf Persons [Recodified.]	6
Chapter 8B - Interpreters for Deaf Persons	6
Chapter 8C - Evidence Code	6
Chapter 9 - Jurors	6
Chapter 10 - Notaries [Repealed.]	6
Chapter 10A - Notaries [Recodified.]	6
Chapter 10B - Notaries	6
Chapter 11 - Oaths	6
Chapter 12 - Statutory Construction	6
Chapter 13 - Citizenship Restored	6
Chapter 14 - Criminal Law	7
Chapter 14 –Criminal Law (Continuation)	8
Chapter 15 - Criminal Procedure	9
Chapter 15A - Criminal Procedure Act (Continuation)	10
Chapter 15A - Criminal Procedure Act (Continuation)	11
Chapter 15B - Victims Compensation	11
Chapter 15C - Address Confidentiality Program	11
Chapter 16 - Gaming Contracts and Futures	11
Chapter 17 - Habeas Corpus	11

Chapter 17A - Law-Enforcement Officers [Recodified.]	11
Chapter 17B - North Carolina Criminal Justice Education and Training System [Recodified.] Chapter 17C - North Carolina Criminal Justice Education and Training Standards Commission	11
	11
Chapter 17D - North Carolina Justice Academy	11
Chapter 17E - North Carolina Sheriffs' Education and Training Standards Commission	11
Chapter 18 - Regulation of Intoxicating Liquors [Repealed.]	12
Chapter 18A - Regulation of Intoxicating Liquors [Repealed.]	12
Chapter 18B - Regulation of Alcoholic Beverages	12
Chapter 18C - North Carolina State Lottery	12
Chapter 19 - Offenses against Public Morals	12
Chapter 19A - Protection of Animals	12
Chapter 20 - Motor Vehicles	13
Chapter 20 - Motor Vehicles (Continuation)	14
Chapter 20 - Motor Vehicles (Continuation)	15
Chapter 20 - Motor Vehicles (Continuation)	16
Chapter 21 - Bills of Lading	17
Chapter 22 - Contracts Requiring Writing	17
Chapter 22A - Signatures	17
Chapter 22B - Contracts Against Public Policy	17
Chapter 22C - Payments to Subcontractors	17
Chapter 23 - Debtor and Creditor	17
Chapter 24 – Interest	17
Chapter 25 – Uniform Commercial Code	18
Chapter 25 – Uniform Commercial Code (Continuation)	19
Chapter 25A – Retail Installment Sales Act	20
Chapter 25B - Credit	20
Chapter 25C - Sales of Artwork	20
Chapter 26 - Suretyship	20
Chapter 27 - Warehouse Receipts [Repealed.]	20
Chapter 28 - Administration [Repealed.]	20
Chapter 28A - Administration of Decedents' Estates	20
Chapter 28B - Estates of Absentees in Military Service	20
Chapter 28C - Estates of Missing Persons	20
Chapter 29 - Intestate Succession	21
Chapter 30 - Surviving Spouses	21
Chapter 31 - Wills	21
Chapter 31A - Acts Barring Property Rights	21
Chapter 31B - Renunciation of Property and Renunciation of Fiduciary Powers Act	21
Chapter 31C - Uniform Disposition of Community Property Rights at Death Act	21
Chapter 32 - Fiduciaries	21
Chapter 32A - Powers of Attorney	21
Chapter 33 - Guardian and Ward [Repealed and Recodified.]	21

Chapter 33A - North Carolina Uniform Transfers to Minors Act	21
Chapter 33B - North Carolina Uniform Custodial Trust Act	21
Chapter 34 - Veterans' Guardianship Act	22
Chapter 35 - Sterilization Procedures	22
Chapter 35A - Incompetency and Guardianship	22
Chapter 36 - Trusts and Trustees [Repealed.]	22
Chapter 36A - Trusts and Trustees	22
Chapter 36B - Uniform Management of Institutional Funds Act [Repealed.]	22
Chapter 36C - North Carolina Uniform Trust Code	22
Chapter 36D - North Carolina Community Third Party Trusts, Pooled Trusts	23
Chapter 36E - Uniform Prudent Management of Institutional Funds Act	23
Chapter 37 - Allocation of Principal and Income [Repealed.]	23
Chapter 37A - Uniform Principal and Income Act	23
Chapter 38 - Boundaries	23
Chapter 38A - Landowner Liability	23
Chapter 38B - Trespasser Responsibility	23
Chapter 39 - Conveyances	23
Chapter 39A - Transfer Fee Covenants Prohibited	23
Chapter 40 - Eminent Domain [Repealed.]	23
Chapter 40A - Eminent Domain	23
Chapter 41 - Estates	23
Chapter 41A - State Fair Housing Act	23
Chapter 42 - Landlord and Tenant	23
Chapter 42A - Vacation Rental Act	23
Chapter 43 - Land Registration	23
Chapter 44 - Liens	24
Chapter 44A - Statutory Liens and Charges	24
Chapter 45 - Mortgages and Deeds of Trust	24
Chapter 45A - Good Funds Settlement Act	24
Chapter 46 - Partition	24
Chapter 47 - Probate and Registration	25
Chapter 47A - Unit Ownership	25
Chapter 47B - Real Property Marketable Title Act	25
Chapter 47C - North Carolina Condominium Act	25
Chapter 47D - Notice of Settlement Act [Expired.]	25
Chapter 47E - Residential Property Disclosure Act	25
Chapter 47F - North Carolina Planned Community Act	25
Chapter 47G - Option to Purchase Contracts	25
Chapter 47H - Contracts for Deed	25
Chapter 48 - Adoptions	26
Chapter 48A - Minors	26
Chapter 49 - Bastardy	26
Chapter 49A - Rights of Children	26
Chapter 50 - Divorce and Alimony	26

Chapter 50A - Uniform Child-Custody Jurisdiction and Enforcement Act	26
Chapter 50B - Domestic Violence	26
Chapter 50C - Civil No-Contact Orders	26
Chapter 51 - Marriage	26
Chapter 52 - Powers and Liabilities of Married Persons	27
Chapter 52A - Uniform Reciprocal Enforcement of Support Act [Repealed.]	27
Chapter 52B - Uniform Premarital Agreement Act	27
Chapter 52C - Uniform Interstate Family Support Act	27
Chapter 53 - Banks	27
Chapter 53A - Business Development Corporations and North Carolina Capital Resource Corporations	28
Chapter 53B - Financial Privacy Act	28
Chapter 54 - Cooperative Organizations	28
Chapter 54A - Capital Stock Savings and Loan Associations [Repealed.]	28
Chapter 54B - Savings and Loan Associations	29
Chapter 54C - Savings Banks	29
Chapter 55 - North Carolina Business Corporation Act	30
Chapter 55A - North Carolina Nonprofit Corporation Act	31
Chapter 55B - Professional Corporation Act	31
Chapter 55C - Foreign Trade Zones	31
Chapter 55D - Filings, Names, and Registered Agents for Corporations, Nonprofit Corporations, and Partnerships	31
Chapter 56 - Electric, Telegraph and Power Companies [Repealed.]	31
Chapter 57 - Hospital, Medical and Dental Service Corporations [Recodified.]	31
Chapter 57A - Health Maintenance Organization Act [Recodified.]	31
Chapter 57B - Health Maintenance Organization Act [Recodified.]	31
Chapter 57C - North Carolina Limited Liability Company Act.	31
Chapter 58 - Insurance.	32
Chapter 58 - Insurance (Continuation)	33
Chapter 58 - Insurance (Continuation)	34
Chapter 58 - Insurance (Continuation)	35
Chapter 58 - Insurance (Continuation)	36
Chapter 58 - Insurance (Continuation)	37
Chapter 58 - Insurance (Continuation)	38
Chapter 58A - North Carolina Health Insurance Trust Commission [Recodified.]	38
Chapter 59 - Partnership.	39
Chapter 59B - Uniform Unincorporated Nonprofit Association Act.	39
Chapter 60 - Railroads and Other Carriers [Repealed and Transferred.]	39
Chapter 61 - Religious Societies	39
Chapter 62 - Public Utilities	39

Chapter 62 - Public Utilities (Continuation)	40
Chapter 62A - Public Safety Telephone Service And Wireless Telephone Service	40
Chapter 63 - Aeronautics	40
Chapter 63A - North Carolina Global TransPark Authority	40
Chapter 64 - Aliens	40
Chapter 65 – Cemeteries	40
Chapter 66 - Commerce and Business	41
Chapter 67 - Dogs	41
Chapter 68 - Fences and Stock Law	41
Chapter 69 - Fire Protection	41
Chapter 70 - Indian Antiquities, Archaeological Resources and Unmarked Human Skeletal Remains Protection	42
Chapter 71 - Indians [Repealed.]	42
Chapter 71A - Indians	42
Chapter 72 - Inns, Hotels and Restaurants	42
Chapter 73 - Mills	42
Chapter 74 - Mines and Quarries	42
Chapter 74A - Company Police [Repealed.]	42
Chapter 74B - Private Protective Services Act [Repealed.]	42
Chapter 74C - Private Protective Services	42
Chapter 74D - Alarm Systems	42
Chapter 74E - Company Police Act	42
Chapter 74F - Locksmith Licensing Act	42
Chapter 74G - Campus Police Act	42
Chapter 75 - Monopolies, Trusts and Consumer Protection	42
Chapter 75A - Boating and Water Safety	43
Chapter 75B - Discrimination in Business	43
Chapter 75C - Motion Picture Fair Competition Act	43
Chapter 75D - Racketeer Influenced and Corrupt Organizations	43
Chapter 75E - Unlawful Activities in Connection With Certain Corporate Transactions	43
Chapter 76 - Navigation	43
Chapter 76A - Navigation and Pilotage Commissions	43
Chapter 77 - Rivers, Creeks, and Coastal Waters	43
Chapter 78 - Securities Law [Repealed.]	43
Chapter 78A - North Carolina Securities Act	43
Chapter 78B - Tender Offer Disclosure Act [Repealed.]	43
Chapter 78C - Investment Advisers	43
Chapter 78D - Commodities Act	43
Chapter 79 - Strays [Repealed.]	43
Chapter 80 - Trademarks, Brands, etc.	44
Chapter 81 - Weights and Measures [Recodified.]	44
Chapter 81A - Weights and Measures Act of 1975.	44
Chapter 82 - Wrecks [Repealed.]	44
Chapter 83 - Architects [Recodified.]	44

Chapter 83A - Architects	44
Chapter 84 - Attorneys-at-Law	44
Chapter 84A - Foreign Legal Consultants	44
Chapter 85 - Auctions and Auctioneers [Repealed.]	44
Chapter 85A - Bail Bondsmen and Runners [Recodified.]	44
Chapter 85B - Auctions and Auctioneers	44
Chapter 85C - Bail Bondsmen and Runners [Recodified.]	44
Chapter 86 - Barbers [Recodified.]	44
Chapter 86A - Barbers	44
Chapter 87 - Contractors	44
Chapter 88 - Cosmetic Art [Repealed.]	44
Chapter 88A - Electrolysis Practice Act	44
Chapter 88B - Cosmetic Art	45
Chapter 89 - Engineering and Land Surveying [Recodified.]	45
Chapter 89A - Landscape Architects	45
Chapter 89B - Foresters	45
Chapter 89C - Engineering and Land Surveying	45
Chapter 89D - Landscape Contractors	45
Chapter 89E - Geologists Licensing Act	45
Chapter 89F - North Carolina Soil Scientist Licensing Act	45
Chapter 89G - Irrigation Contractors	45
Chapter 90 - Medicine and Allied Occupations	45
Chapter 90 - Medicine and Allied Occupations (Continuation)	46
Chapter 90 - Medicine and Allied Occupations (Continuation)	47
Chapter 90 - Medicine and Allied Occupations (Continuation)	48
Chapter 90A - Sanitarians and Water and Wastewater Treatment Facility Operators	48
Chapter 90B - Social Worker Certification and Licensure Act	48
Chapter 90C - North Carolina Recreational Therapy Licensure Act	48
Chapter 90D - Interpreters and Transliterators	48
Chapter 91 - Pawnbrokers [Repealed.]	48
Chapter 91A - Pawnbrokers Modernization Act of 1989	48
Chapter 92 - Photographers [Deleted.]	48
Chapter 93 - Certified Public Accountants	48
Chapter 93A - Real Estate License Law	49
Chapter 93B - Occupational Licensing Boards	49
Chapter 93C - Watchmakers [Repealed.]	49
Chapter 93D - North Carolina State Hearing Aid Dealers and Fitters Board.	49
Chapter 93E - North Carolina Appraisers Act	49
Chapter 94 - Apprenticeship	49
Chapter 95 - Department of Labor and Labor Regulations	49
Chapter 95 - Department of Labor and Labor Regulations (Continuation)	50
Chapter 96 - Employment Security	50
Chapter 97 - Workers' Compensation Act	50
Chapter 97 - Workers' Compensation Act (Continuation)	51

Chapter 98 - Burnt and Lost Records	51
Chapter 99 - Libel and Slander	51
Chapter 99A - Civil Remedies for Criminal Actions	51
Chapter 99B - Products Liability	51
Chapter 99C - Actions Relating to Winter Sports Safety and Accidents	51
Chapter 99D - Civil Rights	51
Chapter 99E - Special Liability Provisions	51
Chapter 100 - Monuments, Memorials and Parks	51
Chapter 101 - Names of Persons	51
Chapter 102 - Official Survey Base	51
Chapter 103 - Sundays, Holidays and Special Days	51
Chapter 104 - United States Lands	51
Chapter 104A - Degrees of Kinship	51
Chapter 104B - Hurricanes or Other Acts of Nature	51
Chapter 104C - Atomic Energy, Radioactivity and Ionizing Radiation [Repealed and Recodified.]	51
Chapter 104D - Southern States Energy Compact	51
Chapter 104E - North Carolina Radiation Protection Act	51
Chapter 104F - Southeast Interstate Low-Level Radioactive Waste Management Compact [Repealed]	51
Chapter 104G - North Carolina Low-Level Radioactive Waste Management Authority Act of 1987 [Repealed]	51
Chapter 105 - Taxation	51
Chapter 105 - Taxation (Continuation)	52
Chapter 105 - Taxation (Continuation)	53
Chapter 105 - Taxation (Continuation)	54
Chapter 105A - Setoff Debt Collection Act	55
Chapter 105B - Defaulted Student Loan Recovery Act	55
Chapter 106 - Agriculture	55
Chapter 106 - Agriculture (Continue)	56
Chapter 106 - Agriculture (Continue)	57
Chapter 107 - Agricultural Development Districts [Repealed.]	57
Chapter 108 - Social Services [Repealed and Recodified.]	57
Chapter 108A - Social Services	57
Chapter 108B - Community Action Programs	58
Chapter 108C Medicaid and Health Choice Provider Requirements.	58
Chapter 108D Medicaid Managed Care for Behavioral Health Services.	58
Chapter 109 - Bonds [Recodified.]	58
Chapter 110 - Child Welfare	58
Chapter 111 - Aid to the Blind	58
Chapter 112 - Confederate Homes and Pensions [Repealed.]	58
Chapter 113 - Conservation and Development	58
Chapter 113 - Conservation and Development (Continuation)	59

Chapter	Page
Chapter 113A - Pollution Control and Environment	59
Chapter 113A - Pollution Control and Environment (Continuation)	60
Chapter 113B - North Carolina Energy Policy Act of 1975	60
Chapter 114 - Department of Justice	60
Chapter 115 - Elementary and Secondary Education [Repealed.]	60
Chapter 115A - Community Colleges, Technical Institutes, and Industrial Education Centers [Repealed.]	60
Chapter 115B - Tuition and Fee Waivers	60
Chapter 115C - Elementary and Secondary Education	60
Chapter 115C - Elementary and Secondary Education (Continuation)	61
Chapter 115C - Elementary and Secondary Education (Continuation)	62
Chapter 115C - Elementary and Secondary Education (Continuation)	63
Chapter 115D - Community Colleges	63
Chapter 115E - Private Educational Facilities Finance Act [Recodified]	63
Chapter 116 - Higher Education	63
Chapter 116 - Higher Education (Continuation)	63
Chapter 116A - Escheats and Abandoned Property [Repealed.]	64
Chapter 116B - Escheats and Abandoned Property	64
Chapter 116C - Continuum of Education Programs	64
Chapter 116D - Higher Education Bonds	64
Chapter 117 - Electrification	64
Chapter 118 - Firemen's and Rescue Squad Workers' Relief and Pension Funds [Recodified.]	64
Chapter 118A - Firemen's Death Benefit Act [Repealed.]	64
Chapter 118B - Members of a Rescue Squad Death Benefit Act [Repealed.]	64
Chapter 119 - Gasoline and Oil Inspection and Regulation	64
Chapter 120 - General Assembly	65
Chapter 120 - General Assembly (Continuation)	66
Chapter 120 - General Assembly (Continuation)	67
Chapter 120C - Lobbying	67
Chapter 121 - Archives and History	67
Chapter 122 - Hospitals for the Mentally Disordered [Repealed.]	67
Chapter 122A - North Carolina Housing Finance Agency	67
Chapter 122B - North Carolina Agricultural Facilities Finance Act [Repealed.]	67
Chapter 122C - Mental Health, Developmental Disabilities, and Substance Abuse Act of 1985	67
Chapter 122C - Mental Health, Developmental Disabilities, and Substance Abuse Act of 1985 (Continuation)	68
Chapter 122D - North Carolina Agricultural Finance Act	68

Chapter 122E - North Carolina Housing Trust and Oil Overcharge Act	68
Chapter 123 - Impeachment	69
Chapter 123A - Industrial Development [Repealed.]	69
Chapter 124 - Internal Improvements	69
Chapter 125 - Libraries	69
Chapter 126 - State Personnel System	69
Chapter 127 - Militia [Repealed.]	69
Chapter 127A - Militia	69
Chapter 127B - Military Affairs	69
Chapter 127C - Advisory Commission on Military Affairs	69
Chapter 128 - Offices and Public Officers	69
Chapter 128 - Offices and Public Officers (Continuation)	70
Chapter 129 - Public Buildings and Grounds	70
Chapter 130 - Public Health [Repealed.]	70
Chapter 130A - Public Health	70
Chapter 130A - Public Health (Continuation)	71
Chapter 130A - Public Health (Continuation)	72
Chapter 130B - Hazardous Waste Management Commission [Repealed.]	72
Chapter 131 - Public Hospitals [Repealed.]	72
Chapter 131A - Health Care Facilities Finance Act	72
Chapter 131B - Licensing of Ambulatory Surgical Facilities [Repealed.]	72
Chapter 131C - Charitable Solicitation Licensure Act [Repealed.]	72
Chapter 131D - Inspection and Licensing of Facilities	72
Chapter 131E - Health Care Facilities and Services	72
Chapter 131E - Health Care Facilities and Services (Continuation)	73
Chapter 131F - Solicitation of Contributions	73
Chapter 132 - Public Records	73
Chapter 133 - Public Works	74
Chapter 134 - Youth Development [Recodified.]	74
Chapter 134A - Youth Services [Repealed.]	74
Chapter 135 - Retirement System for Teachers and State Employees; Social Security; Health Insurance Program for Children	74
Chapter 135 - Retirement System for Teachers and State Employees; Social Security; Health Insurance Program for Children	75
Chapter 136 - Transportation	75
Chapter 136 - Transportation (Continuation)	76
Chapter 137 - Rural Rehabilitation [Repealed.]	76
Chapter 138 - Salaries, Fees and Allowances	76
Chapter 138A - State Government Ethics Act	76
Chapter 139 - Soil and Water Conservation Districts	76

Chapter	Page
Chapter 140 - State Art Museum; Symphony and Art Societies	76
Chapter 140A - State Awards System	76
Chapter 141 - State Boundaries	76
Chapter 142 - State Debt	76
Chapter 143 - State Departments, Institutions, and Commissions	77
Chapter 143 - State Departments, Institutions, and Commissions (Continuation)	78
Chapter 143 - State Departments, Institutions, and Commissions (Continuation)	79
Chapter 143 - State Departments, Institutions, and Commissions (Continuation)	80
Chapter 143A - State Government Reorganization	80
Chapter 143B - Executive Organization Act of 1973	80
Chapter 143B - Executive Organization Act of 1973 (Continuation)	81
Chapter 143B - Executive Organization Act of 1973 (Continuation)	82
Chapter 143C - State Budget Act	83
Chapter 143D - The State Governmental Accountability and Internal Control Act	83
Chapter 144 - State Flag, Official Governmental Flags, Motto, and Colors	83
Chapter 145 - State Symbols and Other Official Adoptions.	83
Chapter 146 - State Lands	83
Chapter 147 - State Officers	83
Chapter 148 - State Prison System	84
Chapter 149 - State Song and Toast	84
Chapter 150 - Uniform Revocation of Licenses [Repealed.]	84
Chapter 150A - Administrative Procedure Act [Recodified.]	84
Chapter 150B - Administrative Procedure Act	84
Chapter 151 - Constables [Repealed.]	84
Chapter 152 - Coroners	84
Chapter 152A - County Medical Examiner [Repealed.]	84
Chapter 152A - County Medical Examiner [Repealed.] (Continuation)	85
Chapter 153 - Counties and County Commissioners [Repealed.]	85
Chapter 153A - Counties	85
Chapter 153B - Mountain Resources Planning Act	85
Chapter 153C - Uwharrie Regional Resources Act	85
Chapter 154 - County Surveyor [Repealed.]	85
Chapter 155 - County Treasurer [Repealed.]	85
Chapter 156 - Drainage	85
Chapter 156 – Drainage (Continuation)	86

Chapter 157 - Housing Authorities and Projects	86
Chapter 157A - Historic Properties Commissions [Transferred.]	86
Chapter 158 - Local Development	86
Chapter 159 - Local Government Finance	86
Chapter 159 - Local Government Finance (Continuation)	87
Chapter 159A - Pollution Abatement and Industrial Facilities Financing Act [Unconstitutional.]	87
Chapter 159B - Joint Municipal Electric Power and Energy Act	87
Chapter 159C - Industrial and Pollution Control Facilities Financing Act	87
Chapter 159D - The North Carolina Capital Facilities Financing Act	87
Chapter 159E - Registered Public Obligations Act	87
Chapter 159F - North Carolina Energy Development Authority [Repealed.]	87
Chapter 159G - Water Infrastructure	87
Chapter 159H - [Reserved.]	87
Chapter 159I - Solid Waste Management Loan Program and Local Government Special Obligation Bonds	87
Chapter 160 - Municipal Corporations [Repealed And Transferred.]	87
Chapter 160A - Cities and Towns	88
Chapter 160A - Cities and Towns (Continuation)	89
Chapter 160B - Consolidated City-County Act	89
Chapter 160C - Baseball Park Districts [Repealed.]	90
Chapter 161 - Register of Deeds	90
Chapter 162 - Sheriff	90
Chapter 162A - Water and Sewer Systems	90
Chapter 162B Continuity of Local Government in Emergency.	90
Chapter 163 Elections and Election Laws.	90
Chapter 163 Elections and Election Laws. (Continuation)	91
Chapter 164 Concerning the General Statutes of North Carolina.	92
Chapter 165 Veterans.	92
Chapter 166 Civil Preparedness Agencies [Repealed.]	92
Chapter 166A North Carolina Emergency Management Act.	92
Chapter 167 State Civil Air Patrol [Repealed.]	92
Chapter 168 Persons with Disabilities.	92
Chapter 168A Persons With Disabilities Protection Act.	92

§§ 48-1 through 48-38: Repealed by Session Laws 1995, c. 457, s. 1.

Chapter 48.

Adoptions.

Article 1.

General Provisions.

§ 48-1-100. Legislative findings and intent; construction of Chapter.

(a) The General Assembly finds that it is in the public interest to establish a clear judicial process for adoptions, to promote the integrity and finality of adoptions, to encourage prompt, conclusive disposition of adoption proceedings, and to structure services to adopted children, biological parents, and adoptive parents that will provide for the needs and protect the interests of all parties to an adoption, particularly adopted minors.

(b) With special regard for the adoption of minors, the General Assembly declares as a matter of legislative policy that:

(1) The primary purpose of this Chapter is to advance the welfare of minors by (i) protecting minors from unnecessary separation from their original parents, (ii) facilitating the adoption of minors in need of adoptive placement by persons who can give them love, care, security, and support, (iii) protecting minors from placement with adoptive parents unfit to have responsibility for their care and rearing, and (iv) assuring the finality of the adoption; and

(2) Secondary purposes of this Chapter are (i) to protect biological parents from ill-advised decisions to relinquish a child or consent to the child's adoption, (ii) to protect adoptive parents from assuming responsibility for a child about whose heredity or mental or physical condition they know nothing, (iii) to protect the privacy of the parties to the adoption, and (iv) to discourage unlawful trafficking in minors and other unlawful placement activities.

(c) In construing this Chapter, the needs, interests, and rights of minor adoptees are primary. Any conflict between the interests of a minor adoptee and those of an adult shall be resolved in favor of the minor.

(d) This Chapter shall be liberally construed and applied to promote its underlying purposes and policies. (1949, c. 300; 1983, c. 454, ss. 1, 6; 1995, c. 457, s. 2.)

§ 48-1-101. Definitions.

In this Chapter, the following definitions apply:

(1) "Adoptee" means an individual who is adopted, is placed for adoption, or is the subject of a petition for adoption properly filed with the court.

(2) "Adoption" means the creation by law of the relationship of parent and child between two individuals.

(3) "Adult" means an individual who has attained 18 years of age, or if under the age of 18, is either married or has been emancipated under the applicable State law.

(3a) "Adoption facilitator" means an individual or a nonprofit entity that assists biological parents in locating and evaluating prospective adoptive parents without charge.

(4) "Agency" means a public or private association, corporation, institution, or other person or entity that is licensed or otherwise authorized by the law of the jurisdiction where it operates to place minors for adoption. "Agency" also means a county department of social services in this State.

(4a) "Agency identified adoption" means a placement where an agency has agreed to place the minor with a prospective adoptive parent selected by the parent or guardian.

(5) "Child" means a son or daughter, whether by birth or adoption.

(5a) "Confidential intermediary" means an agency that may act as a third party to facilitate the sharing of information authorized by G.S. 48-9-104.

(5b) "Criminal history" means a county, State, or federal conviction of a felony by a court of competent jurisdiction or a pending felony indictment of a crime for child abuse or neglect, spousal abuse, a crime against a child, including child pornography, or for a crime involving violence, including rape, sexual assault, or homicide, other than physical assault or battery; a county, State, or federal conviction of a felony by a court of competent jurisdiction or a pending felony indictment for physical assault, battery, or a drug-related offense, if the offense was committed within the past five years; or similar crimes under federal law or under the laws of other states.

(6) "Department" means the North Carolina Department of Health and Human Services.

(7) "Division" means the Division of Social Services of the Department.

(8) "Guardian" means an individual, other than a parent, appointed by a clerk of court in North Carolina to exercise all of the powers conferred by G.S. 35A-1241, including a standby guardian appointed under Article 21 of Chapter 35A of the General Statutes whose authority has actually commenced; and also means an individual, other than a parent, appointed in another jurisdiction according to the law of that jurisdiction who has the power to consent to adoption under the law of that jurisdiction.

(9) "Legal custody" of an individual means the general right to exercise continuing care of and control over the individual as authorized by law, with or without a court order, and:

a. Includes the right and the duty to protect, care for, educate, and discipline the individual;

b. Includes the right and the duty to provide the individual with food, shelter, clothing, and medical care; and

c. May include the right to have physical custody of the individual.

(9a) Repealed by Session Laws 2010-116, s. 1, effective October 1, 2010.

(10) "Minor" means an individual under 18 years of age who is not an adult.

(11) "Party" means a petitioner, adoptee, or any person whose consent to an adoption is necessary under this Chapter but has not been obtained.

(12) "Physical custody" means the physical care of and control over an individual.

(13) "Placement" means transfer of physical custody of a minor to the selected prospective adoptive parent. Placement may be either:

a. Direct placement by a parent or the guardian of the minor; or

b. Placement by an agency.

(14) "Preplacement assessment" means a document, whether prepared before or after placement, that contains the information required by G.S. 48-3-303 and any rules adopted by the Social Services Commission.

(15) "Relinquishment" means the voluntary surrender of a minor to an agency for the purpose of adoption.

(16) "Report to the court" means a document prepared in accordance with G.S. 48-2-501, et seq.

(17) "State" means a state as defined in G.S. 12-3(11).

(18) "Stepparent" means an individual who is the spouse of a parent of a child, but who is not a legal parent of the child. (1949, c. 300; 1953, c. 880; 1957, c. 778, s. 1; 1961, c. 241; 1969, c. 982; 1971, c. 157, ss. 1, 2; c. 1231, s. 1; 1973, c. 476, s. 138; 1975, c. 321, s. 2; 1977, c. 879, s. 1; 1981, c. 924, s. 1; 1985, c. 758, s. 4; 1995, c. 457, s. 2; 1997-215, s. 11(e); 1997-443, s. 11A.118(a); 1998-229, s. 12; 2001-150, s. 1; 2007-262, s. 2; 2007-276, s. 7; 2010-116, s. 1.)

§ 48-1-102. Parent includes adoptive parent.

As used in this Article, the term "parent" includes one who has become a parent by adoption. (1949, c. 300; 1953, c. 880; 1957, c. 778, s. 1; 1961, c. 241; 1969, c. 982; 1971, c. 157, ss. 1, 2; c. 1231, s. 1; 1973, c. 476, s. 138; 1975, c. 321, s. 2; 1977, c. 879, s. 1; 1981, c. 924, s. 1; 1985, c. 758, s. 4; 1995, c. 457, s. 2.)

§ 48-1-103. Who may adopt.

Any adult may adopt another individual as provided in this Chapter, but spouses may not adopt each other. (1949, c. 300; 1963, c. 699; 1967, c. 619, ss. 1-3; c. 693; c. 880, s. 3; 1969, c. 21, ss. 3-6; 1971, c. 395; c. 1231, s. 1; 1973, c. 849, s. 3; c. 1354, ss. 1-4; 1975, c. 91; 1979, c. 107, s. 6; 1981, c. 657; 1983, c. 454, s. 6; 1989, c. 208; c. 727, s. 219(4); 1993, c. 553, s. 14; 1995, c. 457, s. 2.)

§ 48-1-104. Who may be adopted.

Any individual may be adopted as provided in this Chapter. (1949, c. 300; 1957, c. 778, s. 2; 1967, c. 880, ss. 2, 3; 1969, c. 21, ss. 3-6; 1971, c. 1231, s. 1; 1973, c. 849, s. 3; 1975, c. 91; 1981, c. 657; 1987, c. 716, s. 1; 1989, c. 208; c. 727, s. 219(4); 1993, c. 539, s. 410; c. 553, s. 14; 1994, Ex. Sess., c. 24, s. 14(c); 1995, c. 457, s. 2.)

§ 48-1-105. Name of adoptee after adoption.

When a decree of adoption becomes final, the name of the adoptee shall become the name designated in the decree. (1949, c. 300; 1951, c. 730, ss. 1-4; 1955, c. 951, s. 1; 1967, c. 880, s. 3; c. 1042, ss. 1-3; 1969, c. 21, s. 2-6; c. 977; 1971, c. 1231, s. 1; 1973, c. 476, s. 128; c. 849, ss. 1-3; 1975, c. 91; 1981, c. 657; 1983, c. 454, s. 6; 1989, c. 208; c. 727, s. 219(3), (4); 1993, c. 553, s. 14; 1995, c. 457, s. 2.)

§ 48-1-106. Legal effect of decree of adoption.

(a)   A decree of adoption effects a complete substitution of families for all legal purposes after the entry of the decree.

(b)   A decree of adoption establishes the relationship of parent and child between each petitioner and the individual being adopted. From the date of the signing of the decree, the adoptee is entitled to inherit real and personal property by, through, and from the adoptive parents in accordance with the statutes on intestate succession and has the same legal status, including all legal rights and obligations of any kind whatsoever, as a child born the legitimate child of the adoptive parents.

(c) A decree of adoption severs the relationship of parent and child between the individual adopted and that individual's biological or previous adoptive parents. After the entry of a decree of adoption, the former parents are relieved of all legal duties and obligations due from them to the adoptee, except that a former parent's duty to make past-due payments for child support is not terminated, and the former parents are divested of all rights with respect to the adoptee.

(d) Notwithstanding any other provision of this section, neither an adoption by a stepparent nor a readoption pursuant to G.S. 48-6-102 has any effect on the relationship between the child and the parent who is the stepparent's spouse.

(e) In any deed, grant, will, or other written instrument executed before October 1, 1985, the words "child", "grandchild", "heir", "issue", "descendant", or an equivalent, or any other word of like import, shall be held to include any adopted person after the entry of the decree of adoption, unless a contrary intention plainly appears from the terms of the instrument, whether the instrument was executed before or after the entry of the decree of adoption. The use of the phrase "hereafter born" or similar language in any such instrument to establish a class of persons shall not by itself be sufficient to exclude adoptees from inclusion in the class. In any deed, grant, will, or other written instrument executed on or after October 1, 1985, any reference to a natural person shall include any adopted person after the entry of the decree of adoption unless the instrument explicitly states that adopted persons are excluded, whether the instrument was executed before or after the entry of the decree of adoption.

(f) Nothing in this Chapter deprives a biological grandparent of any visitation rights with an adopted minor available under G.S. 50-13.2(b1), 50-13.2A, and 50-13.5(j). (1949, c. 300; 1953, c. 824; 1955, c. 813, s. 5; 1957, c. 778, s. 5; 1963, c. 967; 1967, c. 619, s. 5; c. 880, s. 3; 1969, c. 21, ss. 3-6; c. 911, s. 6; 1971, c. 1093, s. 13; c. 1231, s. 1; 1973, c. 849, s. 3; c. 1354, s. 5; 1975, c. 91; 1981, c. 657; 1983, c. 30; c. 454, ss. 2, 6; 1985, c. 67, ss. 1-4; c. 575, s. 1; 1989, c. 208; c. 727, s. 219(4); 1993, c. 553, s. 14; 1995, c. 457, s. 2.)

§ 48-1-107. Other rights of adoptee.

A decree of adoption does not divest any vested property interest owned by the adoptee immediately prior to the decree of adoption including any public assistance benefit or child support payment due on or before the date of the decree. An adoption divests any property interest, entitlement, or other interest contingent on an ongoing family relationship with the adoptee's former family. (1949, c. 300; 1953, c. 824; 1955, c. 813, s. 5; 1963, c. 967; 1967, c. 619, s. 5; c. 880, s. 3; 1969, c. 21, ss. 3-6; 1971, c. 1231, s. 1; 1973, c. 849, s. 3; 1975, c. 91; 1981, c. 657; 1983, c. 454, s. 6; 1985, c. 67, ss. 1-4; c. 575, s. 1; 1989, c. 208; c. 727, s. 219(4); 1993, c. 553, s. 14; 1995, c. 457, s. 2.)

§ 48-1-108. Adoptees subject to Indian Child Welfare Act.

If the individual is an Indian child as defined in the Indian Child Welfare Act, 25 U.S.C. § 1901, et seq., then the provisions of that act shall control the individual's adoption. (1995, c. 457, s. 2.)

§ 48-1-109. Which agencies may prepare assessments and reports to the court.

(a) Except as authorized in subsections (b) and (c) of this section, only a county department of social services in this State or an agency licensed by the Department may prepare preplacement assessments pursuant to Article 3 of this Chapter or reports to the court pursuant to Article 2 of this Chapter.

(b) A preplacement assessment prepared in another state may be used in this State only if:

(1) The prospective adoptive parent resided in the state where it was prepared; and

(2) The person or entity that prepared it was authorized by the law of that state to gather the necessary information.

An assessment prepared in another state that does not meet the requirements of this section and G.S. 48-3-303(c) through (h) must be updated by a county department of social services in this State, an agency licensed by the Department, or a person or entity authorized to gather the necessary information pursuant to the laws of the state where the prospective adoptive parent resides before being used in this State.

(c) An order for a report to the court must be sent to a county department of social services in this State, an agency licensed by the Department, or a person or entity authorized to prepare home assessments for the purpose of adoption proceedings under the laws of the petitioner's state of residence. If the petitioner moves to a different state before the agency completes the report, the agency shall request a report pursuant to the Interstate Compact on the Placement of Children under Article 38 of Chapter 7B of the General Statutes from a person or entity authorized to prepare home assessments for the purpose of adoption proceedings under the laws of the petitioner's new state residence. (1949, c. 300; 1961, c. 186; 1969, c. 982; 1973, c. 476, s. 138; 1983, c. 454, s. 5; 1991, c. 335, s. 2; 1995, c. 457, s. 2; 1998-202, s. 13(h); 2009-185, s. 1.)

Article 2.

General Adoption Procedure.

Part 1. Jurisdiction and Venue.

§ 48-2-100. Jurisdiction.

(a) Adoption shall be by a special proceeding before the clerk of superior court.

(b) Except as provided in subsection (c) of this section, jurisdiction over adoption proceedings commenced under this Chapter exists if, at the commencement of the proceeding:

(1) The adoptee has lived in this State for at least the six consecutive months immediately preceding the filing of the petition or from birth;

(2) The prospective adoptive parent has lived in or been domiciled in this State for at least the six consecutive months immediately preceding the filing of the petition; or

(3) An agency licensed by this State or a county department of social services in this State has legal custody of the adoptee.

(c) The courts of this State shall not exercise jurisdiction under this Chapter if at the time the petition for adoption is filed, a court of any other state is exercising jurisdiction substantially in conformity with the Uniform Child-Custody Jurisdiction and Enforcement Act, Article 2 of Chapter 50A of the General Statutes. However, this subsection shall not apply if within 60 days after the date the petition for adoption is filed, the court of the other state dismisses its proceeding or releases its exclusive, continuing jurisdiction. (1949, c. 300; 1963, c. 699; 1967, c. 619, ss. 1-3; c. 693; c. 880, s. 3; 1969, c. 21, ss. 3-6; 1971, c. 233, s. 1; c. 395; c. 1231, s. 1; 1973, c. 849, s. 3; c. 1354, ss. 1-4; 1975, c. 91; 1979, c. 107, s. 6; 1981, c. 657; 1983, c. 454, s. 6; 1989, c. 208; c. 727, s. 219(4); 1993, c. 553, s. 14; 1995, c. 88, ss. 3, 4; c. 457, s. 2; 1999-223, s. 8; 2007-151, s. 2.)

§ 48-2-101. Venue.

A petition for adoption may be filed with the clerk of the superior court in the county in which:

(1) A petitioner lives, or is domiciled, at the time of filing;

(2) The adoptee lives; or

(3) An office of the agency that placed the adoptee is located. (1949, c. 300; 1967, c. 880, s. 3; 1969, c. 21, ss. 3-6; 1971, c. 233, s. 1; c. 1231, s. 1; 1973, c. 849, s. 3; 1975, c. 91; 1981, c. 657; 1989, c. 208; c. 727, s. 219(4); 1993, c. 553, s. 14; 1995, c. 88, s. 4; c. 457, s. 2.)

§ 48-2-102. Transfer, stay, or dismissal.

(a) If the court, on its own motion or on motion of a party, finds in the interest of justice that the matter should be heard in another county where venue lies under G.S. 48-2-101, the court may transfer, stay, or dismiss the proceeding.

(b) If an adoptee is also the subject of a pending proceeding under Chapter 7B of the General Statutes, then the district court having jurisdiction under

Chapter 7B shall retain jurisdiction until the final order of adoption is entered. The district court may waive jurisdiction for good cause. (1949, c. 300; 1971, c. 233, s. 1; 1995, c. 88, s. 4; c. 457, s. 2; 1998-202, s. 13(i).)

Part 2. General Procedural Provisions.

§ 48-2-201. Appointment of attorney or guardian ad litem.

(a)   The court may appoint an attorney to represent a parent or alleged parent who is unknown or whose whereabouts are unknown and who has not responded to notice of the adoption proceeding as provided in Part 4 of this Article.

(b)   The court on its own motion may appoint an attorney or a guardian ad litem to represent the interests of the adoptee in a contested proceeding brought under this Chapter. (1995, c. 457, s. 2.)

§ 48-2-202. No right to jury.

All proceedings under this Chapter must be heard by the court without a jury. (1995, c. 457, s. 2.)

§ 48-2-203. Confidentiality of proceedings under Chapter.

A judicial hearing in any proceeding pursuant to this Chapter shall be held in closed court. (1995, c. 457, s. 2.)

§ 48-2-204. Death of a joint petitioner or stepparent pending final decree.

(a)   When spouses have petitioned jointly to adopt and one spouse dies before entry of a final decree, the adoption may proceed in the names of both spouses. Upon completion of the adoption, the name of the deceased spouse shall be entered as one of the adoptive parents on the new birth certificate prepared pursuant to Article 9 of this Chapter. For purposes of inheritance, testate or intestate, the adoptee shall be treated as a child of the deceased spouse.

(b)   When a stepparent who has petitioned to adopt dies before entry of a final decree, the adoption may proceed in the name of the petitioning stepparent if the court causes to be mailed to any individual who executed a consent to adoption a notice advising that the petitioning stepparent has died and the individual may, within 15 days from the date the individual receives notice, request a hearing on the adoption. Notice is complete when mailed to the individual at the address given in the consent. Upon completion of the adoption, the name of the petitioning stepparent shall be entered as one of the adoptee's parents on the new birth certificate prepared in accordance with Article 9 of this Chapter. For purposes of inheritance, testate or intestate, the adoptee shall be treated as a child of the deceased stepparent. (1949, c. 300; 1995, c. 457, s. 2; 2013-236, s. 2.)

§ 48-2-205. Recognition of adoption decrees from other jurisdictions.

A final adoption decree issued by any other state must be recognized in this State. Where a minor child has been previously adopted in a foreign country by a petitioner or petitioners seeking to readopt the child under the laws of North Carolina, the adoption order entered in the foreign country may be accepted in lieu of the consent of the biological parent or parents or the guardian of the child to the readoption. A man and a woman who adopted a minor child in a foreign country while married to one another must readopt jointly, regardless of whether they have since divorced. If either does not join in the petition, he or she must be joined as a necessary party as provided in G.S. 1A-1, Rule 19. (1975, c. 262; 1983, c. 454, s. 6; 1995, c. 457, s. 2; 2009-185, s. 2.2.)

§ 48-2-206. Prebirth determination of right to consent.

(a)   At any time after six months from the date of conception as reasonably determined by a physician, the biological mother, agency, or adoptive parents chosen by the biological mother may file a special proceeding with the clerk requesting the court to determine whether consent of the biological father is required. The biological father shall be served with notice of the intent of the biological mother to place the child for adoption, allowing the biological father 15 days after service to assert a claim that his consent is required.

(b) The notice required under subsection (a) of this section shall contain the special proceeding case caption and file number and shall be substantially similar to the following language:

"[Name of the biological mother], the biological mother, is expected to give birth to a child on or about [birth due date]. You have been identified as the biological father. It is the intention of the biological mother to place the child for adoption. It is her belief that your consent to the adoption is not required. If you believe your consent to the adoption of this child is required pursuant to G.S. 48-3-601, you must notify the court in writing no later than 15 days from the date you received this notice that you believe your consent is required. A copy of your notice to the court must also be sent to the person or agency that sent you this notice. If you fail to notify the court within 15 days that you believe your consent is required, the court will rule that your consent is not required."

(c) If the biological father fails to respond within the time required, the court shall enter an order that the biological father's consent is not required for the adoption. A biological father who fails to respond within the time required under this section is not entitled to notice under G.S. 48-2-401(c) of an adoption petition filed within three months of the birth of the minor or to participate in the adoption proceeding.

(d) If the biological father notifies the court within 15 days of his receipt of the notice required by subsection (a) of this section that he believes his consent to the adoption is required, on motion of the petitioner, the court shall hold a hearing to determine whether the consent of the biological father is required. Promptly on receipt of the petitioner's motion, the court shall set a date for the hearing no earlier than 60 days nor later than 70 days after the biological father received the notice required by subsection (a) of this section and shall notify the petitioner and the biological father of the date, time, and place of the hearing. The notice of hearing to the biological father shall include a statement substantially similar to the following:

"To the biological father named above: You have told the court that you believe your consent is necessary for the adoption of the child described in the notice sent to you earlier. This hearing is being held to decide whether your consent is in fact necessary. Before the date of the hearing, you must have taken steps under G.S. 48-3-601 to establish that your consent is necessary or this court will decide that your consent is not necessary and the child can be adopted without it."

During the hearing, the court may take such evidence as necessary and enter an order determining whether or not the consent of the biological father is necessary. If the court determines that the consent of the biological father is not required, that individual is not entitled to receive notice under G.S. 48-2-401(c) of an adoption petition filed within three months of the birth of the minor or to participate in the adoption proceeding.

(e) The manner of service under this section shall be the same as set forth in G.S. 48-2-402.

(f) The jurisdiction provisions of Article 6A of Chapter 1 of the General Statutes and the venue provisions of Article 7 of Chapter 1 of the General Statutes rather than the provisions of Part 1 of this Article apply to proceedings under this section.

(g) Computation of periods of time provided for in this section shall be calculated as set forth in G.S. 1A-1, Rule 6.

(h) Transfer under G.S. 1-301.2 and appeal under G.S. 1-279.1 shall be as for an adoption proceeding.

(i) A determination by the court under this section that the consent of the biological father is not required shall only apply to an adoption petition filed within three months of the birth of the minor. (1997-215, s. 14; 2002-159, s. 11; 2005-166, s. 1.)

§ 48-2-207. Necessity of consent post-petition.

(a) If any individual who is described in G.S. 48-3-601 or entitled to notice under G.S. 48-2-401(c)(3) is served with notice of the filing of the petition in accordance with G.S. 48-2-402 and fails to respond within the time specified in the notice, the court, upon motion by the petitioner, shall enter an order under G.S. 48-3-603(a)(7) that the individual's consent is not required for the adoption.

(b) The court shall hold a hearing to take evidence and determine whether an individual's consent to an adoption is required if any of the following:

(1) Any individual described in G.S. 48-2-401(c)(3) who has been served with notice of the filing of the petition in accordance with G.S. 48-2-402 notifies the court within the time specified in the notice that he believes his consent to the adoption is required.

(2) Any individual who has not been served with the notice of the filing of the petition intervenes in the adoption proceeding alleging that his or her consent to the adoption is required.

(c) If the court determines that the consent of any individual is required, the adoption cannot proceed until such individual's consent is obtained or such individual's parental rights are terminated. If the individual whose consent is required did not have physical custody of the minor immediately prior to the placement of the minor with the prospective adoptive parents, a finding that such individual's consent is required does not entitle such individual to physical custody of the minor.

(d) If the court determines that the consent of any individual described in G.S. 48-2-401(c)(3) is not required, such individual shall not be entitled to receive notice of, or to participate in, further proceedings in the adoption. (2005-166, s. 2; 2013-236, s. 3.)

Part 3. Petition for Adoption.

§ 48-2-301. Petition for adoption; who may file.

(a) A prospective adoptive parent may file a petition for adoption pursuant to Article 3 of this Chapter only if a minor has been placed with the prospective adoptive parent pursuant to Part 2 of Article 3 of this Chapter unless the requirement of placement is waived by the court for cause.

(b) Except as authorized by Articles 4 and 6 of this Chapter, the spouse of a petitioner must join in the petition, unless the spouse has been declared incompetent or unless this requirement is otherwise waived by the court for cause.

(c) If the individual who files the petition is unmarried, no other individual may join in the petition, except that a man and a woman who jointly adopted a minor child in a foreign country while married to one another must readopt jointly as provided in G.S. 48-2-205. (1949, c. 300; 1963, c. 699; 1967, c. 619, ss. 1-3; c. 693; c. 880, s. 3; 1969, c. 21, ss. 3-6; 1971, c. 395; c. 1231, s. 1; 1973, c. 849, s. 3; c. 1354, ss. 1-4; 1975, c. 91; 1979, c. 107, s. 6; 1981, c. 657; 1983, c. 454, s. 6; 1989, c. 208; c. 727, s. 219(4); 1993, c. 553, s. 14; 1995, c. 88, s. 3; c. 457, s. 2; 2009-185, s. 2.1.)

§ 48-2-302. Concurrent petitions to adopt and terminate parental rights.

(a)   Repealed by Session Laws 2012-16, s. 1, effective October 1, 2012.

(b)   Repealed by Session Laws 2013-236, s. 4, effective July 3, 2013.

(c)   A petition for adoption may be filed concurrently with a petition to terminate parental rights. (1949, c. 300; 1957, c. 90; c. 778, s. 3; 1971, c. 1185, s. 17; 1975, c. 321, s. 1; 1977, c. 879, s. 2; 1979, c. 107, s. 7; 1985, c. 758, ss. 5-9; 1987, c. 371, s. 1; 1995, c. 457, s. 2; 2012-16, s. 1; 2013-236, s. 4.)

§ 48-2-303. Caption of petition for adoption.

The caption of the petition shall be substantially as follows:

STATE OF NORTH CAROLINA

       IN THE DISTRICT COURT

_____ COUNTY

       BEFORE THE CLERK

_____ |

*(Full name of petitioning father) |

       and |

| _____ | PETITION FOR
ADOPTION

*(Full name of petitioning mother) |

      and |

FOR THE ADOPTION OF |

_____ |

*(Full name by which the adoptee is to be known if the adoption is granted). (1949, c. 300; 1961, c. 186; 1969, c. 982; 1973, c. 476, s. 138; 1995, c. 88, s. 5; c. 457, s. 2; 1997-215, s. 9(d).)

§ 48-2-304. Petition for adoption; content.

(a)   The original petition for adoption must be signed and verified by each petitioner, and the original and two exact or conformed copies shall be filed with the clerk of court. The petition shall state:

(1)   Each petitioner's full name, current address, place of domicile if different from current address, and whether each petitioner has resided or been domiciled in this State for the six months immediately preceding the filing of the petition;

(2)   The marital status and gender of each petitioner;

(3)   The sex and, if known, the date and state or country of birth of the adoptee;

(4)   The full name by which the adoptee is to be known if the petition is granted;

(5)   That the petitioner desires and agrees to adopt and treat the adoptee as the petitioner's lawful child; and

(6) If the adoptee is a minor or an adult who has been adjudicated incompetent, a description and estimate of the value of any property of the adoptee.

(b) Any petition to adopt a minor shall also state:

(1) The length of time the adoptee has been in the physical custody of the petitioner.

(2) If the adoptee is not in the physical custody of the petitioner, the reason why the petitioner does not have physical custody and the date and manner in which the petitioner intends to acquire custody.

(3) That the petitioner has the resources, including those available under a subsidy for an adoptee with special needs, to provide for the care and support of the adoptee.

(4) Any information required by the Uniform Child-Custody Jurisdiction and Enforcement Act, Article 2 of Chapter 50A of the General Statutes, which is known to the petitioner.

(5) That any required assessment has been completed or updated within the 18 months before the placement.

(6) That all necessary consents, relinquishments, or terminations of parental rights have been obtained and will be filed as additional documents with the petition; or that the necessary consents, relinquishments, and terminations of parental rights that have been obtained will be filed as additional documents with the petition, along with the document listing the names of any other individuals whose consent, relinquishment, or termination of rights may be necessary but has not been obtained.

(c) A petition to adopt a minor under Article 3 of this Chapter shall also state all of the following:

(1) A description of the source of placement and the date of placement of the adoptee with the petitioner.

(2) That the provisions of the Interstate Compact on the Placement of Children, Article 38 of Chapter 7B of the General Statutes, were followed if the adoptee was brought into this State from another state for purposes of adoption,

or that a statement is attached describing the circumstances of any noncompliance.

(d) A petition to adopt a minor under Article 4 of this Chapter shall also state:

(1) The date of the petitioner's marriage, the name of the petitioner's spouse, and whether the spouse is deceased or has been adjudicated incompetent;

(2) The length of time the petitioner's spouse or the petitioner has had legal custody of the adoptee and the circumstances under which custody was acquired; and

(3) That the adoptee has resided primarily with the petitioner or with the petitioner and the petitioner's spouse during the six months immediately preceding the filing of the petition.

(e) Any petition to adopt an adult shall also state:

(1) The name, age, and last known address of any child of the prospective adoptive parent, including a child previously adopted by the prospective adoptive parent or the adoptive parent's spouse, and the date and place of the adoption; and

(2) The name, age, and last known address of any living parent, spouse, or child of the adoptee.

(f) The Department may promulgate a standard adoption petition. (1949, c. 300; 1961, c. 186; 1969, c. 982; 1973, c. 476, s. 138; 1995, c. 88, s. 5; c. 457, s. 2; 1998-202, s. 13(k); 1999-223, s. 9; 2001-150, s. 2; 2005-166, s. 3; 2012-16, s. 2.)

§ 48-2-305. Petition for adoption; additional documents.

The petitioner shall file or cause to be filed the following documents:

(1) Any required affidavit of parentage executed under G.S. 48-3-206.

(2) Any required consent or relinquishment that has been executed.

(3)   A certified copy of any court order terminating the rights and duties of a parent or a guardian of the adoptee.

(4)   A certified copy of any court order or pleading in a pending proceeding concerning custody of or visitation with the adoptee.

(5)   A copy of any required preplacement assessment certified by the agency that prepared the assessment or an affidavit from the petitioner stating why the assessment is not available.

(6)   A copy of any document containing the information required under G.S. 48-3-205 concerning the health, social, educational, and genetic history of the adoptee and the adoptee's original family which the petitioner received before the placement or at any later time, certified by the person who prepared it, or if this document is not available, an affidavit stating the reason why it is not available.

(7)   Any signed copy of the form required by the Interstate Compact on the Placement of Children, Article 38 of Chapter 7B of the General Statutes, authorizing a minor to come into this State, or any statement required by G.S. 48-2-304(c) describing the circumstances of any noncompliance.

(8)   A writing that states the name of any individual whose consent is or may be required, but who has not executed a consent or a relinquishment or whose parental rights have not been legally terminated, and any fact or circumstance that may excuse the lack of consent or relinquishment.

(9)   In an adoption pursuant to Article 4 of this Chapter, a copy of any agreement to release past-due child support payments.

(10)   Any consent to an agency by a placing parent and adopting parents to release identifying information under G.S. 48-9-109.

(11)   A certificate as required by G.S. 48-3-307(c), if the person who placed the minor executes a consent before receiving a copy of the preplacement assessment.

(12)   A certified copy of any judgment of conviction of a crime specified under G.S. 48-3-603(a)(9) establishing that an individual's consent to adoption is not required.

Any document required under this section that is available to the petitioner when the petition is filed shall be filed with the petition. Any document required under this section that is not available when the petition is filed shall be filed as the document becomes available. The petitioner may also file any other document necessary or helpful to the court's determination. (1949, c. 300; 1953, c. 906; 1961, c. 186; 1969, c. 911, s. 7; c. 982; 1975, c. 702, ss. 1-3; 1977, c. 879, s. 5; 1985, c. 758, ss. 10, 11; 1995, c. 457, s. 2; 1997-215, s. 1; 1998-202, s. 13(m); 2001-150, s. 3; 2005-166, s. 4; 2013-236, s. 5.)

§ 48-2-306. Omission of required information.

(a) Before entry of a decree of adoption, the court may require or allow the filing of any additional information required by this Chapter.

(b) After entry of a decree of adoption, omission of any information required by G.S. 48-2-304 and G.S. 48-2-305 does not invalidate the decree. (1995, c. 457, s. 2.)

Part 4. Notice of Pendency of Proceedings.

§ 48-2-401. Notice by petitioner.

(a) No later than 30 days after a petition for adoption is filed pursuant to Part 3 of this Article, the petitioner shall initiate service of notice of the filing on the persons required to receive notice under subsections (b), (c), and (d) of this section.

(b) In all adoptions, the petitioner shall serve notice of the filing on each of the following:

(1) Any individual whose consent to the adoption is required but has not been obtained, has been revoked in accord with this Chapter, or has become void as provided in this Chapter.

(2) The spouse of the petitioner if that spouse is required to join in the petition and petitioner is requesting that the joinder requirement be waived, provided the court for cause may waive this notice requirement.

(3) Any individual who has executed a consent or relinquishment, but who the petitioner has actually been informed has filed an action to set it aside for fraud or duress.

(4) Any other person designated by the court who can provide information relevant to the proposed adoption.

(c) In the adoption of a minor, the petitioner shall also serve notice of the filing on each of the following:

(1) A minor whose consent is dispensed with under G.S. 48-3-603(b)(2).

(2) Any agency that placed the adoptee.

(3) A man who to the actual knowledge of the petitioner claims to be or is named as the biological or possible biological father of the minor, and any biological or possible biological fathers who are unknown or whose whereabouts are unknown, but notice need not be served upon a man who has executed a consent, a relinquishment, or a notarized statement denying paternity or disclaiming any interest in the minor, a man whose parental rights have been legally terminated or who has been judicially determined not to be the minor's parent, a man whose consent to the adoption is not required under G.S. 48-3-603(a)(9) due to his conviction of a specified crime, or, provided the petition is filed within three months of the birth of the minor, a man whose consent to the adoption has been determined not to be required under G.S. 48-2-206.

(4) Any individual who the petitioner has been actually informed has legal or physical custody of the minor or who has a right of visitation or communication with the minor under an existing court order issued by a court in this State or another state.

(d) In the adoption of an adult, the petitioner shall also serve notice of the filing on any adult children of the prospective adoptive parent and any parent, spouse, or adult child of the adoptee who are listed in the petition to adopt; provided the court for cause may waive the requirement of notice to a parent of an adult adoptee.

(e)   Only those persons identified in subsections (b), (c), and (d) of this section are entitled to notice of the proceeding.

(f)   A notice required under this section must state that the person served must file a response to the petition within 30 days after service in order to participate in and to receive further notice of the proceeding, including notice of the time and place of any hearing.

(g)   Issuance of a summons is not required to commence an adoption proceeding under this Chapter. (1949, c. 300; 1957, c. 778, s. 5; 1969, c. 911, s. 6; 1971, c. 1093, s. 13; 1973, c. 1354, s. 5; 1983, c. 30; c. 454, ss. 2, 6; 1995, c. 457, s. 2; 1997-215, s. 2; 2001-208, s. 12; 2001-487, s. 101; 2005-166, s. 5; 2009-185, s. 3; 2012-16, s. 3; 2013-236, s. 6.)

§ 48-2-402. Manner of service.

(a)   Service of the notice required under G.S. 48-2-401 must be made as provided by G.S. 1A-1, Rule 4, for service of process.

(b)   In the event that the identity of a biological or possible biological parent cannot be ascertained and notice is required, the parent or possible parent shall be served by publication pursuant to G.S. 1A-1, Rule 4 (j1). The time for response shall be the time provided in the rule. The words "In re Doe" may be substituted for the title of the action in the notice as long as the notice contains the correct docket number. The notice shall be directed to "the unknown father [or mother] of" the adoptee, and the adoptee shall be described by sex, date of birth, and place of birth. The notice shall contain any information known to the petitioner that would allow an unknown parent or possible parent to identify himself or herself as the individual being addressed, such as the approximate date and place of conception, any name by which the other biological parent was known to the unknown parent or possible parent, and any fact about the unknown parent or possible parent known to or believed by the other biological parent. The notice shall also state that any parental rights the unknown parent or possible parent may have will be terminated upon entry of the order of adoption.

(c)   In an agency placement under Article 3 of this Chapter, the agency or other proper person shall file a petition to terminate the parental rights of an unknown parent or possible parent instead of serving notice under subsection

(b) of this section, and the court shall stay any adoption proceeding already filed, except that nothing in this subsection shall require that the agency or other proper person file a petition to terminate the parental rights of any known or possible parent who has been served notice as provided under G.S. 1A-1, Rule 4(j)(1) of the Rules of Civil Procedure. (1949, c. 300; 1957, c. 778, s. 5; 1969, c. 911, s. 6; 1971, c. 1093, s. 13; 1973, c. 1354, s. 5; 1983, c. 30; c. 454, ss. 2, 6; 1995, c. 457, s. 2; 2001-150, s. 4.)

§ 48-2-403. Notice of proceedings by clerk.

No later than five days after a petition is filed, the clerk of the court shall mail or otherwise deliver notice of the adoption proceeding to any agency that has undertaken but not yet completed a preplacement assessment and any agency ordered to make a report to the court pursuant to Part 5 of this Article. (1995, c. 457, s. 2; 1997-215, s. 3.)

§ 48-2-404. Notice of proceedings by court to alleged father.

If, at any time in the proceeding, it appears to the court that there is an alleged father of a minor adoptee as described in G.S. 48-2-401(c)(3) who has not been given notice, the court shall require notice of the proceeding to be given to him pursuant to G.S. 48-2-402. (1995, c. 457, s. 2.)

§ 48-2-405. Rights of persons entitled to notice.

Except as provided in G.S. 48-2-206(c), 48-2-206(d), and 48-2-207(d), a person entitled to notice whose consent is not required may appear and present evidence only as to whether the adoption is in the best interest of the adoptee. (1995, c. 457, s. 2; 2005-166, s. 6.)

§ 48-2-406. Waiver of notice; effect.

(a) If notice is required under this Part, it may be waived in open court by the person entitled to receive it or by an agent authorized by that person; it may also be waived at any time in a writing signed by the person entitled to receive the notice.

(b) A person who has executed a consent or relinquishment or otherwise waived notice is not a necessary party and, except as provided in subsection (c) of this section, is not entitled to appear in any subsequent proceeding related to the petition.

(c) A parent who has executed a consent or relinquishment may appear in the adoption proceeding for the limited purpose of moving to set aside the consent or relinquishment on the grounds that it was obtained by fraud or duress. (1949, c. 300; 1957, c. 778, s. 5; 1969, c. 911, s. 6; 1971, c. 1093, s. 13; 1973, c. 1354, s. 5; 1983, c. 30; c. 454, ss. 2, 6; 1995, c. 457, s. 2.)

§ 48-2-407. Filing proof of service.

Proof of service of notice on each person entitled to receive notice under this Part, or a certified copy of each waiver of notice, must be filed with the court before the hearing on the adoption begins. (1995, c. 457, s. 2.)

Part 5. Report to the Court.

§ 48-2-501. Report to the court during proceeding for adoption of a minor.

(a) Whenever a petition for adoption of a minor is filed, the court shall order a report to the court made to assist the court to determine if the proposed adoption of the minor by the petitioner is in the minor's best interest.

(b) Consistent with G.S. 48-1-109, the court shall order the report to be prepared:

(1) By the agency that placed the minor;

(2) By the agency that made the preplacement assessment pursuant to Part 3 of Article 3 of this Chapter; or

(3) By another agency.

(c) The court shall provide the individual who prepares the report with copies of:

(1) The petition to adopt; and

(2) The documents filed with it.

(d) The following exceptions apply in this section:

(1) In any stepparent adoption under Article 4 of this Chapter in which the minor has lived with the stepparent for at least the two consecutive years immediately preceding the filing of the petition, the court may order a report. However, the court is not required to order a report unless the minor's consent is to be waived, the minor has revoked a consent, or both of the minor's parents are dead.

(2) In any adoption of a minor by the minor's grandparent in which the minor has lived with the grandparent for at least the two consecutive years immediately preceding the filing of the petition, the court may order a report. However, the court is not required to order a report unless the minor's consent is to be waived, the minor has revoked a consent, or the minor is eligible for adoption assistance pursuant to G.S. 108A-49. (1949, c. 300; 1961, c. 186; 1969, c. 982; 1973, c. 476, s. 138; 1983, c. 454, s. 5; 1991, c. 335, s. 2; 1995, c. 457, s. 2; 1997-215, s. 12(a); 2009-185, s. 4.)

§ 48-2-502. Preparation and content of report.

(a) In preparing a report to the court, the agency shall conduct a personal interview with each petitioner in the petitioner's residence and at least one additional interview with each petitioner and the adoptee, and shall observe the relationship between the adoptee and the petitioner or petitioners.

(b) The report must be in writing and contain:

(1) An account of the petitioner's marital or family status, physical and mental health, home environment, property, income, and financial obligations; if

there has been a preplacement assessment, the account may be limited to any changes since the filing of the preplacement assessment;

(2) All reasonably available nonidentifying information concerning the physical, mental, and emotional condition of the adoptee required by G.S. 48-3-205 which is not already included in the document prepared under that section;

(3) Copies of any court order, judgment, decree, or pending legal proceeding affecting the adoptee, the petitioner, or any child of the petitioner relevant to the welfare of the adoptee;

(4) A list of the expenses, fees, or other charges incurred, paid, or to be paid in connection with the adoption that can reasonably be ascertained by the agency;

(5) Any fact or circumstance known to the agency that raises a specific concern about whether the proposed adoption is contrary to the best interest of the adoptee because it poses a significant risk of harm to the well-being of the adoptee;

(6) A finding by the agency concerning the suitability of the petitioner and the petitioner's home for the adoptee;

(7) A recommendation concerning the granting of the petition; and

(8) Such other information as may be required by rules adopted pursuant to subsection (c) of this section.

In an agency adoption, the report shall be written in such a way as to exclude all information that could reasonably be expected to lead directly to the identity of the adoptee at birth or any former parent or family member of the adoptee, and any copies of documents included pursuant to subdivision (3) of this subsection shall be redacted to exclude this information.

(c) The Social Services Commission may adopt rules to implement the provisions of this section. (1949, c. 300; 1961, c. 186; 1969, c. 982; 1973, c. 476, s. 138; 1983, c. 454, s. 5; 1991, c. 335, s. 2; 1995, c. 457, s. 2; 1997-215, s. 4.)

§ 48-2-503. Timing and filing of report.

(a)   The agency shall complete a written report and file it with the court within 60 days after the mailing or delivery of the order under G.S. 48-2-501 unless the court extends the time for filing. The agency shall have three additional days to complete and file the report if the order was mailed.

(b)   If the agency identifies a specific concern about the suitability of the petitioner or the petitioner's home for the adoptee, the agency must file an interim report immediately, which must contain an account of the specific concern. The agency shall indicate in the final report whether its concerns have been satisfied and in what manner.

(b1)   When an agency identifies a specific concern in a final report and the court extends the time for a final hearing or disposition to allow resolution of these concerns, the agency shall file a supplemental report indicating whether its concerns have been satisfied and in what manner.

(c)   The agency shall give the petitioner a copy of each report filed with the court, and the agency shall retain a copy. (1949, c. 300; 1961, c. 186; 1969, c. 982; 1973, c. 476, s. 138; 1983, c. 454, s. 5; 1991, c. 335, s. 2; 1995, c. 457, s. 2; 1997-215, s. 5(a)-(c).)

§ 48-2-504. Fee for report.

(a)   An agency that prepares a report to the court may charge the petitioner a reasonable fee for preparing and writing the report. No fee may be charged except pursuant to a written fee agreement which must be signed by the parties to be charged prior to the beginning of the preparation. The fee agreement may not be based on the outcome of the report or the adoption proceeding.

(b)   A fee for a report is subject to review by the court pursuant to G.S. 48-2-602 and G.S. 48-2-603.

(c)   The Department shall set the maximum fees, based on ability to pay and other factors, which may be charged by county departments of social services. The Department shall require waiver of fees for those unable to pay. Fees collected under this section shall be applied to the costs of preparing and writing reports and shall be used by the county department of social services to supplement and not to supplant appropriated funds. (1995, c. 457, s. 2.)

Part 6. Dispositional Hearing; Decree of Adoption.

§ 48-2-601. Hearing on, or disposition of, adoption petition; transfer of adoption proceeding; timing.

(a) If it appears to the court that a petition to adopt a minor is not contested, the court may dispose of the petition without a formal hearing.

(a1) If an issue of fact, an equitable defense, or a request for equitable relief is raised before the clerk, the clerk shall transfer the proceeding to the district court under G.S. 1-301.2.

(b) No later than 90 days after a petition for adoption has been filed, the court shall set a date and time for hearing or disposing of the petition.

(c) The hearing or disposition must take place no later than six months after the petition is filed, but the court for cause may extend the time for the hearing or disposition. (1949, c. 300; 1953, c. 571; 1959, cc. 340, 561; 1961, cc. 186, 384; 1967, c. 19; c. 619, s. 4; 1969, c. 982; 1973, c. 1354, s. 6; 1989 (Reg. Sess., 1990), c. 977, s. 1; 1995, c. 457, s. 2; 1997-215, s. 10(a); 2002-159, s. 12.)

§ 48-2-602. Disclosure of fees and charges.

At least 10 days before the date of the hearing or disposition, each petitioner shall file with the court an affidavit accounting for any payment or disbursement of money or anything of value made or agreed to be made by or on behalf of each petitioner in connection with the adoption, or pursuant to Article 10, including the amount of each payment or disbursement made or to be made and the name and address of each recipient. The court in its discretion may request a more specific statement of any fees, charges, or payments made or to be made by any petitioner in connection with the adoption. (1995, c. 457, s. 2.)

§ 48-2-603. Hearing on, or disposition of, petition to adopt a minor.

(a) At the hearing on, or disposition of, a petition to adopt a minor, the court shall grant the petition upon finding by a preponderance of the evidence that the adoption will serve the best interest of the adoptee, and upon finding the following:

(1) At least 90 days have elapsed since the filing of the petition for adoption, unless the court for cause waives this requirement.

(2) The adoptee has been in the physical custody of the petitioner for at least 90 days, unless the court for cause waives this requirement.

(3) Notice of the filing of the petition has been served on any person entitled to receive notice under Part 4 of this Article.

(4) Each necessary consent, relinquishment, waiver, or judicial order terminating parental rights, has been obtained and filed with the court and the time for revocation has expired.

(5) Any assessment required by this Chapter has been filed with and considered by the court.

(6) If applicable, the requirements of the Interstate Compact on the Placement of Children, Article 38 of Chapter 7B of the General Statutes, have been met.

(7) Any motion to dismiss the proceeding has been denied.

(8) Each petitioner is a suitable adoptive parent.

(9) Any accounting and affidavit required under G.S. 48-2-602 has been reviewed by the court, and the court has denied, modified, or ordered reimbursement of any payment or disbursement that violates Article 10 or is unreasonable when compared with the expenses customarily incurred in connection with an adoption.

(10) The petitioner has received information about the adoptee and the adoptee's biological family if required by G.S. 48-3-205.

(10a) Any certificate of service required by G.S. 48-3-307 has been filed.

(11) There has been substantial compliance with the provisions of this Chapter.

(b) If the Court finds a violation of this Chapter pursuant to Article 10 or of the Interstate Compact on the Placement of Children, Article 38 of Chapter 7B of the General Statutes, but determines that in every other respect there has been substantial compliance with the provisions of this Chapter, and the adoption will serve the best interest of the adoptee, the court shall:

(1) Grant the petition to adopt; and

(2) Impose the sanctions provided by this Chapter against any individual or entity who has committed a prohibited act or report the violations to the appropriate legal authorities.

(c) The court on its own motion may continue the hearing for further evidence. (1949, c. 300; 1953, c. 571; 1959, cc. 340, 561; 1961, cc. 186, 384; 1967, c. 19; c. 619, s. 4; 1969, c. 982; 1973, c. 476, s. 138; c. 1354, s. 6; 1989 (Reg. Sess., 1990), c. 977, s. 1; 1995, c. 457, s. 2; 1998-202, s. 13(l); 2001-150, s. 5.)

§ 48-2-604. Denying petition to adopt a minor.

(a) If at any time between the filing of a petition to adopt a minor and the issuance of the final order completing the adoption it appears to the court that the minor should not be adopted by the petitioners or the petition should be dismissed for some other reason, the court may dismiss the proceeding.

(b) The court, before entering an order to dismiss the proceeding, shall give at least five days' notice of the motion to dismiss to the parties, to the agency that made the report to the court, and to the Department of Health and Human Services. The parties and agency entitled to notice under this subsection, and the Department, shall be entitled to a hearing on the issue of dismissing the proceeding.

(c) If the court denies the petition, the custody of the minor shall revert to any agency or person having custody immediately before the filing of the petition. If the placement of the minor was a direct placement under Article 3 of this Chapter, the court shall notify the director of social services of the county in which the petition was filed of the dismissal, and the director of social services shall be responsible for taking appropriate action for the protection of the minor. (1949, c. 300; 1961, c. 186; 1969, c. 982; 1973, c. 476, s. 138; 1983, c. 454, s. 6.; 1995, c. 457, s. 2; 1997-215, s. 6(a); 1997-443, s. 11A.118(b).)

§ 48-2-605. Hearing on petition to adopt an adult.

(a) At the hearing on a petition to adopt an adult, the prospective adoptive parent and the adoptee shall both appear in person, unless the court waives this requirement for cause, in which event an appearance may be made for either or both of them by an attorney authorized in writing to make the appearance.

(b) At the hearing, the court shall grant the petition for adoption upon finding by a preponderance of the evidence all of the following:

(1) At least 30 days have elapsed since the filing of the petition for adoption, but the court for cause may waive this requirement;

(2) Notice of the petition has been served on any person entitled to receive notice under Part 4 of this Article;

(3) Each necessary consent, waiver, document, or judicial order has been obtained and filed with the court;

(4) The adoption is entered into freely and without duress or undue influence for the purpose of creating the relation of parent and child between each petitioner and the adoptee, and each petitioner and the adoptee understand the consequences of the adoption; and

(5) There has been substantial compliance with the provisions of this Chapter. (1967, c. 880, s. 3; 1969, c. 21, ss. 3-6; 1971, c. 1231, s. 1; 1973, c. 849, s. 3; 1975, c. 91; 1981, c. 657; 1989, c. 208; c. 727, s. 219(4); 1993, c. 553, s. 14; 1995, c. 457, s. 2.)

§ 48-2-606. Decree of adoption.

(a) A decree of adoption must state at least:

(1) The name and gender of each petitioner for adoption;

(2) Whether the petitioner is married, a stepparent, or single;

(3) The name by which the adoptee is to be known;

(4) Information to be incorporated in a new standard certificate of birth to be issued by the State Registrar;

(5) The adoptee's date and place of birth, if known, or as determined under subsection (b) of this section in the case of an adoptee born outside the United States;

(6) The effect of the decree of adoption as set forth in G.S. 48-1-106; and

(7) That the adoption is in the best interest of the adoptee.

(b) In stating the date and place of birth of an adoptee born outside the United States, the court shall:

(1) Enter the date and place of birth as stated in the certificate of birth from the country of origin, the United States Department of State's report of birth abroad, or the documents of the United States Immigration and Naturalization Service;

(2) If the exact place of birth is unknown, enter the information that is known, including the country of origin; and

(3) If the exact date of birth is unknown, determine and enter a date of birth based upon medical evidence by affidavit or testimony as to the probable chronological age of the adoptee and other evidence the court finds appropriate to consider.

(c) A decree of adoption must not contain the name of a former parent of the adoptee. (1949, c. 300; 1973, c. 476, s. 138.; 1983, c. 454, s. 6; 1995, c. 457, s. 2.)

§ 48-2-607. Appeals.

(a)   Except as provided in subsections (b) and (c) of this section, after the final order of adoption is entered, no party to an adoption proceeding nor anyone claiming under such a party may question the validity of the adoption because of any defect or irregularity, jurisdictional or otherwise, in the proceeding, but shall be fully bound by the order. No adoption may be attacked either directly or collaterally because of any procedural or other defect by anyone who was not a party to the adoption. The failure on the part of the court or an agency to perform duties or acts within the time required by the provisions of this Chapter shall not affect the validity of any adoption proceeding.

(b)   A party to an adoption proceeding may appeal a final decree of adoption entered by a clerk of superior court to district court by giving notice of appeal as provided in G.S. 1-301.2. A party to an adoption proceeding may appeal a judgment or order entered by a judge of district court by giving notice of appeal as provided in G.S. 1-279.1.

(c)   A parent or guardian whose consent or relinquishment was obtained by fraud or duress may, within six months of the time the fraud or duress is or ought reasonably to have been discovered, move to have the decree of adoption set aside and the consent declared void. A parent or guardian whose consent was necessary under this Chapter but was not obtained may, within six months of the time the omission is or ought reasonably to have been discovered, move to have the decree of adoption set aside. Any action for damages against an adoptee or the adoptive parents for fraud or duress in obtaining a consent must be brought within six months of the time the fraud or duress is or ought reasonably to have been discovered. (1949, c. 300; 1961, c. 186; 1969, c. 982; 1983, c. 454, s. 6; 1995, c. 457, s. 2; 1999-216, s. 11.1.)

Article 3.

Adoption of Minors.

Part 1. General Provisions.

§ 48-3-100. Application of Article.

This Article shall apply to the adoption of minors by adults who are not their stepparents. (1995, c. 457, s. 2.)

Part 2. Placement of Minors for Adoption.

§ 48-3-201. Who may place minors for adoption.

(a) Only the following may place the minor for adoption:

(1) An agency,

(2) A guardian,

(3) Both parents acting jointly, if

a. Both parents are married to each other and living together, or

b. One parent has legal custody of a minor and the other has physical custody but neither has both, or

(4) A parent with legal and physical custody of a minor, except as provided in subdivision (3) of this subsection.

(b) A parent, guardian, or agency that places a minor directly for adoption shall execute a consent to the minor's adoption pursuant to Part 6 of this Article.

(c) A parent or guardian of a minor who wants an agency to place the minor for adoption must execute a relinquishment to the agency pursuant to Part 7 of this Article before the agency can place the minor.

(d) An agency having legal and physical custody of a minor may place the minor for adoption at any time after a relinquishment is executed by anyone as permitted by G.S. 48-3-701. The agency may place the minor for adoption even if other consents are required before an adoption can be granted, unless an individual whose consent is required notifies the agency in writing of the individual's objections before the placement. The agency shall act promptly after accepting a relinquishment to obtain all other necessary consents, relinquishments, or terminations of any guardian's authority pursuant to Chapter 35A of the General Statutes or parental rights pursuant to Article 11 of Chapter 7B of the General Statutes. (1995, c. 457, s. 2; 1997-215, s. 11(b); 1998-202, s. 13(j).)

§ 48-3-202. Direct placement for adoption.

(a)   In a direct placement, a parent or guardian must personally select a prospective adoptive parent, but a parent or guardian may obtain assistance from another person or entity, or an adoption facilitator, in locating or evaluating a prospective adoptive parent, subject to the limitations of Article 10 of this Chapter.

(b)   Information about a prospective adoptive parent shall be provided to a parent or guardian by the prospective adoptive parent, the prospective adoptive parent's attorney, or a person or entity assisting the parent or guardian. Except as otherwise provided in this subsection, this information shall include the preplacement assessment prepared pursuant to Part 3 of this Article, and may include additional information requested by the parent or guardian. The agency preparing the preplacement assessment may redact from the preplacement assessment provided to a placing parent or guardian detailed information reflecting the prospective adoptive parent's financial account balances and detailed information about the prospective adoptive parent's extended family members, including surnames, names of employers, names of schools attended, social security numbers, telephone numbers and addresses, and other similarly detailed information about extended family members obtained under G.S. 48-3-303. (1995, c. 457, s. 2; 2001-150, s. 6.)

§ 48-3-203. Agency placement adoption.

(a)   An agency may acquire legal and physical custody of a minor for purposes of adoptive placement only by means of a relinquishment pursuant to Part 7 of this Article or by a court order terminating the rights and duties of a parent or guardian of the minor.

(b)   An agency shall give any individual, upon request, a written statement of the services it provides, its procedure for selecting a prospective adoptive parent for a minor, including the role of the minor's parent or guardian in the selection process, and the procedure for an agency identified adoption and the disclosures permitted under G.S. 48-9-109. This statement shall include a schedule of any fee or expenses charged or required to be paid by the agency and a summary of the provisions of this Chapter that pertain to the requirements and consequences of a relinquishment and to the selection of a prospective adoptive parent.

(c) An agency may notify the parent when a placement has occurred and when an adoption decree is issued.

(d) An agency may place a minor for adoption only with an individual for whom a favorable preplacement assessment has been prepared. Placement shall be made as follows:

(1) If the agency has agreed to place the minor with the prospective adoptive parent selected by the parent or guardian, the minor shall be placed with the individual selected by the parent or guardian.

(2) If the agency has not agreed to place the minor with the prospective adoptive parent selected by the parent or guardian, the minor shall be placed with the prospective adoptive parent selected by the agency on the basis of the preplacement assessment. The selection may not be delegated, but may be based on criteria requested by a parent who relinquishes the child to the agency.

(d1) A minor who is in the custody or placement responsibility of a county department of social services shall not be placed with a selected prospective adoptive parent prior to the completion of an investigation of the individual's criminal history pursuant to G.S. 48-3-309 or G.S. 131D-10.3A and, based on the criminal history, a determination as to the individual's fitness to have responsibility for the safety and well-being of children.

(e) In addition to the authority granted in G.S. 131D-10.5, the Social Services Commission may adopt rules for placements by agencies consistent with the purposes of this Chapter.

(f) An agency may release identifying information as provided in G.S. 48-9-104. (1949, c. 300; 1953, c. 906; 1961, c. 186; 1969, c. 911, s. 7; c. 982; 1975, c. 702, ss. 1-3; 1977, c. 879, s. 5; 1985, c. 758, ss. 10, 11; 1995, c. 457, s. 2; 1998-229, s. 13; 2001-150, s. 7.)

§ 48-3-204. Recruitment of adoptive parents.

(a) The Social Services Commission may adopt rules requiring agencies to adopt and follow appropriate recruitment plans for prospective adoptive parents.

(b) The Division may maintain a statewide photo-listing service for all agencies within this State as a means of recruiting adoptive parents for minors who have been legally freed for adoption.

(c) Agencies and the Division shall cooperate with similar agencies in other states, and with national adoption exchanges in an effort to recruit suitable adoptive parents. (1995, c. 457, s. 2.)

§ 48-3-205. Disclosure of background information.

(a) Notwithstanding any other provision of law, before placing a minor for adoption, an individual or agency placing the minor, or the individual's agent, must compile and provide to the prospective adoptive parent a written document containing the following information:

(1) The date of the birth of the minor and the minor's weight at birth and any other reasonably available nonidentifying information about the minor that is relevant to the adoption decision or to the minor's development and well-being;

(2) Age of the biological parents in years at the time of the minor's birth;

(3) Heritage of the biological parents, which shall consist of nationality, ethnic background, and race;

(4) Education of the biological parents, which shall be the number of years of school completed by the biological parents at the time of the minor's birth; and

(5) General physical appearance of the biological parents.

In addition, the written document must also include all reasonably available nonidentifying information about the health of the minor, the biological parents, and other members of the biological parents' families that is relevant to the adoption decision or to the minor's health and development. This health-related information shall include each such individual's present state of physical and mental health, health and genetic histories, and information concerning any history of emotional, physical, sexual, or substance abuse. This health-related information shall also include an account of the prenatal and postnatal care received by the minor. The information described in this subsection, if known, shall, upon written request of the minor, be made available to the minor upon the minor reaching age 18 or upon the minor's marriage or emancipation.

(b) Information provided under this section, or any information directly or indirectly derived from such information, may not be used against the provider or against an individual described in subsection (a) of this section who is the subject of the information in any criminal action or any civil action for damages. In addition, information provided under this section may not be admitted in evidence against the provider or against an individual described in subsection (a) of this section who is the subject of the information in any other action or proceeding.

(c) The agency placing the minor shall receive and preserve any additional health-related information obtained after the preparation of the document described in subsection (a) of this section.

(d) The Division shall develop and make available forms designed to collect the information described in subsection (a) of this section. However, forms reasonably equivalent to those provided by the Division may be substituted. (1949, c. 300; 1957, c. 778, s. 7; 1961, c. 186; 1969, c. 982; 1973, c. 476, s. 138; 1979, c. 739, ss. 1, 2; 1981, c. 924, ss. 2, 3; 1983, c. 454, s. 6; 1993, c. 539, s. 411; 1994, Ex. Sess., c. 24, s. 14(c); 1995, c. 457, s. 2; 2012-16, s. 4.)

§ 48-3-206. Affidavit of parentage.

(a) To assist the court in determining that a direct placement was valid and all necessary consents have been obtained, the parent or guardian who placed the minor shall execute an affidavit setting out names, last known addresses, and marital status of the minor's parents or possible parents. If the placing parent or guardian is unavailable to execute the affidavit, the affidavit may be prepared by a knowledgeable individual who shall sign the affidavit and indicate the source of the individual's knowledge.

(b)   In an agency placement, the agency shall obtain from at least one individual who relinquishes a minor to the agency an affidavit setting out the information required in subsection (a) of this section. This affidavit is not necessary when the agency acquires legal and physical custody of a minor for purposes of adoptive placement by a court order terminating the parental rights of a parent or guardian. (1949, c. 300; 1977, c. 879, s. 6; 1983, c. 454, s. 6; 1995, c. 457, s. 2; 2001-208, s. 14; 2001-487, s. 101.)

§ 48-3-207. Interstate placements.

An interstate placement of a minor for purposes of adoption shall comply with the Interstate Compact on the Placement of Children, Article 38 of Chapter 7B of the General Statutes. (1995, c. 457, s. 2; 1998-202, s. 13(n).)

Part 3. Preplacement Assessment.

§ 48-3-301. Preplacement assessment required.

(a)   Except as provided in subsection (b) of this section, placement of a minor may occur only if a written preplacement assessment:

(1)   Has been completed or updated within the 18 months immediately preceding the placement; and

(2)   Contains a finding that the individual who is the subject of the assessment is suitable to be an adoptive parent, either in general or for a specific minor.

(b)   A preplacement assessment is not required when a parent or guardian places a minor directly with a grandparent, sibling, first cousin, aunt, uncle, great-aunt, great-uncle, or great-grandparent of the minor.

(c)   If a direct placement is made in violation of this section:

(1) The prospective adoptive parent shall request any preplacement assessment already commenced to be expedited, and if none has been commenced, shall obtain a preplacement assessment from an agency as authorized by G.S. 48-1-109; in either case, the assessment shall include the fact and date of placement;

(2) The court may not enter a decree of adoption until both a favorable preplacement assessment and a report to the court have been completed and filed, and the court may not order a report to the court for at least 30 days after the preplacement assessment has been completed; and

(3) If the person who placed the minor executes a consent before receiving a copy of the preplacement assessment, G.S. 48-3-608 shall determine the time within which that person may revoke. (1949, c. 300; 1957, c. 778, s. 2; 1967, c. 880, s. 2; 1987, c. 716, s. 1; 1993, c. 539, s. 410; 1994, Ex. Sess., c. 24, s. 14(c); 1995, c. 457, s. 2; 1997-215, s. 19(a).)

§ 48-3-302. Request for preplacement assessment.

(a) An individual seeking to adopt may request a preplacement assessment at any time by an agency authorized by G.S. 48-1-109 to prepare preplacement assessments.

(b) An individual requesting a preplacement assessment need not have located a prospective adoptee when the request is made.

(c) An individual may have more than one preplacement assessment or may request that an assessment, once initiated, not be completed.

(d) If an individual is seeking to adopt a minor from a particular agency, the agency may require the individual to be assessed by its own employee, even if the individual has already had a favorable preplacement assessment completed by another agency.

(e) If an individual requesting a preplacement assessment has identified a prospective adoptive child and has otherwise been unable to obtain a preplacement assessment, the county department of social services must, upon request, prepare or contract for the preparation of the preplacement assessment. As used in this subsection, "unable to obtain a preplacement assessment" includes the inability to obtain a preplacement assessment at the fee the county department of social services is permitted to charge the individual. Except as provided in this subsection, no agency is required to conduct a preplacement assessment unless it agrees to do so. (1949, c. 300; 1957, c. 778, s. 2; 1967, c. 880, s. 2; 1987, c. 716, s. 1; 1993, c. 539, s. 410; 1994, Ex. Sess., c. 24, s. 14(c); 1995, c. 457, s. 2; 1997-215, s. 15.)

§ 48-3-303. Content and timing of preplacement assessment.

(a)   A preplacement assessment shall be completed within 90 days after a request has been accepted.

(b)   The preplacement assessment must be based on at least one personal interview with each individual being assessed in the individual's residence and any report received pursuant to subsection (c) of this section.

(c)   The preplacement assessment shall, after a reasonable investigation, report on the following about the individual being assessed:

(1)   Age and date of birth, nationality, race, or ethnicity, and any religious preference;

(2)   Marital and family status and history, including the presence of any children born to or adopted by the individual and any other children in the household;

(3)   Physical and mental health, including any addiction to alcohol or drugs;

(4)   Educational and employment history and any special skills;

(5)   Property and income, and current financial information provided by the individual;

(6)   Reason for wanting to adopt;

(7)   Any previous request for an assessment or involvement in an adoptive placement and the outcome of the assessment or placement;

(8) Whether the individual has ever been a respondent in a domestic violence proceeding or a proceeding concerning a minor who was allegedly abused, dependent, neglected, abandoned, or delinquent, and the outcome of the proceeding;

(9) Whether the individual has ever been convicted of a crime other than a minor traffic violation;

(10) Whether the individual has located a parent interested in placing a child with the individual for adoption and a brief, nonidentifying description of the parent and the child; and

(11) Any other fact or circumstance that may be relevant to a determination of the individual's suitability to be an adoptive parent, including the quality of the environment in the home and the functioning of any children in the household.

(12) The agency preparing the preplacement assessment may redact from the preplacement assessment provided to a placing parent or guardian detailed information reflecting the prospective adoptive parent's income and financial account balances and social security numbers, and detailed information about the prospective adoptive parent's extended family members, including surnames, names of employers, names of schools attended, social security numbers, telephone numbers and addresses, and other similarly detailed information about extended family members obtained under subsections (b) and (c) of this section.

When any of the above is not reasonably available, the preplacement assessment shall state why it is unavailable.

(d) The agency shall conduct an investigation for any criminal record as permitted by law. If a prospective adoptive parent is seeking to adopt a minor who is in the custody or placement responsibility of a county department of social services, a county department of social services shall have the prospective adoptive parent's criminal history and the criminal histories of all individuals 18 years of age or older who reside in the prospective adoptive home investigated pursuant to G.S. 48-3-309, and in accordance with G.S. 48-3-309(b), make a determination as to the prospective adoptive parent's fitness to have responsibility for the safety and well-being of children and as to whether other individuals required to be checked are fit for an adoptive child to reside with them in the home.

(e) In the preplacement assessment, the agency shall review the information obtained pursuant to subsections (b), (c), and (d) of this section and evaluate the individual's strengths and weaknesses to be an adoptive parent. The agency shall then determine whether the individual is suitable to be an adoptive parent.

(f) If the agency determines that the individual is suitable to be an adoptive parent, the preplacement assessment shall include specific factors which support that determination.

(g) If the agency determines that the individual is not suitable to be an adoptive parent, the replacement assessment shall state the specific concerns which support that determination. A specific concern is one that reasonably indicates that placement of any minor, or a particular minor, in the home of the individual would pose a significant risk of harm to the well-being of the minor.

(h) In addition to the information and finding required by subsections (c) through (g) of this section, the preplacement assessment must contain a list of the sources of information on which it is based.

(i) The Social Services Commission shall have authority to establish by rule additional standards for preplacement assessments. (1995, c. 457, s. 2; 1998-229, s. 14; 2001-150, s. 8; 2005-114, s. 2; 2007-276, s. 8; 2012-16, s. 5.)

§ 48-3-304. Fees for preplacement assessment.

(a) An agency that prepares a preplacement assessment may charge a reasonable fee for doing so, even if the individual being assessed requests that it not be completed. No fee may be charged except pursuant to a written agreement which must be signed by the individual to be charged prior to the beginning of the assessment. The fee agreement may not be based on the outcome of the assessment or any adoption.

(b) An assessment fee is subject to review by the court pursuant to G.S. 48-2-602 and G.S. 48-2-603 if the person who is assessed files a petition to adopt.

(c) The Department shall set the maximum fees, based on the individual's ability to pay and other factors, which may be charged by county departments of social services. The Department shall require waiver of fees for those unable to pay. Fees collected under this section shall be applied to the costs of preparing preplacement assessments and shall be used by the county department of social services to supplement and not to supplant appropriated funds. (1995, c. 457, s. 2.)

§ 48-3-305. Agency disposition of preplacement assessments.

(a)   The agency shall give a copy of any completed or incomplete preplacement assessment to the individual who was the subject of the assessment. If the assessment contains a finding that an individual is not suitable to be an adoptive parent, the agency shall contemporaneously file the original with the Division.

(b)   The agency shall retain a copy of a completed or incomplete preplacement assessment for at least five years. (1995, c. 457, s. 2.)

§ 48-3-306. Favorable preplacement assessments.

An individual who receives a preplacement assessment containing a finding that the individual is suitable to be an adoptive parent shall provide a copy of the assessment to any person or agency considering the placement of a minor with the individual for adoption and shall also attach a copy of the assessment to any petition to adopt. (1995, c. 457, s. 2.)

§ 48-3-307. Assessments completed after placement.

(a)   If a placement occurs before a preplacement assessment is completed, the prospective adoptive parent shall deliver a copy of the assessment when completed, whether favorable or unfavorable, to the parent or guardian who placed the minor. A prospective adoptive parent, who cannot after the exercise of due diligence personally locate the parent or guardian who placed the minor, may deposit a copy of the preplacement assessment in the United States mail, return receipt requested, addressed to the address of the parent or guardian given in the consent, and the date of receipt by the parent or guardian for purposes of G.S. 48-3-608 shall be deemed to be the date of delivery or last attempted delivery.

(b)   If a petition for adoption is filed before the preplacement assessment is completed, the prospective adoptive parent shall attach to the petition an affidavit explaining why the assessment has not been completed and, upon completion of the assessment, shall file it with the court in which the petition is pending.

(c)   A prospective adoptive parent shall file or cause to be filed a certificate indicating that the prospective adoptive parent has delivered a copy of the assessment to the parent or guardian who placed the minor for adoption. (1995, c. 457, s. 2; 2001-150, s. 9.)

§ 48-3-308. Response to unfavorable preplacement assessment.

(a)   Each agency shall have a procedure for allowing an individual who has received an unfavorable preplacement assessment to have the assessment reviewed by the agency. In addition to the authority in G.S. 131D-10.5, the Social Services Commission shall have authority to adopt rules implementing this section.

(b)   An individual who receives an unfavorable preplacement assessment may, after exhausting the agency's procedures for internal review, prepare and file a written response with the Division and the agency. The Division shall attach the response to the unfavorable assessment.

(c)   The Division shall acknowledge receipt of the response but shall have no authority to take any action with respect to the response.

(d)   If an unfavorable preplacement assessment is completed and filed with the Division and a minor has been placed with a prospective adoptive parent who is the subject of the unfavorable assessment, the Division shall notify the county department of social services, which shall take appropriate action.

(e)   An unfavorable preplacement assessment and any response filed with the Division under this section shall not be public records as set forth in Chapter 132 of the General Statutes. (1995, c. 457, s. 2.)

§ 48-3-309. Mandatory preplacement criminal checks of prospective adoptive parents seeking to adopt a minor who is in the custody or placement responsibility of a county department of social services and mandatory preplacement criminal checks of all individuals 18 years of age or older who reside in the prospective adoptive home.

(a) The Department shall ensure that the criminal histories of all prospective adoptive parents seeking to adopt a minor who is in the custody or placement responsibility of a county department of social services and the criminal histories of all individuals 18 years of age or older who reside in the prospective adoptive home are checked prior to placement and, based on the criminal history, a determination is made as to the prospective adoptive parent's fitness to have responsibility for the safety and well-being of children and whether other individuals required to be checked are fit for an adoptive child to reside with them in the home. The Department shall ensure that all individuals required to be checked are checked prior to placement for county, state, and federal criminal histories.

(b) A county department of social services shall issue an unfavorable preplacement assessment to a prospective adoptive parent if an individual required to submit to a criminal history check pursuant to subsection (a) of this section has a criminal history. A county department of social services shall issue an unfavorable preplacement assessment to a prospective adoptive parent if the county department of social services determines, pursuant to G.S. 48-3-303(e), that, based on other criminal convictions, whether felony or misdemeanor, the prospective adoptive parent is unfit to have responsibility for the safety and well-being of children or other individuals required to be checked are unfit for an adoptive child to reside with them in the home.

(c) The Department of Justice shall provide to the Department of Health and Human Services the criminal history of any individual required to be checked under subsection (a) of this section as requested by the Department and obtained from the State and National Repositories of Criminal Histories. The Department shall provide to the Department of Justice, along with the request, the fingerprints of any individual to be checked, any additional information required by the Department of Justice, and a form consenting to the check of the criminal record and to the use of fingerprints and other identifying information required by the State or National Repositories signed by the individual to be checked. The fingerprints of any individual to be checked shall be forwarded to the State Bureau of Investigation for a search of the State's criminal history record file, and the State Bureau of Investigation shall forward a set of fingerprints to the Federal Bureau of Investigation for a national criminal history record check.

(d)   At the time of the request for a preplacement assessment or at a subsequent time prior to placement, any individual whose criminal history is to be checked shall be furnished with a statement substantially similar to the following:

"NOTICE

MANDATORY CRIMINAL HISTORY CHECK: NORTH CAROLINA LAW REQUIRES THAT A CRIMINAL HISTORY CHECK BE CONDUCTED PRIOR TO PLACEMENT ON PROSPECTIVE ADOPTIVE PARENTS SEEKING TO ADOPT A MINOR WHO IS IN THE CUSTODY OR PLACEMENT RESPONSIBILITY OF A COUNTY DEPARTMENT OF SOCIAL SERVICES AND ON ALL PERSONS 18 YEARS OF AGE OR OLDER WHO RESIDE IN THE PROSPECTIVE ADOPTIVE HOME.

"Criminal history" means a county, State, or federal conviction of a felony by a court of competent jurisdiction or a pending felony indictment of a crime for child abuse or neglect, spousal abuse, a crime against a child, including child pornography, or for a crime involving violence, including rape, sexual assault, or homicide, other than physical assault or battery; a county, State, or federal conviction of a felony by a court of competent jurisdiction or a pending felony indictment for physical assault, battery, or a drug-related offense, if the offense was committed within the past five years; or similar crimes under federal law or under the laws of other states. Your fingerprints will be used to check the criminal history records of the State Bureau of Investigation (SBI) and the Federal Bureau of Investigation (FBI).

If it is determined, based on your criminal history, that you are unfit to have responsibility for the safety and well being of children or have an adoptive child reside with you, you shall have the opportunity to complete, or challenge the accuracy of, the information contained in the SBI or FBI identification records.

If the prospective adoptive parent is denied a favorable preplacement assessment by a county department of social services as a result of a criminal history check as required under G.S. 48-3-309(a), the prospective adoptive parent may request a review of the assessment pursuant to G.S. 48-3-308(a).

Any person who intentionally falsifies any information required to be furnished to conduct the criminal history is guilty of a Class 2 misdemeanor."

Refusal to consent to a criminal history check by any individual required to be checked under G.S. 48-3-309(a) is grounds for the issuance by a county department of social services of an unfavorable preplacement assessment. Any person who intentionally falsifies any information required to be furnished to conduct the criminal history is guilty of a Class 2 misdemeanor.

(e)   The Department shall notify the prospective adoptive parent's supervising county department of social services of the results of the criminal history check. In accordance with the federal and State law regulating the dissemination of the contents of the criminal history file, the Department shall not release or disclose any portion of an individual's criminal history to the prospective adoptive parent or any other individual required to be checked. The Department, however, shall ensure that the prospective adoptive parent or any other individual required to be checked is notified of the individual's right to review the criminal history information, the procedure for completing or challenging the accuracy of the criminal history, and the prospective adoptive parent's right to contest the preplacement assessment of the county department of social services.

A prospective adoptive parent who disagrees with the preplacement assessment of the county department of social services may request a review of the assessment pursuant to G.S. 48-3-308(a).

(f)   All the information that the Department receives through the checking of the criminal history is privileged information and is not a public record but is for the exclusive use of the Department and those persons authorized under this section to receive the information. The Department may destroy the information after it is used for the purposes authorized by this section after one calendar year.

(g)   There is no liability for negligence on the part of a State or local agency, or the employees of a State or local agency, arising from any action taken or omission by any of them in carrying out the provisions of this section. The immunity established by this subsection shall not extend to gross negligence, wanton conduct, or intentional wrongdoing that would otherwise be actionable. The immunity established by this subsection shall be deemed to have been waived to the extent of indemnification by insurance, indemnification under

Article 31A of Chapter 143 of the General Statutes, and to the extent sovereign immunity is waived under the Tort Claims Act, as set forth in Article 31 of Chapter 143 of the General Statutes.

(h) The Department of Justice shall perform the State and national criminal history checks on prospective adoptive parents seeking to adopt a minor in the custody or placement responsibility of a county department of social services and all individuals 18 years of age or older who reside in the prospective adoptive home and shall charge the Department of Health and Human Services a reasonable fee only for conducting the checks of the national criminal history records authorized by this section. The Division of Social Services, Department of Health and Human Services, shall bear the costs of implementing this section. (1998-229, s. 15; 2005-114, s. 1; 2007-276, ss. 9, 10.)

Part 4. Transfer of Physical Custody of Minor by Health Care Facility or Attending Practitioner for Purposes of Adoption.

§ 48-3-401. "Health care facility" and "attending practitioner" defined.

As used in this Article:

(1) "Health care facility" includes a hospital and maternity home; and

(2) "Attending practitioner" includes a physician, licensed nurse, or other licensed professional provider of health care who assists in a birth. (1995, c. 457, s. 2.)

§ 48-3-402. Authorization required to transfer physical custody.

(a) A health care facility or attending practitioner who has physical custody may release a minor for the purpose of adoption to a prospective adoptive parent or agency not legally entitled to the custody of the minor if, in the presence of an employee of the health care facility or the attending practitioner:

(1) A parent, guardian, or other person or entity having legal custody of the minor signs an authorization of the transfer of physical custody; and

(2) The authorization states that the release is for the purpose of adoption.

(b) The health care facility or attending practitioner shall retain the authorization described in subsection (a) of this section for at least one year. (1995, c. 457, s. 2.)

Part 5. Custody of Minors Pending Final Decree of Adoption.

§ 48-3-501. Petitioner entitled to custody in direct placement adoptions.

Unless the court orders otherwise, when a parent or guardian places the adoptee directly with the petitioner, the petitioner acquires that parent's or guardian's right to legal and continuing physical custody of the adoptee and becomes a person responsible for the care and support of the adoptee, after the earliest of:

(1) The execution of consent by the parent or guardian who placed the adoptee;

(2) The filing of a petition for adoption by the petitioner; or

(3) The execution of a document by a parent or guardian having legal and physical custody of a minor temporarily transferring custody to the petitioner, pending the execution of a consent. (1949, c. 300; 1995, c. 457, s. 2.)

§ 48-3-502. Agency entitled to custody in placement by agency.

(a) Unless the court orders otherwise, during a proceeding for adoption in which an agency places the adoptee with the petitioner:

(1) The agency retains legal but not physical custody of the adoptee until the adoption decree becomes final; but

(2) The agency may delegate to the petitioner responsibility for the care and support of the adoptee.

(b) Before a decree of adoption becomes final, the agency may for cause petition the court to dismiss the adoption proceeding and to restore full legal and physical custody of the minor to the agency; and the court may grant the petition on finding that it is in the best interest of the minor. (1995, c. 457, s. 2.)

Part 6. Consent to Adoption.

§ 48-3-601. Persons whose consent to adoption is required.

Unless consent is not required under G.S. 48-3-603, a petition to adopt a minor may be granted only if consent to the adoption has been executed by:

(1) The minor to be adopted if 12 or more years of age;

(2) In a direct placement, by:

a. The mother of the minor;

b. Any man who may or may not be the biological father of the minor but who:

1. Is or was married to the mother of the minor if the minor was born during the marriage or within 280 days after the marriage is terminated or the parties have separated pursuant to a written separation agreement or an order of separation entered under Chapters 50 or 50B of the General Statutes or a similar order of separation entered by a court in another jurisdiction;

2. Attempted to marry the mother of the minor before the minor's birth, by a marriage solemnized in apparent compliance with law, although the attempted marriage is or could be declared invalid, and the minor is born during the attempted marriage, or within 280 days after the attempted marriage is terminated by annulment, declaration of invalidity, divorce, or, in the absence of a judicial proceeding, by the cessation of cohabitation;

3. Before the filing of the petition, has legitimated the minor under the law of any state;

4. Before the earlier of the filing of the petition or the date of a hearing under G.S. 48-2-206, has acknowledged his paternity of the minor and

I. Is obligated to support the minor under written agreement or by court order;

II. Has provided, in accordance with his financial means, reasonable and consistent payments for the support of the biological mother during or after the term of pregnancy, or the support of the minor, or both, which may include the payment of medical expenses, living expenses, or other tangible means of support, and has regularly visited or communicated, or attempted to visit or communicate with the biological mother during or after the term of pregnancy, or with the minor, or with both; or

III. After the minor's birth but before the minor's placement for adoption or the mother's relinquishment, has married or attempted to marry the mother of the minor by a marriage solemnized in apparent compliance with law, although the attempted marriage is or could be declared invalid; or

5. Before the filing of the petition, has received the minor into his home and openly held out the minor as his biological child; or

6. Is the adoptive father of the minor; and

c. A guardian of the minor; and

(3) In an agency placement by:

a. The agency that placed the minor for adoption; and

b. Each individual described in subdivision (2) of this section who has not relinquished the minor pursuant to Part 7 of Article 3 of this Chapter. (1949, c. 300; 1953, c. 906; 1957, c. 90; c. 778, ss. 3-5; 1961, c. 186; 1969, c. 534, s.1; c. 911, ss. 6, 7; c. 982; 1971, c. 1093, s. 13; c. 1185, s. 17; 1973, c. 1354, s. 5; 1975, c. 321, s. 1; c. 702, ss. 1-3; c. 714; 1977, c. 879, ss. 2, 3, 5; 1979, c. 107, s. 7; 2nd Sess., c. 1088, s. 1; 1983, cc. 30, 292; c. 454, ss. 2, 6; 1985, c. 758, ss. 5-11; 1987, c. 371, s. 1; 1995, c. 457, s. 2; 1997-215, s. 16.)

§ 48-3-602. Consent of incompetent parents.

If a parent as described in G.S. 48-3-601 has been adjudicated incompetent, then the court shall appoint a guardian ad litem for that parent and, unless the child already has a guardian, a guardian ad litem for the child to make a full investigation as to whether the adoption should proceed. The investigation shall include an evaluation of the parent's current condition and any reasonable likelihood that the parent will be restored to competency, the relationship between the child and the incompetent parent, alternatives to adoption, and any other relevant fact or circumstance. If the court determines after a hearing on the matter that it will be in the best interest of the child for the adoption to proceed, the court shall order the guardian ad litem of the parent to execute for that parent a consent as provided in this Part or a relinquishment as provided in Part 7 of this Article. (1949, c. 300; 1953, c. 906; 1961, c. 186; 1969, c. 911, s. 7; c. 982; 1975, c. 702, ss. 1-3; 1977, c. 879, s. 5; 1985, c. 758, ss. 10, 11; 1995, c. 457, s. 2; 1997-215, s. 11(d); 2012-16, s. 6.)

§ 48-3-603. Persons whose consent is not required.

(a) Consent to an adoption of a minor is not required of a person or entity whose consent is not required under G.S. 48-3-601, or any of the following:

(1) An individual whose parental rights and duties have been terminated under Article 11 of Chapter 7B of the General Statutes or by a court of competent jurisdiction in another state.

(2) A man described in G.S. 48-3-601(2), other than an adoptive father, if (i) the man has been judicially determined not to be the father of the minor to be adopted, or (ii) another man has been judicially determined to be the father of the minor to be adopted.

(3) Repealed by Session Laws 1997-215, s. 11(a).

(4) An individual who has relinquished parental rights or guardianship powers, including the right to consent to adoption, to an agency pursuant to Part 7 of this Article.

(5) A man who is not married to the minor's birth mother and who, after the conception of the minor, has executed a notarized statement denying paternity or disclaiming any interest in the minor.

(6) A deceased parent or the personal representative of a deceased parent's estate.

(7) An individual listed in G.S. 48-3-601 who has not executed a consent or a relinquishment and who fails to respond to a notice of the adoption proceeding within 30 days after the service of the notice.

(8) An individual notified under G.S. 48-2-206 who does not respond in a timely manner or whose consent is not required as determined by the court.

(9) (See editor's note) An individual whose actions resulted in a conviction under G.S. 14-27.2, G.S. 14-27.2A, or G.S. 14-27.3 and the conception of the minor to be adopted.

(b) The court may issue an order dispensing with the consent of the following:

(1) A guardian or an agency that placed the minor upon a finding that the consent is being withheld contrary to the best interest of the minor.

(2) A minor 12 or more years of age upon a finding that it is not in the best interest of the minor to require the consent. (1949, c. 300; 1957, c. 90; c. 778, ss. 3, 4; 1969, c. 534, s. 1; 1971, c. 1185, s. 17; 1975, c. 321, s. 1; c. 714; 1977, c. 879, ss. 2, 3; 1979, c. 107, s. 7; 2nd Sess., c. 1088, s. 1; 1983, c. 292; 1985, c. 758, ss. 5-9; 1987, c. 371, s. 1; 1995, c. 457, s. 2; 1997-215, ss. 11(a), 17; 1998-202, s. 13(o); 2004-128, s. 9; 2013-236, s. 7.)

§ 48-3-604. Execution of consent: timing.

(a) A man whose consent is required under G.S. 48-3-601 may execute a consent to adoption either before or after the child is born.

(b) The mother of a minor child may execute a consent to adoption at any time after the child is born but not sooner.

(c) A guardian of a minor to be adopted may execute a consent to adoption at any time.

(d) An agency licensed by the Department or a county department of social services in this State that places a minor for adoption shall execute its consent no later than 30 days after being served with notice of the proceeding for adoption.

(e) A minor to be adopted who is 12 years of age or older may execute a consent at any time. (1995, c. 457, s. 2.)

§ 48-3-605. Execution of consent: procedures.

(a) A consent executed by a parent or guardian or by a minor to be adopted who is 12 years of age or older must conform substantially to the requirements in G.S. 48-3-606 and must be signed and acknowledged under oath before an individual authorized to administer oaths or take acknowledgments.

(b) A parent who has not reached the age of 18 years shall have legal capacity to give consent to adoption and to release that parent's rights in a child, and shall be as fully bound as if the parent had attained 18 years of age.

(c) An individual before whom a consent is signed and acknowledged under subsection (a) of this section shall certify in writing that to the best of the individual's knowledge or belief, the parent, guardian, or minor to be adopted executing the consent has met each of the following:

(1) Read, or had read to him or her, and understood the consent.

(2) Signed the consent voluntarily.

(3) Been given an original or a copy of his or her fully executed consent.

(4) Been advised that counseling services may be available through county departments of social services or licensed child-placing agencies.

(d) A consent by an agency must be executed by the executive head or another authorized employee and must be signed and acknowledged under oath in the presence of an individual authorized to administer oaths or take acknowledgments.

(e)   A consent signed in another state or in another country in accord with the procedure of that state or country shall not be invalid solely because of failure to comply with the formalities set out in this Chapter.

(f)   A consent to the adoption of an Indian child, as that term is defined in the Indian Child Welfare Act, 25 U.S.C. § 1901 et seq., must meet the requirements of that Act. (1949, c. 300; 1971, c. 1231, s. 1; 1995, c. 457, s. 2; 2013-236, s. 8.)

§ 48-3-606. Content of consent; mandatory provisions.

A consent required from a minor to be adopted, a parent, or a guardian under G.S. 48-3-601 must be in writing and state each of the following:

(1)   The date and place of the execution of the consent.

(2)   The name, date of birth, and permanent address of the individual executing the consent.

(3)   The date of birth or the expected delivery date, the sex, and the name of the minor to be adopted, if known.

(4)   That the individual executing the document is voluntarily consenting to the transfer of legal and physical custody to, and the adoption of the minor to be adopted by, the identified prospective adoptive parent.

(5)   The name of a person and an address where any notice of revocation may be sent.

(6)   That the individual executing the document understands that after the consent is signed and acknowledged in accord with the procedures set forth in G.S. 48-3-605, it may be revoked in accord with G.S. 48-3-608, but that it is otherwise final and irrevocable and may not be withdrawn or set aside except under a circumstance set forth in G.S. 48-3-609.

(7)   That the consent shall be valid and binding and is not affected by any oral or separate written agreement between the individual executing the consent and the adoptive parent.

(8) That the individual executing the consent has not received or been promised any money or anything of value for the consent, and has not received or been promised any money or anything of value in relation to the adoption of the child except for lawful payments that are itemized on a schedule attached to the consent.

(9) That the individual executing the consent understands that when the adoption is final, all rights and obligations of the adoptee's former parents or guardian with respect to the adoptee will be extinguished, and every aspect of the legal relationship between the adoptee and the former parent or guardian will be terminated.

(10) The name and address of the court, if known, in which the petition for adoption has been or will be filed.

(11) That the individual executing the consent waives notice of any proceeding for adoption.

(12) If the individual executing the document is the minor to be adopted or the person placing the minor for adoption, a statement that the adoption shall be by a specific named adoptive parent.

(13) If the individual executing the document is the person placing the minor for adoption, that the individual executing the consent has provided the prospective adoptive parent, or the prospective adoptive parent's attorney, with the written document required by G.S. 48-3-205.

(14) That the person executing the consent has:

a. Repealed by Session Laws 2013-236, s. 9, effective July 3, 2013.

b. Been advised that counseling services may be available through county departments of social services or licensed child-placing agencies; and

c. Been advised of the right to employ independent legal counsel. (1995, c. 457, s. 2; 2013-236, s. 9.)

§ 48-3-607. Consequences of consent.

(a) A consent executed pursuant to G.S. 48-3-605 and G.S. 48-3-606 may be revoked as provided in G.S. 48-3-608. A consent is otherwise final and irrevocable except under a circumstance set forth in G.S. 48-3-609.

(b) Except as provided in subsection (c) of this section, the consent of a parent, guardian, or agency that placed a minor for adoption pursuant to Part 2 of this Article vests legal and physical custody of the minor in the prospective adoptive parent and empowers this individual to petition the court to adopt the minor.

(c) Any other parental right and duty of a parent who executed a consent is not terminated until either the decree of adoption becomes final or the relationship of parent and child is otherwise terminated, whichever comes first. Until termination, the minor remains the child of a parent who executed a consent for purposes of any inheritance, succession, insurance, arrears of child support, and other benefit or claim that the minor may have from, through, or against the parent. (1949, c. 300; 1957, c. 778, s. 6; 1961, c. 186; 1969, c. 982; 1983, cc. 83, 688; 1985, c. 758, s. 12; 1987, c. 541, s. 1; 1991, c. 667, s. 1; 1995, c. 457, s. 2.)

§ 48-3-608. Revocation of consent.

(a) A consent to the adoption of any infant who is in utero or any minor may be revoked within seven days following the day on which it is executed, inclusive of weekends and holidays. If the final day of the revocation period falls on a Saturday, Sunday, or a legal holiday when North Carolina courthouses are closed for transactions, then the revocation period extends to the next business day. The individual who gave the consent may revoke by giving written notice to the person specified in the consent. Notice may be given by personal delivery, overnight delivery service, or registered or certified mail, return receipt requested. If notice is given by mail, notice is deemed complete when it is deposited in the United States mail, postage prepaid, addressed to the person to whom consent was given at the address specified in the consent. If notice is given by overnight delivery service, notice is deemed complete on the date it is deposited with the service as shown by the receipt from the service, with delivery charges paid by the sender, addressed to the person to whom consent was given at the address specified in the consent.

(b) In a direct placement, if:

(1) A preplacement assessment is required, and

(2) Placement occurs before the preplacement assessment is given to the parent or guardian who is placing the minor,

then that individual's time under subsection (a) of this section to revoke any consent previously given shall be either five business days after the date the individual receives the preplacement assessment prepared substantially in conformance with the requirements of G.S. 48-3-303, or the remainder of the time provided in subsection (a) of this section, whichever is longer. The date of receipt is the earlier of the date of actual receipt or the date established pursuant to G.S. 48-3-307.

(c) If a person who has physical custody places the minor with the prospective adoptive parent and thereafter revokes a consent pursuant to this section, the prospective adoptive parent shall, immediately upon request, return the minor to that person. The revocation restores the right to physical custody and any right to legal custody to the person who placed the minor and divests the prospective adoptive parent of any right to legal or physical custody and any further responsibility for the care and support of the minor. In any subsequent proceeding, the court shall award reasonable attorneys' fees to the person who revoked if the prospective adoptive parent fails upon request to return the minor.

(d) If a person other than a person described in subsection (c) of this section revokes a consent pursuant to this section and this person's consent is required, the adoption cannot proceed until another consent is obtained or the person's parental rights are terminated. The person who revoked consent is not thereby entitled to physical custody of the minor. If the minor whose consent is required revokes consent, the county department of social services shall be notified for appropriate action.

(e) A second consent to adoption by the same adoptive parents is irrevocable. (1949, c. 300; 1957, c. 778, s. 6; 1961, c. 186; 1969, c. 982; 1983, cc. 83, 688; 1985, c. 758, s. 12; 1987, c. 541, s. 1; 1991, c. 667, s. 1; 1995, c. 457, s. 2; 1997-215, s. 8(a); 2001-150, s. 10; 2009-185, s. 5; 2012-16, s. 7.)

§ 48-3-609. Challenges to validity of consent.

(a) A consent shall be void if:

(1) Before the entry of the adoption decree, the individual who executed the consent establishes by clear and convincing evidence that it was obtained by fraud or duress;

(2) The prospective adoptive parent and the individual who executed the consent mutually agree in writing to set it aside;

(3) The petition to adopt is voluntarily dismissed with prejudice; or

(4) The court dismisses the petition to adopt and no appeal has been taken, or the dismissal has been affirmed on appeal and all appeals have been exhausted.

(b) If the consent of an individual who previously had legal and physical custody of a minor becomes void under subsection (a) of this section and no grounds exist under G.S. 48-3-603 for dispensing with this individual's consent, the court shall order the return of the minor to the custody of that individual and shall dismiss any pending adoption proceeding. If the court has reasonable cause to believe that the return will be detrimental to the minor, the court shall not order the return of the minor but shall notify the county department of social services for appropriate action.

(c) If the consent of an individual who did not previously have physical custody of a minor becomes void under subsection (a) of this section and no ground exists under G.S. 48-3-603 for dispensing with this individual's consent, the court shall dismiss any pending proceeding for adoption. If return of the minor is not ordered under subsection (b) of this section, the court shall notify the county department of social services for appropriate action. (1995, c. 457, s. 2.)

§ 48-3-610. Collateral agreements.

If a person executing a consent and the prospective adoptive parent or parents enter into an agreement regarding visitation, communication, support, and any other rights and duties with respect to the minor, this agreement shall not be a condition precedent to the consent itself, failure to perform shall not invalidate a consent already given, and the agreement itself shall not be enforceable. (1995, c. 457, s. 2.)

Part 7. Relinquishment of Minor for Adoption.

§ 48-3-701. Individuals who may relinquish minor; timing.

(a) A parent or guardian may relinquish all parental rights or guardianship powers, including the right to consent to adoption, to an agency. If both parents are married to each other and living together, both parents must act jointly in relinquishing a child to an agency.

(b) The mother of a minor child may execute a relinquishment at any time after the child is born but not sooner. A man whose consent is required under G.S. 48-3-601 may execute a relinquishment either before or after the child is born.

(c) A guardian may execute a relinquishment at any time. (1949, c. 300; 1953, c. 906; 1961, c. 186; 1969, c. 911, s. 7; c. 982; 1975, c. 702, ss. 1-3; 1977, c. 879, s. 5; 1985, c. 758, ss. 10, 11; 1995, c. 457, s. 2.)

§ 48-3-702. Procedures for relinquishment.

(a) A relinquishment executed by a parent or guardian must conform substantially to the requirements in this Part and must be signed and acknowledged under oath before an individual authorized to administer oaths or take acknowledgments.

(b) The provisions of G.S. 48-3-605(b), (e), and (f), also apply to a relinquishment executed under this Part.

(b1) An individual before whom a relinquishment is signed and acknowledged under subsection (a) of this section shall certify in writing that to the best of the individual's knowledge or belief, the parent, guardian, or minor to be adopted executing the relinquishment has met each of the following:

(1) Read, or had read to him or her, and understood the relinquishment.

(2) Signed the relinquishment voluntarily.

(3) Been given an original or copy of his or her fully executed relinquishment.

(4) Been advised that counseling services are available through the agency to which the relinquishment is given.

(c) An agency that accepts a relinquishment shall furnish each parent or guardian who signs the relinquishment a letter or other writing indicating the agency's willingness to accept that person's relinquishment. (1995, c. 457, s. 2; 1997-215, s. 7(a); 2013-236, s. 10.)

§ 48-3-703. Content of relinquishment; mandatory provisions.

(a) A relinquishment executed by a parent or guardian under G.S. 48-3-701 must be in writing and state the following:

(1) The date and place of the execution of the relinquishment.

(2) The name, date of birth, and permanent address of the individual executing the relinquishment.

(3) The date of birth or the expected delivery date, the sex, and the name of the minor, if known.

(4) The name and address of the agency to which the minor is being relinquished.

(5) That the individual voluntarily consents to the permanent transfer of legal and physical custody of the minor to the agency for the purposes of adoption, and

a. The placement of the minor for adoption with a prospective adoptive parent selected by the agency; or

b. The placement of the minor for adoption with a prospective adoptive parent selected by the agency and agreed upon by the individual executing the relinquishment.

(6) That the individual executing the relinquishment understands that after the relinquishment is signed and acknowledged in the manner provided in G.S. 48-3-702, it may be revoked in accord with G.S. 48-3-706 but that it is otherwise final and irrevocable except under the circumstances set forth in G.S. 48-3-707.

(7) That the relinquishment shall be valid and binding and shall not be affected by any oral or separate written agreement between the individual executing the consent and the agency.

(8) That the individual executing the relinquishment understands that when the adoption is final, all rights and duties of the individual executing the relinquishment with respect to the minor will be extinguished and all other aspects of the legal relationship between the minor child and the parent will be terminated.

(9) That the individual executing the relinquishment has not received or been promised any money or anything of value for the relinquishment of the minor, and has not received or been promised any money or anything of value in relation to the relinquishment or the adoption of the minor except for lawful payments that are itemized on a schedule attached to the relinquishment.

(10) That the individual executing the relinquishment waives notice of any proceeding for adoption.

(11) That the individual executing the relinquishment has provided the agency with the written document required by G.S. 48-3-205, or that the individual has provided the agency with signed releases that will permit the agency to compile the information required by G.S. 48-3-205.

(12) That the individual executing the relinquishment has:

a. Repealed by Session Laws 2013-236, s. 9, effective July 3, 2013.

b. Been advised that counseling services are available through the agency to which the relinquishment is given; and

c. Been advised of the right to employ independent legal counsel.

(b) Reserved. (1995, c. 457, s. 2; 2013-236, s. 11.)

§ 48-3-704. Content of relinquishment; optional provisions.

In addition to the mandatory provisions listed in G.S. 48-3-703, a relinquishment may also state that the relinquishment may be revoked upon notice by the agency that an adoption by a specific prospective adoptive parent, named or described in the relinquishment is not completed. In this event the parent's time to revoke a relinquishment is 10 days, inclusive of weekends and holidays, from the date the parent receives such notice from the agency. The revocation shall be in writing and delivered in a manner specified in G.S. 48-3-706(a) for revocation of relinquishments. An agency, which after the exercise of due diligence cannot personally locate the parent entitled to this notice, may deposit a copy of the notice in the United States mail, return receipt requested, addressed to the address of the parent given in the relinquishment, and the date of receipt by the parent is deemed to be the date of delivery or last attempted delivery. If a parent does not revoke the relinquishment in the time and manner provided in this section, the relinquishment is deemed a general relinquishment to the agency, and the agency may place the child for adoption with a prospective adoptive parent selected by the agency. (1995, c. 457, s. 2; 1997-215, s. 19.1(a); 2001-208, s. 15; 2001-487, s. 101.)

§ 48-3-705. Consequences of relinquishment.

(a) A relinquishment executed pursuant to G.S. 48-3-702 through G.S. 48-3-704 may be revoked as provided in G.S. 48-3-706 and is otherwise final and irrevocable except under a circumstance set forth in G.S. 48-3-707.

(b) Upon execution, a relinquishment by a parent or guardian entitled under G.S. 48-3-201 to place a minor for adoption:

(1) Vests legal and physical custody of the minor in the agency; and

(2) Empowers the agency to place the minor for adoption with a prospective adoptive parent selected in the manner specified in the relinquishment.

(c) A relinquishment terminates:

(1) Any right and duty of the individual who executed the relinquishment with respect to the legal and physical custody of the minor.

(2) The right to consent to the minor's adoption.

(3) Repealed by Session Laws 1997-215, s. 19.1(b).

(d) Except as provided in subsection (c) of this section, parental rights and duties of a parent who executed a relinquishment are not terminated until the decree of adoption becomes final or the parental relationship is otherwise legally terminated, whichever occurs first. Until termination the minor remains the child of a parent who executed a relinquishment for purposes of any inheritance, succession, insurance, arrears of child support, and other benefit or claim that the minor may have from, through, or against the parent. (1949, c. 300; 1953, c. 906; 1957, c. 778, s. 6; 1961, c. 186; 1967, c. 926, s. 1; 1969, c. 911, ss. 7, 9; c. 982; 1973, c. 476, s. 138; 1975, c. 702, ss. 1-3; 1977, c. 879, s. 5; 1983, c. 454, ss. 4, 7; cc. 83, 688; 1985, c. 758, ss. 10-12; 1987, c. 541, s. 1; 1991, c. 667, s. 1; 1995, c. 457, s. 2; 1997-215, s. 19.1(b).)

§ 48-3-706. Revocation of relinquishments.

(a) A relinquishment of any infant who is in utero or any minor may be revoked within seven days following the day on which it is executed by the infant or minor's parent or guardian, inclusive of weekends and holidays. If the final day of the period falls on a Saturday, Sunday, or a legal holiday when North Carolina courthouses are closed for transactions, then the revocation period extends to the next business day. The individual who gave the relinquishment may revoke by giving written notice to the agency to which the relinquishment was given. Notice may be given by personal delivery, overnight delivery service, or registered or certified mail, return receipt requested. If notice is given by mail, notice is deemed complete when it is deposited in the United States mail, postage prepaid, addressed to the agency at the agency's address as given in the relinquishment. If notice is given by overnight delivery service, notice is deemed complete on the date it is deposited with the service as shown by the receipt from the service, with delivery charges paid by the sender, addressed to the agency at the agency's address as given in the relinquishment.

(b)   If a person who has physical custody relinquishes a minor and thereafter revokes a relinquishment pursuant to this section, the agency shall upon request return the minor to that person. The revocation restores the right to physical custody and any right to legal custody to the person who relinquished the minor and divests the agency of any right to legal or physical custody and any further responsibility for the care and support of the minor. In any subsequent proceeding, the court may award the person who revoked reasonable attorneys' fees from a prospective adoptive parent with whom the minor was placed who refuses to return the minor and from the agency if the agency fails to cooperate in securing the minor's return.

(c)   If a person other than a person described in subsection (b) of this section revokes a relinquishment pursuant to this section and this person's consent is required, the agency may not give consent for the adoption and the adoption cannot proceed until another relinquishment or a consent is obtained or parental rights are terminated. The person who revoked the relinquishment is not thereby entitled to physical custody of the minor.

(d)   A second relinquishment for placement with the same adoptive parent selected by the agency and agreed upon by the person executing the relinquishment, or a second general relinquishment for placement by the agency with any adoptive parent selected by the agency, is irrevocable. (1949, c. 300; 1957, c. 778, s. 6; 1961, c. 186; 1969, c. 982; 1983, cc. 83, 688; 1985, c. 758, s. 12; 1987, c. 541, s. 1; 1991, c. 667, s. 1; 1995, c. 457, s. 2; 1997-456, s. 56.2(a); 2001-150, s. 11; 2009-185, s. 6.)

§ 48-3-707. Challenges to validity of relinquishments.

(a)   A relinquishment shall become void if any of the following occur:

(1)   Before the entry of the adoption decree, the individual who executed the relinquishment establishes by clear and convincing evidence that it was obtained by fraud or duress.

(2)   Before placement with a prospective adoptive parent occurs, the agency and the person relinquishing the minor agree to rescind the relinquishment.

(3) After placement with a prospective adoptive parent occurs, but before the entry of the adoption decree, the agency, the person relinquishing the minor, and the prospective adoptive parent agree to rescind the relinquishment.

(4) Upon motion of a county department of social services or licensed child-placing agency under G.S. 7B-909, the court orders that the relinquishment shall be voided based on a finding that another consent or relinquishment necessary for an adoption cannot be obtained and that no further steps are being taken to terminate the parental rights of the parent from whom the consent or relinquishment has not been obtained.

(b) A relinquishment may be revoked upon the happening of a condition expressly provided for in the relinquishment pursuant to G.S. 48-3-704.

(c) If the relinquishment of an individual who previously had legal and physical custody of a minor is set aside under subsection (a) or (b) of this section and no grounds exist under G.S. 48-3-603 for dispensing with this individual's consent, the court shall order the return of the minor to the custody of that individual, and shall dismiss any pending proceeding for adoption. If the court has reasonable cause to believe that the return will be detrimental to the minor, the court shall not order the return of the minor but shall notify the county department of social services for appropriate action.

(d) If the relinquishment of an individual who did not previously have physical custody of a minor is set aside under subsection (a) or (b) of this section, and no grounds exist under G.S. 48-3-603 for dispensing with this individual's consent, the court shall dismiss any pending proceeding for adoption. If return of the minor is not ordered under subsection (c) of this section, the court shall notify the county department of social services for appropriate action. (1995, c. 457, s. 2; 1997-215, s. 19.1(c); 2012-16, s. 8; 2013-236, s. 12.)

Article 4.

Adoption of a Minor Stepchild by Stepparent.

§ 48-4-100. Application of Article.

This Article shall apply to the adoption of minors by their stepparents. (1995, c. 457, s. 2.)

§ 48-4-101. Who may file a petition to adopt a minor stepchild.

A stepparent may file a petition under this Article to adopt a minor who is the child of the stepparent's spouse if:

(1)   The parent who is the spouse has legal and physical custody of the child, and the child has resided primarily with this parent and the stepparent during the six months immediately preceding the filing of the petition;

(2)   The spouse is deceased or incompetent but, before dying or being adjudicated incompetent, had legal and physical custody of the child, and the child has resided primarily with the stepparent during the six months immediately preceding the filing of the petition; or

(3)   For cause, the court permits a stepparent who does not meet the requirements of subdivisions (1) and (2) of this section to file a petition. (1995, c. 457, s. 2.)

§ 48-4-102. Consent to adoption of stepchild.

Except under circumstances described in G.S. 48-3-603, a petition to adopt a minor stepchild may be granted only if consent to the adoption has been executed by the adoptee if 12 or more years of age; and

(1)   The adoptee's parents as described in G.S. 48-3-601; and

(2)   Any guardian of the adoptee.

The consent of an incompetent parent may be given pursuant to the procedures in G.S. 48-3-602. (1949, c. 300; 1957, c. 778, s. 5; 1969, c. 911, s. 6; 1971, c. 1093, s. 13; 1973, c. 1354, s. 5; 1983, c. 30; c. 454, ss. 2, 6; 1995, c. 457, s. 2; 1997-215, s. 11(c).)

§ 48-4-103. Execution and content of consent to adoption by stepparent.

(a) A consent executed by a parent who is the stepparent's spouse:

(1) Must be signed and acknowledged before an individual authorized to administer oaths or take acknowledgments;

(2) Must be in writing and state or contain:

a. The statements required by G.S. 48-3-606, except for those required by subdivisions (4), (9), (12), and (13) of that section;

b. That the parent executing the consent has legal and physical custody of the child and is voluntarily consenting to the adoption of the child by the stepparent;

c. That the adoption will not terminate the legal relation of parent and child between the parent executing the consent and the child; and

d. That the adoption will terminate the legal relation of parent and child between the adoptee and the adoptee's other parent, including all right of the adoptee to inherit as a child from or through the other parent, and will extinguish any existing court order of custody, visitation, or communication with the adoptee, except that the other parent will remain liable for past-due child support payments unless legally released from this obligation.

(b) A consent executed by a minor stepchild's parent who is not the stepparent's spouse:

(1) Must be signed and acknowledged before an individual authorized to administer oaths or take acknowledgments; and

(2) Must be in writing and state or contain:

a. The statements required by G.S. 48-3-606, except for those required by subdivisions (4), (9), (12), and (13) of that section;

b. That the parent executing the consent is voluntarily consenting to:

1. The transfer of any right the parent has to legal or physical custody of the child to the child's other parent and stepparent, and

2. The adoption of the child by the stepparent; and

c. That the adoption will terminate the legal relation of parent and child between the adoptee and the parent executing the consent, including all rights of the adoptee to inherit as a child from or through the parent, and will extinguish any court order of custody, visitation, or communication with the adoptee, except that the parent executing the consent will remain liable for past-due child support payments unless legally released from this obligation.

(c) A consent executed by the guardian of a minor stepchild:

(1) Must be signed and acknowledged before an individual authorized to administer oaths or take acknowledgments; and

(2) Must be in writing and state or contain:

a. The statements required by G.S. 48-3-606, except for those required by subdivisions (4), (9), (12), and (13) of that section;

b. A statement that the guardian is voluntarily consenting to:

1. The transfer of any right the guardian has to legal or physical custody of the adoptee to the adoptive stepparent; and

2. The adoption of the adoptee by the stepparent;

c. That the adoption will not terminate the legal relation of parent and child between a parent who is or was the stepparent's spouse and the adoptee;

d. That the adoption will terminate the legal relation of parent and child between the adoptee and a parent who is not or has not been the stepparent's spouse, including all right of the adoptee to inherit from or through that parent, and will extinguish any court order of custody, visitation, or communication with the adoptee, except that a parent whose relation to the adoptee is terminated by the adoption will remain liable for past-due child support payments unless legally released from this obligation.

(d) G.S. 48-3-608(a) applies to consents executed pursuant to subsections (a) through (c) of this section. Unless so revoked, the consent is final and irrevocable except under a circumstance set forth in G.S. 48-3-609.

(e) A consent executed by an adoptee in a proceeding for adoption by a stepparent must be signed and acknowledged under oath before an individual authorized to administer oaths or take acknowledgments. The minor may revoke the consent at any time before the decree is entered by filing written notice with the court in which the petition is pending. (1949, c. 300; 1957, c. 778, s. 6; 1961, c. 186; 1969, c. 982; 1983, cc. 83, 688; 1985, c. 758, s. 12; 1987, c. 541, s. 1; 1991, c. 667, s. 1; 1995, c. 457, s. 2.)

§ 48-4-104: Repealed by Session Laws 1997-215, s. 12(b).

§ 48-4-105. Visitation awards to grandparents pursuant to Chapter 50 of the General Statutes.

(a) An adoption under this Article does not terminate or otherwise affect visitation rights awarded to a biological grandparent of a minor pursuant to G.S. 50-13.2.

(b) An adoption under this Article does not affect the right of a biological grandparent to petition for visitation rights pursuant to G.S. 50-13.2A or G.S. 50-13.5(j). (1949, c. 300; 1953, c. 824; 1955, c. 813, s. 5; 1963, c. 967; 1967, c. 619, s. 5; 1983, c. 454, s. 6; 1985, c. 67, ss. 1-4; c. 575, s. 1; 1995, c. 457, s. 2.)

Article 5.

Adoption of Adults.

§ 48-5-100. Application of Article.

This Article shall apply to the adoption of adults, including married and emancipated minors. (1995, c. 457, s. 2.)

§ 48-5-101. Who may file for a petition to adopt an adult.

(a) An adult may adopt another adult, except for the spouse of the adopting adult, pursuant to this Article.

(b) If a prospective adoptive parent is married, both spouses must join in the petition unless the prospective adoptive parent is the adoptee's stepparent or unless the court waives this requirement for cause. (1967, c. 880, s. 3; 1969, c. 21, ss. 3-6; 1971, c. 1231, s. 1; 1973, c. 849, s. 3; 1975, c. 91; 1981, c. 657; 1989, c. 208; c. 727, s. 219(4); 1993, c. 553, s. 14; 1995, c. 457, s. 2.)

§ 48-5-102. Consent to adoption.

(a) Consent to the adoption of an adult is required only of:

(1) The adult being adopted; and

(2) The spouse of the petitioner in an adoption by the adult's stepparent, unless the court waives this requirement for cause.

(b) The consent of the adult being adopted must:

(1) Be in writing and be signed and acknowledged before an individual authorized to administer oaths or take acknowledgments;

(2) State that the adult agrees to assume toward the adoptive parent the legal relation of parent and child and to have all of the rights and be subject to all of the duties of that relationship; and

(3) State that the adult understands the consequences the adoption may have for rights of inheritance, property, or support, including the loss of nonvested inheritance rights which existed prior to the adoption and the acquisition of new inheritance rights.

(c) The consent of the spouse of the petitioner in a stepparent adoption:

(1) Must be in writing and be signed and acknowledged before an individual authorized to administer oaths or take acknowledgments; and

(2) Must state that the spouse:

a. Consents to the proposed adoption;

b. Understands that the adoption may diminish the amount the spouse might take from the petitioner through intestate succession or by dissenting to the petitioner's will and may also diminish the amount of other entitlements that may become due the spouse and any other children of the petitioner through the petitioner; and

c. Believes the adoption will be in the best interest of the adult being adopted and the prospective adoptive parent.

(d) Anyone who gives a consent under this Article may revoke the consent at any time before the entry of the decree of adoption by delivering a written notice of revocation to the individual to whom the consent was given. If a petition to adopt has been filed, the notice of revocation shall also be filed with the clerk of court in the county where the petition is pending. (1967, c. 880, s. 3; 1969, c. 21, ss. 3-6; 1971, c. 1231, s. 1; 1973, c. 849, s. 3; 1975, c. 91; 1981, c. 657; 1989, c. 208; c. 727, s. 219(4); 1993, c. 553, s. 14; 1995, c. 457, s. 2.)

§ 48-5-103. Adoption of incompetent adults.

(a) If an adult being adopted has been adjudicated incompetent, then that adult's guardian shall have authority to consent in place of that adult.

(b) The consent of the guardian must:

(1) Be in writing and signed and acknowledged before an individual authorized to administer oaths or take acknowledgments;

(2) State that the guardian understands that the adoption will terminate the legal relationship of parent and child between the adult being adopted and the adult's former parents, including all rights of the adult to inherit as a child from or through the former parents, unless the adoption is by a stepparent, in which case the adoption will terminate the legal relationship of parent and child

between the adult and the parent who is not married to the stepparent but will have no effect on the relationship between the adult and the parent who is married to the stepparent;

(3)   State that the guardian understands that the adoption will create the legal relationship of parent and child between the adult and the petitioner, including the right of inheritance by, from, and through each other;

(4)   State that the guardian consents to the proposed adoption and believes the adoption will be in the best interest of the adult; and

(5)   State that the guardian understands that the adoption will not terminate the guardian's rights, duties, and powers.

(c)   In any adoption of an adult who has been adjudicated incompetent, the court shall appoint a guardian ad litem other than the guardian to investigate and report to the court on the proposed adoption. (1995, c. 457, s. 2.)

Article 6.

Adoption by a Former Parent.

§ 48-6-100. Application of Article.

This Article shall apply to the adoption of adoptees by a former parent. (1995, c. 457, s. 2.)

§ 48-6-101. Readoption under other Articles.

A former parent may readopt a minor adoptee pursuant to Article 3 of this Chapter or, if applicable, Article 4 of this Chapter. A former parent may readopt an adult adoptee pursuant to Article 5 of this Chapter. (1995, c. 457, s. 2.)

§ 48-6-102. Readoption after a stepparent adoption.

(a) In addition to the methods set out in G.S. 48-6-101, a former parent may petition pursuant to this section to readopt an adoptee adopted by a stepparent.

(b) The petitioner's spouse shall not join the petition.

(c) Consent to the readoption must be executed by:

(1) The adoptee, if 12 or more years of age;

(2) The petitioner's spouse, if any;

(3) The adoptee's adoptive parent, if the adoptee is a minor;

(4) The adoptee's parent who is or was the spouse of the adoptive parent, if the adoptee is a minor; and

(5) Any guardian of the adoptee.

(d) The consent executed by the adoptee shall conform to the requirements of G.S. 48-4-103(e).

(e) The consent executed by the petitioner's spouse shall conform to the requirements of G.S. 48-5-102(c).

(f) The consent executed by the adoptive parent shall conform to the requirements of G.S. 48-4-103(b).

(g) The consent of the adoptee's parent who was the spouse of the adoptive parent shall conform to the requirements of G.S. 48-4-103(a) except for those required by G.S. 48-4-103(a)(2)b.

(h) A consent executed by the guardian of a minor adoptee shall conform to the requirements of G.S. 48-4-103(c).

(i) An adoption under this section does not affect the relationship between the adoptee and the parent who was married to the adoptive parent.

(j) An adoption under this section does not terminate or otherwise affect any existing order of custody. (1949, c. 300; 1983, c. 454, s. 6; 1995, c. 457, s. 2.)

Article 9.

Confidentiality of Records and Disclosure of Information.

§ 48-9-101. Records defined.

(a) For purposes of this Article, "records" means any petition, affidavit, consent or relinquishment, transcript or notes of testimony, deposition, power of attorney, report, decree, order, judgment, correspondence, document, invoice, receipt, certificate, or other printed, written, microfilmed or microfiched, video-taped or tape-recorded material or electronic data processing records regardless of physical form or characteristics pertaining to a proceeding for adoption under this Chapter.

(b) Repealed by Session Laws 2010-116, s. 2, effective October 1, 2010. (1995, c. 457, s. 2; 2007-262, s. 1; 2010-116, s. 2.)

§ 48-9-102. Records confidential and sealed.

(a) All records created or filed in connection with an adoption, except the decree of adoption and the entry in the special proceedings index in the office of the clerk of court, and on file with or in the possession of the court, an agency, the State, a county, an attorney, or other provider of professional services, are confidential and may not be disclosed or used except as provided in this Chapter.

(b) During a proceeding for adoption, records shall not be open to inspection by any person except upon an order of the court finding that disclosure is necessary to protect the interest of the adoptee.

(c) When a decree of adoption becomes final, all records and all indices of records on file with the court, an agency, or this State shall be retained permanently and sealed. Sealed records shall not be open to inspection by any person except as otherwise provided in this Article.

(d) All records filed in connection with an adoption, including a copy of the petition giving the date of the filing of the original petition, the original of each consent and relinquishment, additional documents filed pursuant to G.S. 48-2-305, any report to the court, any additional documents submitted and orders entered and a copy of the final decree, shall be sent by the clerk of superior court to the Division within 10 days after the decree of adoption is entered or 10 days following the final disposition of an appeal pursuant to G.S. 48-2-607(b). The original petition and final decree shall be retained by the clerk.

(e) The Division must cause the papers and reports related to the proceeding to be permanently indexed and filed.

(f) The Division shall transmit a report of each adoption and any name change to the State Registrar if the adoptee was born in this State. In the case of an adoptee who was not born in this State, the Division shall transmit the report and any name change to the appropriate official responsible for issuing birth certificates or their equivalent.

(g) In any adoption, the State Registrar may, in addition to receiving the report from the Division, request a copy of the final order and any separate order of name change directly from the clerk of court. (1949, c. 300; 1957, c. 778, s. 7; 1961, c. 186; 1967, c. 619, ss. 6, 7; c. 880, s. 3; 1969, c. 21, ss. 3-6; c. 982; 1971, c. 1231, s. 1; 1973, c. 476, s. 138; c. 849, s. 3; 1975, c. 91; 1979, c. 739, ss. 1, 2; 1981, c. 657; c. 924, ss. 2, 3; 1983, c. 454, s. 6; 1989, c. 208; c. 727, s. 219(4); 1993, c. 539, s. 411; c. 553, s. 14; 1994, Ex. Sess., c. 24, s. 14(c); 1995, c. 457, s. 2; 1997-215, s. 9(a)-(c); 2001-208, s. 11; 2001-487, s. 101.)

§ 48-9-103. Release of nonidentifying information.

(a) An adoptive parent, an adoptee who is an adult at the time of the request, or a minor adoptee who is a parent or an expectant parent may request a copy of any document prepared pursuant to G.S. 48-3-205 and a copy of any additional nonidentifying health-related information about the adoptee's original family that has been submitted to a court, agency, or the Division. A minor seeking treatment pursuant to G.S. 90-21.1 may request that a copy of this information be sent to the treating physician.

(b) If a request under this section is made to the agency that placed the adoptee or prepared the report to the court, the agency shall furnish the individual making the request or the treating physician named by a minor making the request with a copy of any relevant report or information that is included in the sealed records of the agency. If a request under this section is made to the court that issued the decree of adoption, the court shall refer the individual to the Division, or, if known to the court, the agency that placed the adoptee or prepared the report to the court. The Division may refer the individual to the agency that prepared the report to the court. If the agency no longer exists, the Division may furnish the information to an agency convenient to the requesting party.

(c) Any report or information released under this section shall be edited by the sender to exclude the name, address, or other information that could reasonably be expected to lead directly to the identity of an adoptee at birth or an adoptee's parent at the adoptee's birth or other member of the adoptee's original family and shall contain an express reference to the confidentiality provisions of this Chapter.

(d) An individual who is denied access to a report or information requested under this section may petition the clerk of original jurisdiction for review of the reasonableness of the denial.

(e) If the court or the agency receives information from an adoptee's former parent or from an adoptee's former relative about a health or genetic condition that may affect the health of the adoptee or the adoptee's child, an appropriate employee shall make a reasonable effort to contact and forward the information to an adoptee who is 18 or more years of age, or an adoptive parent of an adoptee who is under 18 years of age.

(f) Nothing in this section shall prohibit an agency from disclosing nonidentifying information about the adoptee's present circumstances, in the nature of information required under G.S. 48-3-205, to a former parent, an adult sibling, or the guardian of a minor sibling on request.

(g) The Department shall prescribe a reasonable procedure for verifying the identity, age, or other relevant characteristics of an individual who requests or provides a report or information under this section and the Department, the court, or agency may charge a reasonable fee for locating and making copies of a report or information.

(h) No request under this section shall be made to the State Registrar of Vital Statistics. (1949, c. 300; 1957, c. 778, s. 7; 1961, c. 186; 1969, c. 982;

1973, c. 476, s. 138; 1979, c. 739, ss. 1, 2; 1981, c. 924, ss. 2, 3; 1983, c. 454, s. 6; 1993, c. 539, s. 411; 1994, Ex. Sess., c. 24, s. 14(c); 1995, c. 457, s. 2.)

§ 48-9-104. Release of identifying information; confidential intermediary services.

(a) Except as provided in this section or in G.S. 48-9-109(2) or (3), no person or entity shall release from any records retained and sealed under this Article the name, address, or other information that reasonably could be expected to lead directly to the identity of an adoptee, an adoptive parent of an adoptee, an adoptee's parent at birth, or an individual who, but for the adoption, would be the adoptee's sibling or grandparent, except upon order of the court for cause pursuant to G.S. 48-9-105.

(b) A child placing agency licensed by the Department or a county department of social services may agree to act as a confidential intermediary for any of the following:

(1) A biological parent.

(2) An adult adoptee.

(3) An adult biological sibling of an adult adoptee.

(4) An adult biological half sibling of an adult adoptee.

(5) An adult family member of a deceased biological parent.

(6) An adult family member of a deceased adoptee.

In order to obtain and share nonidentifying birth family health information, to facilitate contact, or to share identifying information with any person listed in subdivisions (1) through (6) of this subsection, an agency may act as a confidential intermediary without appointment by the court pursuant to G.S. 48-9-105 and with the written consent of all parties to the contact or the sharing of information. Written consent of the biological parent is required if the biological parent is living at the time any party described in subdivisions (2) through (6) of this subsection seeks to contact or share identifying information with any other party described in subdivisions (2) through (6) of this subsection. Further, an agency may agree to act as a confidential intermediary for the adoptive parents of a minor adoptee or the guardian of a minor adoptee, without appointment by the court pursuant to G.S. 48-9-105, to obtain and share nonidentifying birth family health information. An agency providing confidential intermediary services shall contact individuals in a manner reasonably calculated to prevent incidental disclosure of confidential information. An agency that agrees to provide confidential intermediary services may charge a reasonable fee for doing so, which fee must be pursuant to written agreement signed by the individual to be charged. The Division shall establish guidelines for confidential intermediary services.

(c) For purposes of this section only, the term "family member" means a spouse, child, stepchild, parent, stepparent, grandparent, or grandchild.

(d) If an agency providing confidential intermediary services determines that the person who is the subject of the search is deceased, the agency may obtain a copy of the death certificate pursuant to G.S. 130A-93 and deliver it to the person who requested the services. If the agency further determines that a lineal ascendant of the deceased person who is the subject of the search is deceased, the agency may also obtain a copy of the death certificate of the deceased lineal ascendant and deliver it to the person who requested the services. (1949, c. 300; 1957, c. 778, s. 7; 1961, c. 186; 1969, c. 982; 1973, c. 476, s. 138; 1979, c. 739, ss. 1, 2; 1981, c. 924, ss. 2, 3; 1983, c. 454, s. 6; 1993, c. 539, s. 411; 1994, Ex. Sess., c. 24, s. 14(c); 1995, c. 457, s. 2; 2001-150, s. 12; 2007-262, s. 3; 2010-116, s. 3; 2011-237, s. 1.)

§ 48-9-105. Action for release of identifying and other nonidentifying information.

(a) Any information necessary for the protection of the adoptee or the public in or derived from the records, including medical information not otherwise obtainable, may be disclosed to an individual who files a written motion in the cause before the clerk of original jurisdiction. In hearing the petition, the court shall give primary consideration to the best interest of the adoptee, but shall also give due consideration to the interests of the members of the adoptee's original and adoptive family.

(b) The movant must serve a copy of the motion, with written proof of service, upon the Department and the agency that prepared the report for the court. The clerk shall give at least five days' notice to the Department and the agency of every hearing on this motion, whether the hearing is before the clerk or a judge of the district court; and the Department and the agency shall be entitled to appear and be heard in response to the motion.

(c)   In determining whether cause exists for the release of the name or identity of an individual, the court shall consider:

(1)   The reason the information is sought;

(2)   Any procedure available for satisfying the petitioner's request without disclosing the name or identity of another individual, including having the court appoint a representative to contact the individual and request specific information;

(3)   Whether the individual about whom identifying information is sought is alive;

(4)   To the extent known, the preference of the adoptee, the adoptive parents, the adoptee's parents at birth, and other members of the adoptee's original and adoptive families, and the likely effect of disclosure on these individuals;

(5)   The age, maturity, and expressed needs of the adoptee;

(6)   The report or recommendation of any individual appointed by the court to assess the request for identifying information; and

(7)   Any other factor relevant to an assessment of whether the benefit to the petitioner of releasing the information sought will be greater than the benefit to any other individual of not releasing the information.

(d)   An individual who files a motion under this section may also ask the court to authorize the release by the State Registrar of a certified copy of the adoptee's original certificate of birth. (1949, c. 300; 1985, c. 448; 1995, c. 88, s. 6; 1995, c. 457, s. 2.)

§ 48-9-106. Release of original certificate of birth.

Upon receipt of a certified copy of a court order issued pursuant to G.S. 48-9-105 authorizing the release of an adoptee's original certificate of birth, the State Registrar shall give the individual who obtained the order a copy of the original certificate of birth with a certification that the copy is a true copy of a record that is no longer a valid certificate of birth. (1995, c. 457, s. 2.)

§ 48-9-107. New birth certificates.

(a) Upon receipt of a report of the adoption of a minor from the Division, or the documents required by G.S. 48-9-102(g) from the clerk of superior court in the adoption of an adult, or a report of an adoption from another state, the State Registrar shall prepare a new birth certificate for the adoptee that shall contain the adoptee's full adoptive name, sex, state of birth, and date of birth; the full name of the adoptive father, if applicable; the full maiden name of the adoptive mother, if applicable; and any other pertinent information consistent with this section as may be determined by the State Registrar. The new certificate shall contain no reference to the adoption of the adoptee and shall not refer to the adoptive parents in any way other than as the adoptee's parents.

(b) In an adoption by a stepparent, the State Registrar shall prepare a new birth certificate pursuant to subsection (a) of this section except:

(1) The adoptive parent and the parent whose relation with the adoptee remains unchanged shall be listed as the adoptee's mother and father on the new birth certificate; and

(2) The city and county of birth of the adoptee shall be the same on the new birth certificate as on the original certificate.

The names of the adoptee's parents shall not be changed as provided in subdivision (1) of this subsection if the petitioner, the petitioner's spouse, the adoptee if age 12 or older, and any living parent whose parental rights are terminated by the adoption jointly file a request that the parents' names not be changed with the court prior to the entry of the adoption decree. The Division shall send a copy of this request with its report to the State Registrar or other appropriate official in the adoption of a minor stepchild, and the clerk of superior court shall send a copy with the documents required by G.S. 48-9-102(g) in the adoption of an adult stepchild.

(c) The State Registrar shall seal the original certificate of birth and all records in the possession of that office pertaining to the adoption. These records shall not be unsealed except as provided in this Article. The State Registrar shall provide certified typed copies or abstracts of the new certificate of birth of an adoptee prepared pursuant to subsection (a) of this section to the adoptee, the adoptee's children, the adoptive parents, and the adoptee's spouse, brothers, and sisters. For purposes of this subsection, "parent", "brother", and "sister" shall mean the adoptee's adoptive parent, brother, or sister and shall not mean a former parent, brother, or sister.

(d) At the time of preparing the new birth certificate pursuant to subsection (a) of this section, the State Registrar shall notify the register of deeds or appropriate official in the health department in the county of the adoptee's birth to remove the adoptee's birth certificate from the records and forward it to the State Registrar for retention under seal with the original certificate of birth in the State Registrar's office. The register of deeds shall also delete all index entries for that birth certificate. The State Registrar shall not issue copies of birth certificates for adoptees to registers of deeds. Only the State Registrar shall issue certified copies of such records, and these copies shall be prepared as prescribed in subsection (c) of this section.

(e) The State Registrar may by rule prescribe requirements for reports of adoptions from other states. (1949, c. 300; 1951, c. 730, ss. 1-4; 1955, c. 951, s. 1; 1967, c. 880, s. 3; c. 1042, ss. 1-3; 1969, c. 21, s. 2-6; c. 977; 1971, c. 1231, s. 1; 1973, c. 476, s. 128; c. 849, ss. 1-3; 1975, c. 91; 1981, c. 657; 1983, c. 454, s. 6; 1989, c. 208; c. 727, s. 219(3), (4); 1993, c. 553, s. 14; 1995, c. 457, s. 2; 1997-215, s. 18.)

§ 48-9-108. Restoration of original birth certificates if a decree of adoption is set aside.

If a final decree of adoption is set aside, the court shall send a certified copy of the order within 10 days after it becomes final to the State Registrar if the adoptee was born in this State or to the appropriate official responsible for issuing birth certificates or their equivalent if the adoptee was not born in this State. The court shall also send a copy to the Division. If the adoptee desires to have the adoptive name shown on the original birth certificate when it is restored, the order must include this directive. Upon receipt of such an order, the State Registrar shall seal the certificate issued under this section and restore the adoptee's original certificate of birth. This sealed file may subsequently be opened only by direction of a valid court order pursuant to G.S. 48-9-105 and G.S. 48-9-106. (1995, c. 457, s. 2.)

§ 48-9-109. Certain disclosures authorized.

Nothing in this Article shall be interpreted or construed to prevent:

(1) An employee of a court, agency, or any other person from:

a. Inspecting permanent, confidential, or sealed records, other than records maintained by the State Registrar, for the purpose of discharging any obligation under this Chapter.

b. Disclosing the name of the court where a proceeding for adoption occurred, or the name of an agency that placed an adoptee, to an individual described in G.S. 48-9-104(a) who can verify his or her identity.

c. Disclosing or using information contained in permanent and sealed records, other than records maintained by the State Registrar, for statistical or other research purposes as long as the disclosure will not result in identification of a person who is the subject of the information and subject to any further conditions the Department may reasonably impose.

(2) In agency placements, a parent or guardian placing a child for adoption and the adopting parents from authorizing an agency to release information or from releasing information to each other that could reasonably be expected to lead directly to the identity of an adoptee, an adoptive parent of an adoptee, or an adoptee's placing parent or guardian. The consent to the release of identifying information shall be in writing and signed prior to the adoption by any placing parent or guardian and the adopting parents and acknowledged under oath in the presence of an individual authorized to administer oaths or take acknowledgments. Any consent to release identifying information shall be filed under G.S. 48-2-305.

(3) The Division from sharing information from its records regarding the identity of birth parents with an agency acting as a confidential intermediary pursuant to G.S. 48-9-104(b), if the information is needed by the agency to carry out its duties as a confidential intermediary. Any information disclosed to the

agency pursuant to this subdivision shall not be redisclosed by the agency except as allowed by G.S. 48-9-104(b). (1995, c. 457, s. 2; 2001-150, s. 13; 2007-262, s. 4; 2012-16, s. 9.)

Article 10.

Prohibited Practices in Connection with Adoption.

§ 48-10-101. Prohibited activities in placement.

(a) No one other than a person or entity specified in G.S. 48-3-201 may place a minor for adoption. No one other than a person or entity specified in G.S. 48-3-201, or an adoption facilitator, may solicit potential adoptive parents for children in need of adoption. No one other than an agency or an adoption facilitator, or an individual with a completed preplacement assessment that contains a finding that the individual is suitable to be an adoptive parent or that individual's immediate family, may solicit for adoption a potential adoptee.

(b) No one other than a county department of social services, an adoption facilitator, or an agency licensed by the Department in this State may advertise in any periodical or newspaper, or by radio, television, or other public medium, that any person or entity will place or accept a child for adoption.

(b1) Notwithstanding subsections (a) and (b) of this section, this Article shall not prohibit a person from advertising that the person desires to adopt. This subsection shall apply only to a person with a current completed preplacement assessment finding that person suitable to be an adoptive parent. The advertisement may be published only in a periodical or newspaper or on radio, television, cable television, or the Internet. The advertisement shall include a statement that (i) the person has a completed preplacement assessment finding that person suitable to be an adoptive parent, (ii) identifies the name of the agency that completed the preplacement assessment, and (iii) identifies the date the preplacement assessment was completed. Any advertisement under this subsection may state whether the person is willing to provide lawful expenses as permitted by G.S. 48-10-103.

(c) A person who violates subsection (a), (b), or (b1) of this section is guilty of a Class 1 misdemeanor.

(d) The district court may enjoin any person from violating this section. (1975, c. 335, s. 2; 1981, c. 275, s. 6; 1993, c. 539, s. 413; 1994, Ex. Sess., c. 24, s. 14(c); 1995, c. 457, s. 2; 2001-150, s. 14.)

§ 48-10-102. Unlawful payments related to adoption.

(a) Except as provided in G.S. 48-10-103, a person or entity may not pay or give, offer to pay or give, or request, receive or accept any money or anything of value, directly or indirectly, for:

(1) The placement of a minor for adoption;

(2) The consent of a parent, a guardian, or an agency to the adoption of a minor;

(3) The relinquishment of a minor to an agency for purposes of adoption; or

(4) Assisting a parent or guardian in locating or evaluating a potential adoptive parent or in transferring custody of a minor to the adoptive parent.

(b) A person who violates this section is guilty of a Class 1 misdemeanor. For each subsequent violation, a person is guilty of a Class H felony which may include a fine of not more than ten thousand dollars ($10,000).

(c) The district court may enjoin any person or entity from violating this section. (1975, c. 335, s. 1; 1991, c. 335, s. 1; 1993, c. 539, ss. 412, 1264; 1994, Ex. Sess., c. 24, s. 14(c); 1995, c. 457, s. 2.)

§ 48-10-103. Lawful payments related to adoption.

(a) An adoptive parent, or another person acting on behalf of an adoptive parent, may pay the reasonable and actual fees and expenses for:

(1) Services of an agency in connection with an adoption;

(2) Medical, hospital, nursing, pharmaceutical, traveling, or other similar expenses incurred by a mother or her child incident to the pregnancy and birth or any illness of the adoptee;

(3) Counseling services for a parent or the adoptee that are directly related to the adoption and are provided by a licensed psychiatrist, licensed psychologist, licensed marriage and family therapist, licensed professional counselor, licensed or certified social worker, fee-based practicing pastoral counselor or other licensed professional counselor, or an employee of an agency;

(4) Ordinary living expenses of a mother during the pregnancy and for no more than six weeks after the birth;

(5) Expenses incurred in ascertaining the information required under G.S. 48-3-205 about an adoptee and the adoptee's biological family;

(6) Legal services, court costs, and traveling or other administrative expenses connected with an adoption, including any legal service connected with the adoption performed for a parent who consents to the adoption of a minor or relinquishes the minor to an agency; and

(7) Preparation of the preplacement assessment and the report to the court.

(b) A birth parent, or another person acting on the parent's behalf, may receive or accept payments authorized in subsection (a) of this section; or a provider of a service listed in subsection (a) of this section may receive or accept payments for that service.

(c) A payment authorized by subsection (a) of this section may not be made contingent on the placement of the minor for adoption, relinquishment of the minor, consent to the adoption, or cooperation in the completion of the adoption. Except as provided in subsection (d) of this section, if the adoption is not completed, a person who has made payments authorized by subsection (a) of this section may not recover them; but neither is this person liable for any further payment unless the person has agreed in a signed writing with a provider of a service to make this payment regardless of the outcome of the proceeding for adoption.

(d) A prospective adoptive parent may seek to recover a payment if the parent or other person receives or accepts it with the fraudulent intent to prevent the proposed adoption from being completed.

(e) An agency may charge or accept a reasonable fee or other compensation from prospective adoptive parents. In assessing a fee or charge, the agency may take into account the income of adoptive parents and may use a sliding scale related to income in order to provide services to persons of all incomes. (1975, c. 335, s. 1; 1991, c. 335, s. 1; 1993, c. 539, ss. 412, 1264; 1994, Ex. Sess., c. 24, s. 14(c); 1995, c. 457, s. 2; 2001-487, s. 40(c).)

§ 48-10-104. Failure to disclose nonidentifying information.

An adoptive parent, an adoptee, or any person who is the subject of any information required under G.S. 48-3-205 or authorized for release under Article 9 of this Chapter may bring a civil action for equitable or monetary relief or both against a person who fraudulently or intentionally misrepresents or fails to disclose information required under G.S. 48-3-205 or Article 9 of this Chapter. (1995, c. 457, s. 2.)

§ 48-10-105. Unauthorized disclosure of information.

(a) Except as authorized in G.S. 48-3-205 or in Article 9 of this Chapter, no identifying or nonidentifying information contained in a report or records described therein may be disclosed by present or former employees or officials of the court, an agency, the State, a county, an attorney or other provider of professional services, or any person or entity who wrongfully obtains such a report or records.

(b) A person who knowingly makes an unauthorized disclosure of identifying information is guilty of a Class 1 misdemeanor.

(c) The district court may enjoin from further violations any person who makes an unauthorized disclosure.

(d) Notwithstanding the penalties provided in subsection (b) of this section, an individual who is the subject of any of this information may bring a civil action for equitable or monetary relief or both against any person or entity who makes an unauthorized disclosure of the information. (1949, c. 300; 1957, c. 778, s. 7; 1961, c. 186; 1969, c. 982; 1973, c. 476, s. 138; 1979, c. 739, ss. 1, 2; 1981, c. 924, ss. 2, 3; 1983, c. 454, s. 6; 1993, c. 539, s. 411; 1994, Ex. Sess., c. 24, s. 14(c); 1995, c. 457, s. 2.)

Chapter 48A.

Minors.

Article 1.

Age of Majority.

§ 48A-1. Common-law definition of "minor" abrogated.

The common-law definition of minor insofar as it pertains to the age of the minor is hereby repealed and abrogated. (1971, c. 585, s. 1; 2003-207, s. 1.)

§ 48A-2. Age of minors.

A minor is any person who has not reached the age of 18 years. (1971, c. 585, s. 1; 2003-207, s. 1.)

§ 48A-3. Statute of limitations; applicability.

For purposes of determining the applicability of the statute of limitations which has been tolled because of minority or for purposes of determining the applicable period of time for disaffirmance of a contract of a minor upon reaching majority, because of a change in applicable law occasioned by enactment of this Chapter or Chapter 1231 of the 1971 Session Laws, the following rules shall apply:

(1)   For those persons who were 21 on the effective date of applicable law, limitations shall apply as they would prior to amendment;

(2) For those persons 18 years of age but not 21 on the effective date of applicable law, any time periods for disaffirmance or application of the statute of limitations shall run from the effective date of this Chapter, to wit, July 5, 1971.

(3) For those persons not yet 18, any time periods for disaffirmance or application of the statute of limitations shall run from the person's reaching age 18. (1971, c. 1231, s. 3; 2003-207, s. 1.)

§§ 48A-4 through 48A-10. Reserved for future codification purposes.

Article 2.

Certain Contracts of Minors.

§ 48A-11. Applicability.

This Article applies to any of the following contracts entered into between an unemancipated minor and any third party or parties:

(1) A contract pursuant to which a person is employed or agrees to render artistic or creative services, either directly or through a third party, including, but not limited to, a personal services corporation or loan-out company. As used in this Article, the term "artistic or creative services" includes, but is not limited to, services as an actor, actress, dancer, musician, comedian, singer, stunt person, voice-over artist, or other performer or entertainer, or as a songwriter, musical producer or arranger, writer, director, producer, production executive, choreographer, composer, conductor, or designer.

(2) A contract pursuant to which a person agrees to purchase, or otherwise secure, sell, lease, license, or otherwise dispose of literary, musical, or dramatic properties, or use of a person's likeness, voice recording, performance, or story of or incidents in his or her life, either tangible or intangible, or any rights therein for use in motion pictures, television, the production of sound recordings in any format now known or hereafter devised, the legitimate or living stage, or otherwise in the entertainment field.

(3) A contract pursuant to which a person is employed or agrees to render services as a participant or player in a sport.

(4) Where a minor renders services as an extra, background performer, or in a similar capacity, through an agency or service that provides one or more performers for a fee, such as a casting agency, the agency or service shall be considered the minor's employer for the purposes of this Article. (2003-207, s. 2.)

§ 48A-12. No disaffirmance if approved by superior court.

(a) A contract, otherwise valid, of a type described in G.S. 48A-11, entered into during minority, cannot be disaffirmed on that ground either during the minority of the person entering into the contract, or at any time thereafter, if the contract has been approved by the superior court in any county in which the minor resides or is employed or in which any party to the contract has its principal office in this State for the transaction of business.

(b) Approval of the court may be given on petition of any party to the contract, after reasonable notice to all other parties to the contract as is fixed by the court, with opportunity to the other parties to appear and be heard.

(c) Approval of the court given under this section extends to the whole of the contract and all of its terms and provisions, including, but not limited to, any optional or conditional provisions contained in the contract for extension, prolongation, or termination of the term of the contract.

(d) For the purposes of any proceeding under this Article, a parent or legal guardian, as the case may be, entitled to the physical custody, care, and control of the minor at the time of the proceeding shall be considered the minor's guardian ad litem for the proceeding, unless the court shall determine that appointment of a different individual as guardian ad litem is required in the best interests of the minor. (2003-207, s. 2.)

§ 48A-13. Copies of certain documents to be provided.

A parent or guardian, as the case may be, entitled to the physical custody, care, and control of a minor, who enters into a contract of a type described in G.S. 48A-11 shall provide a certified copy of the minor's birth certificate indicating the minor's minority to the other party or parties to the contract and in addition, in the case of a guardian, a certified copy of the court document appointing the person as the minor's legal guardian. (2003-207, s. 2.)

§ 48A-14. Financial safeguards in court orders approving contracts.

(a) Notwithstanding any other statute, in an order approving a minor's contract of a type described in G.S. 48A-11, the court shall require that fifteen percent (15%) of the minor's gross earnings pursuant to the contract be set aside by the minor's employer in trust, in an account or other savings plan, and preserved for the benefit of the minor in accordance with G.S. 48A-16. The court may also require that more than fifteen percent (15%) of the minor's gross earnings be set aside in trust, in an account or other savings plan, and preserved for the benefit of the minor in accordance with G.S. 48A-16, upon request of the minor's parent or legal guardian, or the minor, through his or her guardian ad litem.

(b) The court shall require that at least one parent or legal guardian, as the case may be, entitled to the physical custody, care, and control of the minor at the time the order is issued be appointed as trustee of the funds ordered to be set aside in trust for the benefit of the minor, unless the court shall determine that appointment of a different individual, individuals, entity, or entities as trustee or trustees is required in the best interest of the minor.

(c) The trustee or trustees of the funds ordered to be set aside in trust shall promptly provide the minor's employer with a true and accurate photocopy of the trustee's statement pursuant to G.S. 48A-16(c).

(d) The minor's employer shall deposit or disburse the funds as required by the order within 15 business days of receiving the order and receiving the trustee's statement pursuant to G.S. 48A-16 and thereafter as funds might be received. Notwithstanding any other statute, pending receipt of the trustee's statement, the minor's employer shall hold for the benefit of the minor the percentage ordered by the court of the minor's gross earnings pursuant to the contract.

(e) When making the initial deposit of funds pursuant to the order, the minor's employer shall provide the financial institution with a copy of the order.

(f) Once the minor's employer deposits the set-aside funds pursuant to G.S. 48A-16, in trust, in an account or other savings plan, the minor's employer shall have no further obligation or duty to monitor or account for the funds. The trustee or trustees of the trust shall be the only individual, individuals, entity, or entities with the obligation or duty to monitor and account for those funds once they have been deposited by the minor's employer. The trustee or trustees shall do an annual accounting of the funds held in trust, in an account or other savings plan, in accordance with Article 21 of Chapter 28A of the General Statutes.

(g) The court shall have continuing jurisdiction over the trust established pursuant to the order and may at any time, upon petition of the parent or legal guardian, the minor, through his or her guardian ad litem, or the trustee or trustees, on good cause shown, order that the trust be amended or terminated, notwithstanding the provisions of the declaration of trust. An order amending or terminating a trust may be made only after reasonable notice to the beneficiary, to the parent or guardian, if any, and to the trustee or trustees of the funds if the beneficiary is then a minor, with opportunity for all parties to appear and be heard.

(h) The trustee or trustees of the funds ordered to be set aside shall promptly notify the minor's employer in writing of any change in facts that affect the employer's obligation or ability to set aside the funds in accordance with the order, including, but not limited to, a change of financial institution or account number, or the existence of a new or amended order issued pursuant to subsection (g) of this section amending or terminating the employer's obligations under the original order. The written notification shall include the information set forth in subsection (c) of this section and shall be accompanied by a true and accurate photocopy of the new or amended order. (2003-207, s. 2.)

§ 48A-15. Financial safeguards when no court order.

(a) Notwithstanding any other statute, for any minor's contract of a type described in G.S. 48A-11 that is not being submitted for approval by the court pursuant to G.S. 48A-12, or for which the court has issued a final order denying approval, fifteen percent (15%) of the minor's gross earnings pursuant to the contract shall be set aside by the minor's employer in trust, in an account or other savings plan, and preserved for the benefit of the minor in accordance with G.S. 48A-16. At least one parent or legal guardian, as the case may be, entitled to the physical custody, care, and control of the minor, shall be the trustee of the funds set aside for the benefit of the minor, unless the court, upon petition by the parent or legal guardian, the minor, through his or her guardian ad litem, or the trustee or trustees of the trust, shall determine that appointment of a different individual, individuals, entity, or entities as trustee or trustees is required in the best interest of the minor.

(b) A parent or guardian, as the case may be, entitled to the physical custody, care, and control of the minor shall promptly provide the minor's employer with a true and accurate photocopy of the trustee's statement pursuant to G.S. 48A-16(c) and in addition, in the case of a guardian, a certified copy of the court document appointing the person as the minor's legal guardian.

(c) The minor's employer shall deposit fifteen percent (15%) of the minor's gross earnings pursuant to the contract within 15 business days of receiving the trustee's statement pursuant to G.S. 48A-16(c), or if the court denies approval of the contract, within 15 business days of receiving a final order denying approval of the contract and thereafter as funds might be received. Notwithstanding any other statute, pending receipt of the trustee's statement or the final court order, the minor's employer shall hold for the benefit of the minor the fifteen percent (15%) of the minor's gross earnings pursuant to the contract.

(d) Once the minor's employer deposits the set-aside funds in trust, in an account or other savings plan pursuant to G.S. 48A-16, the minor's employer shall have no further obligation or duty to monitor or account for the funds. The trustee or trustees of the trust shall be the only individual, individuals, entity, or entities with the obligation or duty to monitor and account for those funds once they have been deposited by the minor's employer. The trustee or trustees shall do an annual accounting of the funds held in trust, in an account or other savings plan, in accordance with G.S. 28A-21-1, et seq.

(e) Upon petition of the parent or legal guardian, the minor, through his or her guardian ad litem, or the trustee or trustees of the trust, to the superior court in any county in which the minor resides or in which the trust is established, the court may at any time, on good cause shown, order that the trust be amended or terminated, notwithstanding the provisions of the declaration of trust. An order amending or terminating a trust may be made only after reasonable notice to the beneficiary, to the parent or guardian, if any, and to the trustee or trustees of the funds if the beneficiary is then a minor, with opportunity for all parties to appear and be heard.

(f) A parent or guardian, as the case may be, entitled to the physical custody, care, and control of the minor shall promptly notify the minor's employer in writing of any change in facts that affect the employer's obligation or ability to set aside funds for the benefit of the minor in accordance with this section, including, but not limited to, a change of financial institution or account number, or the existence of a new or amended order issued pursuant to subsection (e) of this section amending or terminating the employer's obligations under this section. The written notification shall be accompanied by a true and accurate photocopy of the trustee's statement and attachments pursuant to subdivision (c) of G.S. 48A-16, or a true and accurate photocopy of the new or amended order.

(g) Where a parent or guardian, as the case may be, is entitled to the physical custody, care, and control of a minor who enters into a contract of a type described in G.S. 48A-11, the relationship between the parent or guardian, as the case may be, and the minor is a fiduciary relationship that is governed by the law of trusts, whether or not a court has issued a formal order to that effect. The parent or guardian, as the case may be, acting in his or her fiduciary relationship, shall, with the earnings and accumulations of the minor under the contract, pay all liabilities incurred by the minor under the contract, including, but not limited to, payments for taxes on all earnings, including taxes on the amounts set aside under this section or G.S. 48A-14 and payments for personal or professional services rendered to the minor or the business related to the contract. Nothing in this subsection shall be construed to alter any other existing responsibilities of a parent or legal guardian to provide for the support of a minor child.

(h) With respect to contracts pursuant to which a person is employed to render services as a musician, singer, songwriter, musical producer, or arranger only, "gross earnings" for purposes of this Article means the amount paid directly to the minor pursuant to the contract, including the payment of any advances to the minor pursuant to the contract, but excluding deductions to offset those advances or other expenses incurred by the employer pursuant to the contract. (2003-207, s. 2.)

§ 48A-16. Trust to be established.

(a)   The trustee or trustees shall establish a trust pursuant to this section at a bank, savings and loan institution, credit union, brokerage firm, or company registered under the Investment Company Act of 1940, 15 U.S.C. § 80a-1, et seq., unless a similar trust has been previously established, for the purpose of preserving for the benefit of the minor the portion of the minor's gross earnings pursuant to G.S. 48A-14(a) or pursuant to G.S. 48A-15(a). The trustee or trustees shall establish the trust pursuant to this section within seven business days after the minor's contract is signed by the minor and the employer.

(b)   Except as otherwise provided in this section, prior to the date on which the beneficiary of the trust attains the age of 18 years or the issuance of a declaration of emancipation of the minor under Article 35 of Chapter 7B of the General Statutes, no withdrawal by the beneficiary or any other individual, individuals, entity, or entities may be made of funds on deposit in trust without written order of the superior court pursuant to G.S. 48A-14(g) or G.S. 48A-15(e). Upon reaching the age of 18 years, the beneficiary may withdraw the funds on deposit in trust only after providing a certified copy of the beneficiary's birth certificate to the financial institution where the trust is located.

(c)   The trustee or trustees shall, within 10 business days after the minor's contract is signed by the minor and the employer, prepare a written statement under penalty of perjury that shall include the name, address, and telephone number of the financial institution, the name of the account, the number of the account, the name of the minor beneficiary, the name of the trustee or trustees of the account, and any additional information needed by the minor's employer to deposit into the account the portion of the minor's gross earnings prescribed by G.S. 48A-14(a) or G.S. 48A-15(a). The trustee or trustees shall attach to the written statement a true and accurate photocopy of any information received from the financial institution confirming the creation of the account, such as an account agreement, account terms, passbook, or other similar writings.

(d)   If the trust is established in the United States, it shall be established either with a financial institution that is and remains insured at all times by the Federal Deposit Insurance Corporation, the Securities Investor Protection Corporation, or the National Credit Union Share Insurance Fund or their respective successors, or with a company that is and remains registered under the Investment Company Act of 1940, 15 U.S.C. § 80a-1, et seq. If the trust is established outside the United States, the financial institution shall be an international banking corporation, as defined in G.S. 53-232.2. The trustee or trustees of the trust shall be the only individual, individuals, entity, or entities with the obligation or duty to ensure that the funds remain in trust, in an account or other savings plan, in a financial institution insured in accordance with this section, or with a company that is and remains registered under the Investment Company Act of 1940, 15 U.S.C. § 80a-1, et seq., as authorized by this section.

(e) Upon application by the trustee or trustees to the financial institution or company where the trust is held, the trust funds may be handled by the trustee or trustees in any of the following methods:

(1) The trustee or trustees may transfer funds to another account or other savings plan at the same financial institution or company, provided that the funds transferred shall continue to be held in trust and subject to this section.

(2) The trustee or trustees may transfer funds to another financial institution or company, provided that the funds transferred shall continue to be held in trust and subject to this Article and that the trustee or trustees have provided written notification to the financial institution or company to which the funds will be transferred that the funds are subject to this section and written notice of the requirements of this Article.

(3) The trustee or trustees may use all or a part of the funds to purchase, in the name of and for the benefit of the minor:

a. Investment funds offered by a company registered under the Investment Company Act of 1940, 15 U.S.C. § 80a-1, et seq., provided that if the underlying investments are equity securities, the investment fund is a broad-based index fund or invests broadly across the domestic or a foreign regional economy, is not a sector fund, and has assets under management of at least two hundred fifty million dollars ($250,000,000); or

b. Government securities and bonds, certificates of deposit, money market instruments, money market accounts, or mutual funds investing solely in those government securities and bonds, certificates, instruments, and accounts that are available at the financial institution where the trust fund or other savings plan is held, provided that the funds remain in trust at a financial institution insured by the Federal Deposit Insurance Corporation, the Securities Investor Protection Corporation, or the National Credit Union Share Insurance Fund if within the United States or maintained in an international banking corporation, as defined in G.S. 53-232.2, if not within the United States; provided that those purchases have a maturity date on or before the date upon which the minor will attain the age of 18 years, and provided further that any proceeds accruing from those purchases be redeposited into that account or accounts or used to further purchase any of those or similar securities, bonds, certificates, instruments, funds, or accounts. (2003-207, s. 2.)

§ 48A-17. Talent agency contracts.

(a) As used in this Article, the term "talent agency" means a person or corporation who engages in the occupation of procuring, offering, promising, or attempting to procure employment or engagements for an artist or artists. Talent agencies may, in addition, counsel or direct artists in the development of their professional careers.

(b) As used in this Article, the term "artists" means actors and actresses rendering services on the legitimate stage and in the production of motion pictures, radio artists, musical artists, musical organizations, directors of legitimate stage, motion picture and radio productions, musical directors, writers, cinematographers, composers, lyricists, arrangers, models, and other artists and persons rendering professional services in motion picture, theatrical, radio, television, and other entertainment enterprises. (2003-207, s. 2.)

§ 48A-18. Disaffirmance of talent agency contracts.

A minor cannot disaffirm a contract, otherwise valid, entered into during minority, either during the actual minority of the minor entering into the contract or at any time thereafter, with a talent agency as defined in G.S. 48A-17, to secure engagements to render artistic or creative services in motion pictures, television, the production of phonograph records, the legitimate or living stage, or otherwise in the entertainment field including, but without being limited to, services as an actor, actress, dancer, musician, comedian, singer, or other performer or entertainer, or as a writer, director, producer, production executive, choreographer, composer, conductor, or designer, where the contract has been approved by the superior court of the county where such minor resides or is employed. This approval may be given by the superior court on the petition of either party to the contract after reasonable notice to the other party thereto as may be fixed by said court, with opportunity to the other party to appear and be heard. (2003-207, s. 2.)

Chapter 49.

Children Born Out of Wedlock.

Article 1.

Support of Children Born Out of Wedlock.

§ 49-1. Title.

This Article shall be referred to as "An act concerning the support of children of parents not married to each other." (1933, c. 228, s. 11.)

§ 49-2. Nonsupport of child born out of wedlock by parents made misdemeanor.

Any parent who willfully neglects or who refuses to provide adequate support and maintain his or her child born out of wedlock shall be guilty of a Class 2 misdemeanor. A child within the meaning of this Article shall be any person less than 18 years of age and any person whom either parent might be required under the laws of North Carolina to support and maintain if the child were the legitimate child of the parent. (1933, c. 228, s. 1; 1937, c. 432, s. 1; 1939, c. 217, ss. 1, 2; 1951, c. 154, s. 1; 1977, c. 3, s. 1; 1993, c. 539, s. 414; 1994, Ex. Sess., c. 24, s. 14(c); 2013-198, s. 17.)

§ 49-3. Place of birth of child no consideration.

The provisions of this Article shall apply whether such child shall have been begotten or shall have been born within or without the State of North Carolina: Provided, that the child to be supported is a bona fide resident of this State at the time of the institution of any proceedings under this Article. (1933, c. 228, s. 2.)

§ 49-4. When prosecution may be commenced.

The prosecution of the reputed father of a child born out of wedlock may be instituted under this Chapter within any of the following periods, and not thereafter:

(1)   Three years next after the birth of the child; or

(2)   Where the paternity of the child has been judicially determined within three years next after its birth, at any time before the child attains the age of 18 years; or

(3)   Where the reputed father has acknowledged paternity of the child by payments for the support thereof within three years next after the birth of the child, three years from the date of the last payment whether the last payment was made within three years of the birth of the child or thereafter: Provided, the action is instituted before the child attains the age of 18 years.

The prosecution of the mother of a child born out of wedlock may be instituted under this Chapter at any time before the child attains the age of 18 years. (1933, c. 228, s. 3; 1939, c. 217, s. 3; 1945, c. 1053; 1951, c. 154, s. 2; 2013-198, s. 18.)

§ 49-5. Prosecution; death of mother no bar; determination of fatherhood.

Proceedings under this Article may be brought by the mother or her personal representative or, if the child is likely to become a public charge, the director of social services or such person as by law performs the duties of such official in said county where the mother resides or the child is found. Proceedings under this Article may be brought in the county where the mother resides or is found, or in the county where the putative father resides or is found, or in the county where the child is found. The fact that the child was born outside of the State of North Carolina shall not be a bar to proceedings against the putative father in any county where he resides or is found, or in the county where the mother resides or the child is found. The death of the mother shall in no wise affect any proceedings under this Article. Preliminary proceedings under this Article to determine the paternity of the child may be instituted prior to the birth of the child but when the judge or court trying the issue of paternity deems it proper, he may continue the case until the woman is delivered of the child. When a continuance is granted, the courts shall recognize the person accused of being the father of the child with surety for his appearance, either at the next session of the court or at a time to be fixed by the judge or court granting a continuance, which shall be after the delivery of the child. (1933, c. 228, s. 4; 1961, c. 186; 1969, c. 982; 1971, c. 1185, s. 18; 1981, c. 599, s. 13.)

§ 49-6. Mother not excused on ground of self-incrimination; not subject to penalty.

No mother of a child born out of wedlock shall be excused, on the ground that it may tend to incriminate her or subject her to a penalty or a forfeiture, from attending and testifying, in obedience to a subpoena of any court, in any suit or proceeding based upon or growing out of the provisions of this Article, but no such mother shall be prosecuted or subjected to any penalty or forfeiture for or on account of any transaction, matter, or thing as to which, in obedience to a subpoena and under oath, she may so testify. (1933, c. 228, s. 5; 1939, c. 217, s. 5; 2013-198, s. 19.)

§ 49-7. Issues and orders.

The court before which the matter may be brought shall determine whether or not the defendant is a parent of the child on whose behalf the proceeding is instituted. After this matter has been determined in the affirmative, the court shall proceed to determine the issue as to whether or not the defendant has neglected or refused to provide adequate support and maintain the child who is the subject of the proceeding. After this matter has been determined in the affirmative, the court shall fix by order, subject to modification or increase from time to time, a specific sum of money necessary for the support and maintenance of the child, subject to the limitations of G.S. 50-13.10. The amount of child support shall be determined as provided in G.S. 50-13.4(c). The order fixing the sum shall require the defendant to pay it either as a lump sum or in periodic payments as the circumstances of the case may appear to the court. The social security number, if known, of the minor child's parents shall be placed in the record of the proceeding. Compliance by the defendant with any or all of the further provisions of this Article or the order or orders of the court requiring additional acts to be performed by the defendant shall not be construed to relieve the defendant of his or her responsibility to pay the sum fixed or any modification or increase thereof.

The court before whom the matter may be brought, on motion of the State or the defendant, shall order that the alleged-parent defendant, the known natural parent, and the child submit to any blood tests and comparisons which have been developed and adapted for purposes of establishing or disproving parentage and which are reasonably accessible to the alleged-parent defendant, the known natural parent, and the child. The results of those blood tests and comparisons, including the statistical likelihood of the alleged parent's parentage, if available, shall be admitted in evidence when offered by a duly qualified, licensed practicing physician, duly qualified immunologist, duly qualified geneticist or other duly qualified person. The evidentiary effect of those blood tests and comparisons and the manner in which the expenses therefor are to be taxed as costs shall be as prescribed in G.S. 8-50.1. In addition, if a jury tries the issue of parentage, they shall be instructed as set out in G.S. 8-50.1. From a finding on the issue of parentage against the alleged-parent defendant, the alleged-parent defendant has the same right of appeal as though he or she had been found guilty of the crime of willful failure to support a child born out of wedlock. (1933, c. 228, s. 6; 1937, c. 432, s. 2; 1939, c. 217, ss. 1, 4; 1944, c. 40; 1947, c. 1014; 1971, c. 1185, s. 19; 1975, c. 449, s. 3; 1977, c. 3, s. 2; 1979, c. 576, s. 2; 1987, c. 739, s. 1; 1989, c. 529, s. 6; 1997-433, s. 4.1; 1998-17, s. 1; 2013-198, s. 20.)

§ 49-8. Power of court to modify orders, suspend sentence, etc.

Upon the determination of the issues set out in G.S. 49-7 and for the purpose of enforcing the payment of the sum fixed, the court is hereby given discretion, having regard for the circumstances of the case and the financial ability and earning capacity of the defendant and his or her willingness to cooperate, to make an order or orders upon the defendant and to modify such order or orders from time to time as the circumstances of the case may in the judgment of the court require subject to the limitations of G.S. 50-13.10. The order or orders made in this regard may include any or all of the following alternatives:

(1)   Repealed By Session Laws 1994, Extra Session, c. 14, s. 35.

(2)   Suspend sentence and continue the case from term to term;

(3)   Release the defendant from custody on probation conditioned upon the defendant's compliance with the terms of the probation and the payment of the sum fixed for the support and maintenance of the child;

(4)   Order the defendant to pay to the mother of the said child the necessary expenses of birth of the child and suitable medical attention for her;

(5)   Require the defendant to sign a recognizance with good and sufficient security, for compliance with any order which the court may make in proceedings under this Article. (1933, c. 228, s. 7; 1939, c. 217, s. 6; 1987, c. 739, s. 2; 1994, Ex. Sess., c. 14, s. 35.)

§ 49-9. Bond for future appearance of defendant.

At the preliminary hearing of any case arising under this Article it shall be the duty of the court, if it finds reasonable cause for holding the accused for a further hearing, to require a bond in the sum of not less than one hundred dollars ($100.00), conditioned upon the reappearance of the accused at the further hearing under this Article. This bond and all other bonds provided for in this Article shall be justified before, and approved by, the court or the clerk thereof. (1933, c. 228, s. 8.)

Article 2.

Legitimation of Children Born Out of Wedlock.

§ 49-10. Legitimation.

The putative father of any child born out of wedlock, whether such father resides in North Carolina or not, may apply by a verified written petition, filed in a special proceeding in the superior court of the county in which the putative father resides or in the superior court of the county in which the child resides, praying that such child be declared legitimate. The mother, if living, and the child shall be necessary parties to the proceeding, and the full names of the father, mother and the child shall be set out in the petition. A certified copy of a certificate of birth of the child shall be attached to the petition. If it appears to the court that the petitioner is the father of the child, the court may thereupon declare and pronounce the child legitimated; and the full names of the father, mother and the child shall be set out in the court order decreeing legitimation of the child. The clerk of the court shall record the order in the record of orders and decrees and it shall be cross-indexed under the name of the father as plaintiff or petitioner on the plaintiff's side of the cross-index, and under the name of the mother, and the child as defendants or respondents on the defendants' side of the cross-index. (Code, s. 39; Rev., s. 263; C.S., s. 277; 1947, c. 663, s. 1; 1971, c. 154; 1977, c. 83, s. 1.)

§ 49-11. Effects of legitimation.

The effect of legitimation under G.S. 49-10 shall be to impose upon the father and mother all of the lawful parental privileges and rights, as well as all of the obligations which parents owe to their lawful issue, and to the same extent as if said child had been born in wedlock, and to entitle such child by succession, inheritance or distribution, to take real and personal property by, through, and from his or her father and mother as if such child had been born in lawful wedlock. In case of death and intestacy, the real and personal estate of such child shall descend and be distributed according to the Intestate Succession Act as if he had been born in lawful wedlock. (Code, s. 40; Rev., s. 264; C.S., s. 278; 1955, c. 540, s. 2; 1959, c. 879, s. 10; 1963, c. 1131.)

§ 49-12. Legitimation by subsequent marriage.

When the mother of any child born out of wedlock and the reputed father of such child shall intermarry or shall have intermarried at any time after the birth of such child, the child shall, in all respects after such intermarriage be deemed and held to be legitimate and the child shall be entitled, by succession, inheritance or distribution, to real and personal property by, through, and from his father and mother as if such child had been born in lawful wedlock. In case of death and intestacy, the real and personal estate of such child shall descend and be distributed according to the Intestate Succession Act as if he had been born in lawful wedlock. (1917, c. 219, s. 1; C.S., s. 279; 1947, c. 663, s. 2; 1955, c. 540, s. 3; 1959, c. 879, s. 11.)

§ 49-12.1. Legitimation when mother married.

(a) The putative father of a child born to a mother who is married to another man may file a special proceeding to legitimate the child. The procedures shall be the same as those specified by G.S. 49-10, except that the spouse of the mother of the child shall be a necessary party to the proceeding and shall be properly served. A guardian ad litem shall be appointed to represent the child if the child is a minor.

(b) The presumption of legitimacy can be overcome by clear and convincing evidence.

(c) The parties may enter a consent order with the approval of the clerk of superior court. The order entered by the clerk shall find the facts and declare the proper person the father of the child and may change the surname of the child.

(d) The effect of legitimation under this section shall be the same as provided by G.S. 49-11.

(e) A certified copy of the order of legitimation under this section shall be sent by the clerk of superior court under his official seal to the State Registrar of Vital Statistics who shall make a new birth certificate bearing the full name of the father of the child and, if ordered by the clerk, changing the surname of the child. (1991, c. 667, s. 2; 1991 (Reg. Sess., 1992), c. 1030, s. 15; 1997-433, s. 4.9; 1998-17, s. 1.)

§ 49-13. New birth certificate on legitimation.

A certified copy of the order of legitimation when issued under the provisions of G.S. 49-10 shall be sent by the clerk of the superior court under his official seal to the State Registrar of Vital Statistics who shall then make the new birth certificate bearing the full name of the father, and change the surname of the child so that it will be the same as the surname of the father.

When a child is legitimated under the provisions of G.S. 49-12, the State Registrar of Vital Statistics shall make a new birth certificate bearing the full name of the father upon presentation of a certified copy of the certificate of marriage of the father and mother and change the surname of the child so that it will be the same as the surname of the father. (1947, c. 663, s. 3; 1955, c. 951, s. 2.)

§ 49-13.1: Repealed by Session Laws 2004-203, s. 3, effective August 17, 2004.

Article 3.

Civil Actions Regarding Children Born Out of Wedlock.

§ 49-14. Civil action to establish paternity; motion to set aside paternity.

(a)   The paternity of a child born out of wedlock may be established by civil action at any time prior to such child's eighteenth birthday. A copy of a certificate of birth of the child shall be attached to the complaint. The establishment of paternity shall not have the effect of legitimation. The social security numbers, if known, of the minor child's parents shall be placed in the record of the proceeding.

(b)   Proof of paternity pursuant to this section shall be by clear, cogent, and convincing evidence.

(c)   No such action shall be commenced nor judgment entered after the death of the putative father, unless the action is commenced either:

(1)   Prior to the death of the putative father;

(2)   Within one year after the date of death of the putative father, if a proceeding for administration of the estate of the putative father has not been commenced within one year of his death; or

(3)   Within the period specified in G.S. 28A-19-3(a) for presentation of claims against an estate, if a proceeding for administration of the estate of the putative father has been commenced within one year of his death.

Any judgment under this subsection establishing a decedent to be the father of a child shall be entered nunc pro tunc to the day preceding the date of death of the father.

(d) If the action to establish paternity is brought more than three years after birth of a child or is brought after the death of the putative father, paternity shall not be established in a contested case without evidence from a blood or genetic marker test.

(e) Either party to an action to establish paternity may request that the case be tried at the first session of the court after the case is docketed, but the presiding judge, in his discretion, may first try any pending case in which the rights of the parties or the public demand it.

(f) When a determination of paternity is pending in a IV-D case, the court shall enter a temporary order for child support upon motion and showing of clear, cogent, and convincing evidence of paternity. For purposes of this subsection, the results of blood or genetic tests shall constitute clear, cogent, and convincing evidence of paternity if the tests show that the probability of the alleged parent's parentage is ninety-seven percent (97%) or higher. If paternity is not thereafter established, then the putative father shall be reimbursed the full amount of temporary support paid under the order.

(g) Invoices for services rendered for pregnancy, childbirth, and blood or genetic testing are admissible as evidence without requiring third party foundation testimony and shall constitute prima facie evidence of the amounts incurred for the services or for testing on behalf of the child.

(h) Notwithstanding the time limitations of G.S. 1A-1, Rule 60 of the North Carolina Rules of Civil Procedure, or any other provision of law, an order of paternity may be set aside by a trial court if each of the following applies:

(1) The paternity order was entered as the result of fraud, duress, mutual mistake, or excusable neglect.

(2) Genetic tests establish the putative father is not the biological father of the child.

The burden of proof in any motion to set aside an order of paternity shall be on the moving party. Upon proper motion alleging fraud, duress, mutual mistake, or excusable neglect, the court shall order the child's mother, the child whose parentage is at issue, and the putative father to submit to genetic paternity testing pursuant to G.S. 8-50.1(b1). If the court determines, as a result of genetic testing, the putative father is not the biological father of the child and the order of paternity was entered as a result of fraud, duress, mutual mistake, or excusable neglect, the court may set aside the order of paternity. Nothing in this subsection shall be construed to affect the presumption of legitimacy where a child is born to a mother and the putative father during the course of a marriage. (1967, c. 993, s. 1; 1973, c. 1062, s. 3; 1977, c. 83, s. 2; 1981, c. 599, s. 14; 1985, c. 208, ss. 1, 2; 1993, c. 333, s. 3; 1995, c. 424, ss. 1, 2; 1997-154, s. 1; 1997-433, ss. 4.2, 4.10; 1998-17, s. 1; 2005-389, s. 3; 2011-328, s. 1.)

§ 49-15. Custody and support of children born out of wedlock when paternity established.

Upon and after the establishment of paternity pursuant to G.S. 49-14 of a child born out of wedlock, the rights, duties, and obligations of the mother and the father so established, with regard to support and custody of the child, shall be the same, and may be determined and enforced in the same manner, as if the child were the legitimate child of the father and mother. When paternity has been established, the father becomes responsible for medical expenses incident to the pregnancy and the birth of the child. (1967, c. 993, s. 1; 2013-198, s. 23.)

§ 49-16. Parties to proceeding.

Proceedings under this Article may be brought by:

(1)   The mother, the father, the child, or the personal representative of the mother or the child.

(2)   When the child, or the mother in case of medical expenses, is likely to become a public charge, the director of social services or such person as by law performs the duties of such official,

    a.   In the county where the mother resides or is found,

    b.   In the county where the putative father resides or is found, or

c. In the county where the child resides or is found. (1967, c. 993, s. 1; 1969, c. 982; 1975, c. 54, s. 2.)

§ 49-17. Jurisdiction over nonresident or nonpresent persons.

(a) The act of sexual intercourse within this State constitutes sufficient minimum contact with this forum for purposes of subjecting the person or persons participating therein to the jurisdiction of the courts of this State for actions brought under this Article for paternity and support of any child who may have been conceived as a result of such act.

(b) The jurisdictional basis in subsection (a) of this section shall be construed in addition to, and not in lieu of, any basis or bases for jurisdiction within G.S. 1-75.4. (1979, c. 542.)

Chapter 49A.

Rights of Children.

Article 1.

Children Conceived by Artificial Insemination.

§ 49A-1. Status of child born as a result of artificial insemination.

Any child or children born as the result of heterologous artificial insemination shall be considered at law in all respects the same as a naturally conceived legitimate child of the husband and wife requesting and consenting in writing to the use of such technique. (1971, c. 260.)

Chapter 50.

Divorce and Alimony.

Article 1.

Divorce, Alimony, and Child Support, Generally.

§ 50-1. Repealed by Session Laws 1971, c. 1185, s. 20.

§ 50-2. Bond for costs unnecessary.

It shall not be necessary for either party to a proceeding for divorce or alimony to give any undertaking to the other party to secure such costs as such other party may recover. (1871-2, c. 193, s. 41; Code, s. 1294; Rev., s. 1558; C.S., s. 1656.)

§ 50-3. Venue; removal of action.

In all proceedings for divorce, the summons shall be returnable to the court of the county in which either the plaintiff or defendant resides.

[In] any action brought under Chapter 50 for alimony or divorce filed in a county where the plaintiff resides but the defendant does not reside, where both parties are residents of the State of North Carolina, and where the plaintiff removes from the State and ceases to be a resident, the action may be removed upon motion of the defendant, for trial or for any motion in the cause, either before or after judgment, to the county in which the defendant resides. The judge, upon such motion, shall order the removal of the action, and the procedures of G.S. 1-87 shall be followed. (1871-2, c. 193, s. 40; Code, s. 1289; Rev., s. 1559; 1915, c. 229, s. 1; C.S., s. 1657; 1977, 2nd Sess., c. 1223.)

§ 50-4. What marriages may be declared void on application of either party.

The district court, during a session of court, on application made as by law provided, by either party to a marriage contracted contrary to the prohibitions contained in the Chapter entitled Marriage, or declared void by said Chapter, may declare such marriage void from the beginning, subject, nevertheless, to G.S. 51-3. (1871-2, c. 193, s. 33; Code, s. 1283; Rev., s. 1560; C.S., s. 1658; 1945, c. 635; 1971, c. 1185, s. 21; 1973, c. 1; 1979, c. 525, s. 10.)

§ 50-5. Repealed by Session Laws 1983, c. 613, s. 1.

§ 50-5.1. Grounds for absolute divorce in cases of incurable insanity.

In all cases where a husband and wife have lived separate and apart for three consecutive years, without cohabitation, and are still so living separate and apart by reason of the incurable insanity of one of them, the court may grant a decree of absolute divorce upon the petition of the sane spouse: Provided, if the insane spouse has been released on a trial basis to the custody of his or her respective spouse such shall not be considered as terminating the status of living "separate and apart" nor shall it be considered as constituting "cohabitation" for the purpose of this section nor shall it prevent the granting of a divorce as provided by this section. Provided further, the evidence shall show that the insane spouse is suffering from incurable insanity, and has been confined or examined for three consecutive years next preceding the bringing of the action in an institution for the care and treatment of the mentally disordered or, if not so confined, has been examined at least three years preceding the institution of the action for divorce and then found to be incurably insane as hereinafter provided. Provided further, that proof of incurable insanity be supported by the testimony of two reputable physicians, one of whom shall be a staff member or the superintendent of the institution where the insane spouse is confined, and one regularly practicing physician in the community wherein such husband and wife reside, who has no connection with the institution in which said insane spouse is confined; and provided further that a sworn statement signed by said staff member or said superintendent of the institution wherein the insane spouse is confined or was examined shall be admissible as evidence of the facts and opinions therein stated as to the mental status of said insane spouse and as to whether or not said insane spouse is suffering from incurable insanity, or the parties according to the laws governing depositions may take the deposition of said staff member or superintendent of the institution wherein the insane spouse is confined; and provided further that incurable insanity may be proved by the testimony of one or more licensed physicians who are members of the staff of one of this State's accredited four-year medical schools or a state-supported mental institution, supported by the testimony of one or more other physicians licensed by the State of North Carolina, that each of them examined the allegedly incurable insane spouse at least three years preceding the institution of the action for divorce and then determined that said spouse was suffering from incurable insanity and that one or more of them examined the allegedly insane spouse subsequent to the institution of the action and that in his or their opinion the said allegedly insane spouse was continuously incurably insane throughout the full period of three years prior to the institution of the said action.

In lieu of proof of incurable insanity and confinement for three consecutive years next preceding the bringing of the action in an institution for the care and treatment of the mentally disordered prescribed in the preceding paragraph, it shall be sufficient if the evidence shall show that the allegedly insane spouse was adjudicated to be insane more than three years preceding the institution of the action for divorce, that such insanity has continued without interruption since such adjudication and that such person has not been adjudicated to be sane since such adjudication of insanity; provided, further, proof of incurable insanity existing after the institution of the action for divorce shall be furnished by the testimony of two reputable, regularly practicing physicians, one of whom shall be a psychiatrist.

In lieu of proof of incurable insanity and confinement for three consecutive years next preceding the bringing of the action in an institution for the care and treatment of the mentally disordered, or the adjudication of insanity, as prescribed in the preceding paragraphs, it shall be sufficient if the evidence shall show that the insane spouse was examined by two or more members of the staff of one of this State's accredited four-year medical schools, both of whom are medical doctors, at least three years preceding the institution of the action for divorce with a determination at that time by said staff members that said spouse is suffering from incurable insanity, that such insanity has continued without interruption since such determination; provided, further, that sworn statements signed by the staff members of the accredited medical school who examined the insane spouse at least three years preceding the commencement of the action shall be admissible as evidence of the facts and opinions therein stated as to the mental status of said insane spouse as to whether or not said insane spouse was suffering from incurable insanity; provided, further, that proof of incurable insanity under this section existing after the institution of the action for divorce shall be furnished by the testimony of two reputable physicians, one of whom shall be a psychiatrist on the staff of one of the State's accredited four-year medical schools, and one a physician practicing regularly in the community wherein such insane person resides.

In all decrees granted under this subdivision in actions in which the insane defendant has insufficient income and property to provide for his or her own care and maintenance, the court shall require the plaintiff to provide for the care and maintenance of the insane defendant for the defendant's lifetime, based upon the standards set out in G.S. 50-16.5(a). The trial court will retain jurisdiction of the parties and the cause, from term to term, for the purpose of making such orders as equity may require to enforce the provisions of the decree requiring plaintiff to furnish the necessary funds for such care and maintenance.

Service of process shall be held upon the regular guardian for said defendant spouse, if any, and if no regular guardian, upon a duly appointed guardian ad litem and also upon the superintendent or physician in charge of the institution wherein the insane spouse is confined. Such guardian or guardian ad litem shall make an investigation of the circumstances and notify the next of kin of the insane spouse or the superintendent of the institution of the action and whenever practical confer with said next of kin before filing appropriate pleadings in behalf of the defendant.

In all actions brought under this subdivision, if the jury finds as a fact that the plaintiff has been guilty of such conduct as has conduced to the unsoundness of mind of the insane defendant, the relief prayed for shall be denied.

The plaintiff or defendant must have resided in this State for six months next preceding institution of any action under this section. (1945, c. 755; 1949, c. 264, s. 5; 1953, c. 1087; 1955, c. 887, s. 15; 1963, c. 1173; 1971, c. 1173, ss. 1, 2; 1975, c. 771; 1977, c. 501, s. 1; 1983, c. 613, s. 1.)

§ 50-6. Divorce after separation of one year on application of either party.

Marriages may be dissolved and the parties thereto divorced from the bonds of matrimony on the application of either party, if and when the husband and wife have lived separate and apart for one year, and the plaintiff or defendant in the suit for divorce has resided in the State for a period of six months. A divorce under this section shall not be barred to either party by any defense or plea based upon any provision of G.S. 50-7, a plea of res judicata, or a plea of recrimination. Notwithstanding the provisions of G.S. 50-11, or of the common law, a divorce under this section shall not affect the rights of a dependent spouse with respect to alimony which have been asserted in the action or any other pending action.

Whether there has been a resumption of marital relations during the period of separation shall be determined pursuant to G.S. 52-10.2. Isolated incidents of sexual intercourse between the parties shall not toll the statutory period required for divorce predicated on separation of one year. (1931, c. 72; 1933, c. 163; 1937, c. 100, ss. 1, 2; 1943, c. 448, s. 3; 1949, c. 264, s. 3; 1965, c. 636, s. 2; 1977, c. 817, s. 1; 1977, 2nd Sess., c. 1190, s. 1; 1979, c. 709, s. 1; 1981, c. 182; 1983, c. 613, s. 2; c. 923, s. 217; 1987, c. 664, s. 2.)

§ 50-7. Grounds for divorce from bed and board.

The court may grant divorces from bed and board on application of the party injured, made as by law provided, in the following cases if either party:

(1)   Abandons his or her family.

(2)   Maliciously turns the other out of doors.

(3)   By cruel or barbarous treatment endangers the life of the other. In addition, the court may grant the victim of such treatment the remedies available under G.S. 50B-1, et seq.

(4)   Offers such indignities to the person of the other as to render his or her condition intolerable and life burdensome.

(5)   Becomes an excessive user of alcohol or drugs so as to render the condition of the other spouse intolerable and the life of that spouse burdensome.

(6)   Commits adultery. (1871-2, c. 193, s. 36; Code, s. 1286; Rev., s. 1562; C.S., s. 1660; 1967, c. 1152, s. 7; 1971, c. 1185, s. 22; 1979, c. 561, s. 5; 1985, c. 574, ss. 1, 2.)

§ 50-8. Contents of complaint; verification; venue and service in action by nonresident; certain divorces validated.

In all actions for divorce the complaint shall be verified in accordance with the provisions of Rule 11 of the Rules of Civil Procedure and G.S. 1-148. The plaintiff shall set forth in his or her complaint that the complainant or defendant has been a resident of the State of North Carolina for at least six months next preceding the filing of the complaint, and that the facts set forth therein as grounds for divorce, except in actions for divorce from bed and board, have existed to his or her knowledge for at least six months prior to the filing of the complaint: Provided, however, that if the cause for divorce is one-year separation, then it shall not be necessary to allege in the complaint that the grounds for divorce have existed for at least six months prior to the filing of the complaint; it being the purpose of this proviso to permit a divorce after such separation of one year without awaiting an additional six months for filing the complaint: Provided, further, that if the complainant is a nonresident of the State action shall be brought in the county of the defendant's residence, and summons served upon the defendant personally or service of summons accepted by the defendant personally in the manner provided in G.S. 1A-1, Rule 4(j)(1). Notwithstanding any other provision of this section, any suit or action for divorce heretofore instituted by a nonresident of this State in which the defendant was personally served with summons or in which the defendant personally accepted service of the summons and the case was tried and final judgment entered in a court of this State in a county other than the county of the defendant's residence, is hereby validated and declared to be legal and proper, the same as if the suit or action for divorce had been brought in the county of the defendant's residence.

In all divorce actions the complaint shall set forth the name and age of any minor child or children of the marriage, and in the event there are no minor children of the marriage, the complaint shall so state.

In all prior suits and actions for divorce heretofore instituted and tried in the courts of this State where the averments of fact required to be contained in the affidavit heretofore required by this section are or have been alleged and set forth in the complaint in said suits or actions and said complaints have been duly verified as required by Rule 11 of the Rules of Civil Procedure, said allegations so contained in said complaints shall be deemed to be, and are hereby made, a substantial compliance as to the allegations heretofore required by this section to be set forth in any affidavit; and all such suits or actions for divorce, as well as the judgments or decrees issued and entered as a result thereof, are hereby validated and declared to be legal and proper judgments and decrees of divorce.

In all suits and actions for divorce heretofore instituted and tried in this State on and subsequent to the 5th day of April, 1951, wherein the statements, averments, or allegations in the verification to the complaint in said suits or actions are not in accordance with the provisions of Rule 11 of the Rules of Civil

Procedure and G.S. 1-148 or the requirements of this section as to verification of complaint or the allegations, statements or averments in the verification contain the language that the facts set forth in the complaint are true "to the best of affiant's knowledge and belief" instead of the language "that the same is true to his (or her) own knowledge" or similar variation in language, said allegations, statements and averments in said verifications as contained in or attached to said complaint shall be deemed to be, and are hereby made, a substantial compliance as to the allegations, averments or statements required by this section to be set forth in any such verifications; and all such suits or actions for divorce, as well as the judgments or decrees issued and entered as a result thereof, are hereby validated and declared to be legal and proper judgments and decrees of divorce. (1868-9, c. 93, s. 46; 1869-70, c. 184; Code, s. 1287; Rev., s. 1563; 1907, c. 1008, s. 1; C.S., s. 1661; 1925, c. 93; 1933, c. 71, ss. 2, 3; 1943, c. 448, s. 1; 1947, c. 165; 1949, c. 264, s. 4; 1951, c. 590; 1955, c. 103; 1965, c. 636, s. 3; c. 751, s. 1; 1967, c. 50; c. 954, s. 3; 1969, c. 803; 1971, c. 415; 1973, c. 39; 1981, c. 599, s. 15; 1997-433, s. 4.3; 1998-17, s. 1; 2013-93, s. 1.)

§ 50-9. Effect of answer of summons by defendant.

In all cases upon an action for a divorce absolute, where judgment of divorce has heretofore been granted and where the plaintiff has caused to be served upon the defendant in person a legal summons, whether by verified complaint or unverified complaint, and such defendant answered such summons, and where the trial of said action was duly and legally had in all other respects and judgments rendered by a judge of the superior court upon issues answered by a judge and jury, in accordance with law, such judgments are hereby declared to have the same force and effect as any judgment upon an action for divorce otherwise had legally and regularly. (1929, c. 290, s. 1; 1947, c. 393.)

§ 50-10. Material facts found by judge or jury in divorce or annulment proceedings; when notice of trial not required; procedure same as ordinary civil actions.

(a)   Except as provided for in subsection (e) of this section, the material facts in every complaint asking for a divorce or for an annulment shall be deemed to be denied by the defendant, whether the same shall be actually denied by pleading or not, and no judgment shall be given in favor of the plaintiff in any such complaint until such facts have been found by a judge or jury.

(b) Nothing herein shall require notice of trial to be given to a defendant who has not made an appearance in the action.

(c) The determination of whether there is to be a jury trial or a trial before the judge without a jury shall be made in accordance with G.S. 1A-1, Rules 38 and 39.

(d) The provisions of G.S. 1A-1, Rule 56, shall be applicable to actions for absolute divorce pursuant to G.S. 50-6, for the purpose of determining whether any genuine issue of material fact remains for trial by jury, but in the event the court determines that no genuine issue of material fact remains for trial by jury, the court must find the facts as provided herein. The court may enter a judgment of absolute divorce pursuant to the procedures set forth in G.S. 1A-1, Rule 56, finding all requisite facts from nontestimonial evidence presented by affidavit, verified motion or other verified pleading.

(e) The clerk of superior court, upon request of the plaintiff, may enter judgment in cases in which the plaintiff's only claim against the defendant is for absolute divorce, or absolute divorce and the resumption of a former name, and the defendant has been defaulted for failure to appear, the defendant has answered admitting the allegations of the complaint, or the defendant has filed a waiver of the right to answer, and the defendant is not an infant or incompetent person. (1868-9, c. 93, s. 47; Code, s. 1288; Rev., s. 1564; C.S., s. 1662; 1963, c. 540, ss. 1, 2; 1965, c. 105; c. 636, s. 4; 1971, c. 17; 1973, cc. 2, 460; 1981, c. 12; 1983 (Reg. Sess., 1984), c. 1037, s. 4; 1985, c. 140; 1991, c. 568, s. 1; 2004-128, s. 6.)

§ 50-11. Effects of absolute divorce.

(a) After a judgment of divorce from the bonds of matrimony, all rights arising out of the marriage shall cease and determine except as hereinafter set out, and either party may marry again without restriction arising from the dissolved marriage.

(b) No judgment of divorce shall cause any child in esse or begotten of the body of the wife during coverture to be treated as a child born out of wedlock.

(c) A divorce obtained pursuant to G.S. 50-5.1 or G.S. 50-6 shall not affect the rights of either spouse with respect to any action for alimony or postseparation support pending at the time the judgment for divorce is granted. Furthermore, a judgment of absolute divorce shall not impair or destroy the right of a spouse to receive alimony or postseparation support or affect any other rights provided for such spouse under any judgment or decree of a court rendered before or at the time of the judgment of absolute divorce.

(d) A divorce obtained outside the State in an action in which jurisdiction over the person of the dependent spouse was not obtained shall not impair or destroy the right of the dependent spouse to alimony as provided by the laws of this State.

(e) An absolute divorce obtained within this State shall destroy the right of a spouse to equitable distribution under G.S. 50-20 unless the right is asserted prior to judgment of absolute divorce; except, the defendant may bring an action or file a motion in the cause for equitable distribution within six months from the date of the judgment in such a case if service of process upon the defendant was by publication pursuant to G.S. 1A-1, Rule 4 and the defendant failed to appear in the action for divorce.

(f) An absolute divorce by a court that lacked personal jurisdiction over the absent spouse or lacked jurisdiction to dispose of the property shall not destroy the right of a spouse to equitable distribution under G.S. 50-20 if an action or motion in the cause is filed within six months after the judgment of divorce is entered. The validity of such divorce may be attacked in the action for equitable distribution. (1871-2, c. 193, s. 43; Code, s. 1295; Rev., s. 1569; 1919, c. 204; C.S., s. 1663; 1953, c. 1313; 1955, c. 872, s. 1; 1967, c. 1152, s. 3; 1981, c. 190; c. 815, s. 2; 1987, c. 844, s. 3; 1991, c. 569, s. 2; 1995, c. 319, s. 8; 1998-217, s. 7(a), (b); 2013-198, s. 24.)

§ 50-11.1. Children born of voidable marriage legitimate.

A child born of voidable marriage or a bigamous marriage is legitimate notwithstanding the annulment of the marriage. (1951, c. 893, s. 2.)

§ 50-11.2. Judgment provisions pertaining to care, custody, tuition and maintenance of minor children.

Where the court has the requisite jurisdiction and upon proper pleadings and proper and due notice to all interested parties the judgment in a divorce action may contain such provisions respecting care, custody, tuition and maintenance of the minor children of the marriage as the court may adjudge; and from time to time such provisions may be modified upon due notice and hearing and a showing of a substantial change in condition; and if there be no minor children, the judgment may so state. The jurisdictional requirements of G.S. 50A-201, 50A-203, or 50A-204 shall apply in regard to a custody decree. (1973, c. 927, s. 1; 1979, c. 110, s. 11; 1999-223, s. 10.)

§ 50-11.3. Certain judgments entered prior to January 1, 1981, validated.

Any judgment of divorce which has been entered prior to January 1, 1981, by a court of competent jurisdiction within the State of North Carolina without a conclusion of law that the plaintiff was entitled to an absolute divorce, but which is proper in all other respects, is hereby rendered valid and of full force and effect. (1977, c. 320; 1981, c. 473.)

§ 50-11.4. Certain judgments of divorce validated.

Any judgment of divorce entered as a result of an action instituted prior to October 1, 1983, upon any grounds abolished by Chapter 613 of the 1983 Session Laws as amended by Section 217(O) of Chapter 923 of the 1983 Session Laws, which is proper in all other respects, is hereby rendered valid and of full force and effect. (1985 (Reg. Sess., 1986), c. 952.)

§ 50-12. Resumption of maiden or premarriage surname.

(a) Any woman whose marriage is dissolved by a decree of absolute divorce may, upon application to the clerk of court of the county in which she resides or where the divorce was granted setting forth her intention to do so, change her name to any of the following:

(1) Her maiden name; or

(2) The surname of a prior deceased husband; or

(3) The surname of a prior living husband if she has children who have that husband's surname.

(a1) A man whose marriage is dissolved by decree of absolute divorce may, upon application to the clerk of court of the county in which he resides or where the divorce was granted setting forth his intention to do so, change the surname he took upon marriage to his premarriage surname.

(b) The application and fee required by subsection (e) of this section shall be presented to the clerk of the court of the county in which such divorced person resides or where the divorce was granted, and shall set forth the full name of the former spouse of the applicant, the name of the county and state in which the divorce was granted, and the term or session of court at which such divorce was granted, and shall be signed by the woman in her full maiden name, or by the man in his full premarriage surname. The clerks of court of the several counties of the State shall record and index such applications in such manner as shall be required by the Administrative Office of the Courts.

(c) If an applicant, since the divorce, has adopted one of the surnames listed in subsection (a) or (a1) of this section, the applicant's use and adoption of that name is validated.

(d) In the complaint, or counterclaim for divorce filed by any person in this State, the person may petition the court to adopt any surname as provided by this section, and the court is authorized to incorporate in the divorce decree an order authorizing the person to adopt that surname.

(e) For support of the General Court of Justice, a fee in the amount of ten dollars ($10.00) shall be assessed against each person requesting the resumption of maiden or premarriage surname in accordance with this section. Sums collected under this section shall be remitted to the State Treasurer. (1937, c. 53; 1941, c. 9; 1951, c. 780; 1957, c. 394; 1971, c. 1185, s. 23; 1981, c. 494, ss. 1-4; 1985, c. 488; 1993 (Reg. Sess., 1994), c. 565, s. 1; 2005-38, s. 1; 2010-31, s. 15.9(a).)

§ 50-13. Repealed by Session Laws 1967, c. 1153, s. 1.

§ 50-13.1. Action or proceeding for custody of minor child.

(a)   (See Editor's note) Any parent, relative, or other person, agency, organization or institution claiming the right to custody of a minor child may institute an action or proceeding for the custody of such child, as hereinafter provided. Any person whose actions resulted in a conviction under G.S. 14-27.2, G.S. 14-27.2A, or G.S. 14-27.3 and the conception of the minor child may not claim the right to custody of that minor child. Unless a contrary intent is clear, the word "custody" shall be deemed to include custody or visitation or both.

(a1)   Notwithstanding any other provision of law, any person instituting an action or proceeding for custody ex parte who has been convicted of a sexually violent offense as defined in G.S. 14-208.6(5) shall disclose the conviction in the pleadings.

(b)   Whenever it appears to the court, from the pleadings or otherwise, that an action involves a contested issue as to the custody or visitation of a minor child, the matter, where there is a program established pursuant to G.S. 7A-494, shall be set for mediation of the unresolved issues as to custody and visitation before or concurrent with the setting of the matter for hearing unless the court waives mediation pursuant to subsection (c). Issues that arise in motions for contempt or for modifications as well as in other pleadings shall be set for mediation unless mediation is waived by the court. Alimony, child support, and other economic issues may not be referred for mediation pursuant to this section. The purposes of mediation under this section include the pursuit of the following goals:

(1)   To reduce any acrimony that exists between the parties to a dispute involving custody or visitation of a minor child;

(2)   The development of custody and visitation agreements that are in the child's best interest;

(3) To provide the parties with informed choices and, where possible, to give the parties the responsibility for making decisions about child custody and visitation;

(4) To provide a structured, confidential, nonadversarial setting that will facilitate the cooperative resolution of custody and visitation disputes and minimize the stress and anxiety to which the parties, and especially the child, are subjected; and

(5) To reduce the relitigation of custody and visitation disputes.

(c) For good cause, on the motion of either party or on the court's own motion, the court may waive the mandatory setting under Article 39A of Chapter 7A of the General Statutes of a contested custody or visitation matter for mediation. Good cause may include, but is not limited to, the following: a showing of undue hardship to a party; an agreement between the parties for voluntary mediation, subject to court approval; allegations of abuse or neglect of the minor child; allegations of alcoholism, drug abuse, or domestic violence between the parents in common; or allegations of severe psychological, psychiatric, or emotional problems. A showing by either party that the party resides more than fifty miles from the court may be considered good cause.

(d) Either party may move to have the mediation proceedings dismissed and the action heard in court due to the mediator's bias, undue familiarity with a party, or other prejudicial ground.

(e) Mediation proceeding shall be held in private and shall be confidential. Except as provided in this Article, all verbal or written communications from either or both parties to the mediator or between the parties in the presence of the mediator made in a proceeding pursuant to this section are absolutely privileged and inadmissible in court. The mediator may assess the needs and interests of the child, and may interview the child or others who are not parties to the proceedings when he or she thinks appropriate.

(f) Neither the mediator nor any party or other person involved in mediation sessions under this section shall be competent to testify to communications made during or in furtherance of such mediation sessions; provided, there is no privilege as to communications made in furtherance of a crime or fraud. Nothing in this subsection shall be construed as permitting an individual to obtain immunity from prosecution for criminal conduct or as excusing an individual from the reporting requirements of Article 3 of Chapter 7B of the General Statutes or G.S. 108A-102.

(g) Any agreement reached by the parties as a result of the mediation shall be reduced to writing, signed by each party, and submitted to the court as soon as practicable. Unless the court finds good reason not to, it shall incorporate the agreement in a court order and it shall become enforceable as a court order. If some or all of the issues as to custody or visitation are not resolved by mediation, the mediator shall report that fact to the court.

(h) If an agreement that results from mediation and is incorporated into a court order is referred to as a "parenting agreement" or called by some similar name, it shall nevertheless be deemed to be a custody order or child custody determination for purposes of Chapter 50A of the General Statutes, G.S. 14-320.1, G.S. 110-139.1, or other places where those terms appear.

(i) If the child whose custody is the subject of an action under this Chapter also is the subject of a juvenile abuse, neglect, or dependency proceeding pursuant to Subchapter 1 of Chapter 7B of the General Statutes, then the custody action under this Chapter is stayed as provided in G.S. 7B-200. (1967, c. 1153, s. 2; 1989, c. 795, s. 15(b); 1998-202, s. 13(p); 2004-128, s. 10; 2005-320, s. 5; 2005-423, s. 4; 2007-462, s. 1; 2011-411, s 4; 2013-236, s. 13.)

§ 50-13.2. Who entitled to custody; terms of custody; visitation rights of grandparents; taking child out of State; consideration of parent's military service.

(a) An order for custody of a minor child entered pursuant to this section shall award the custody of such child to such person, agency, organization or institution as will best promote the interest and welfare of the child. In making the determination, the court shall consider all relevant factors including acts of domestic violence between the parties, the safety of the child, and the safety of either party from domestic violence by the other party and shall make findings accordingly. An order for custody must include findings of fact which support the determination of what is in the best interest of the child. Between the mother and father, whether natural or adoptive, no presumption shall apply as to who will better promote the interest and welfare of the child. Joint custody to the parents shall be considered upon the request of either parent.

(b) An order for custody of a minor child may grant joint custody to the parents, exclusive custody to one person, agency, organization, or institution, or grant custody to two or more persons, agencies, organizations, or institutions. Any order for custody shall include such terms, including visitation, as will best promote the interest and welfare of the child. If the court finds that domestic violence has occurred, the court shall enter such orders that best protect the children and party who were the victims of domestic violence, in accordance with the provisions of G.S. 50B-3(a1)(1), (2), and (3). If a party is absent or relocates with or without the children because of an act of domestic violence, the absence or relocation shall not be a factor that weighs against the party in determining custody or visitation. Absent an order of the court to the contrary, each parent shall have equal access to the records of the minor child involving the health, education, and welfare of the child.

(b1) An order for custody of a minor child may provide visitation rights for any grandparent of the child as the court, in its discretion, deems appropriate. As used in this subsection, "grandparent" includes a biological grandparent of a child adopted by a stepparent or a relative of the child where a substantial relationship exists between the grandparent and the child. Under no circumstances shall a biological grandparent of a child adopted by adoptive parents, neither of whom is related to the child and where parental rights of both biological parents have been terminated, be entitled to visitation rights.

(b2) Any order for custody, including visitation, may, as a condition of such custody or visitation, require either or both parents, or any other person seeking custody or visitation, to abstain from consuming alcohol and may require submission to a continuous alcohol monitoring system, of a type approved by the Division of Adult Correction of the Department of Public Safety, to verify compliance with this condition of custody or visitation. Any order pursuant to this subsection shall include an order to the monitoring provider to report any violation of the order to the court and each party to the action. Failure to comply with this condition shall be grounds for civil or criminal contempt.

(c) An order for custody of a minor child may provide for such child to be taken outside of the State, but if the order contemplates the return of the child to this State, the judge may require the person, agency, organization or institution having custody out of this State to give bond or other security conditioned upon the return of the child to this State in accordance with the order of the court.

(d) If, within a reasonable time, one parent fails to consent to adoption pursuant to Chapter 48 of the General Statutes or parental rights have not been terminated, the consent of the other consenting parent shall not be effective in an action for custody of the child.

(e) An order for custody of a minor child may provide for visitation rights by electronic communication. In granting visitation by electronic communication, the court shall consider the following:

(1) Whether electronic communication is in the best interest of the minor child.

(2) Whether equipment to communicate by electronic means is available, accessible, and affordable to the parents of the minor child.

(3) Any other factor the court deems appropriate in determining whether to grant visitation by electronic communication.

The court may set guidelines for electronic communication, including the hours in which the communication may be made, the allocation of costs between the parents in implementing electronic communication with the child, and the furnishing of access information between parents necessary to facilitate electronic communication. Electronic communication with a minor child may be used to supplement visitation with the child. Electronic communication may not be used as a replacement or substitution for custody or visitation. The amount of time electronic communication is used shall not be a factor in calculating child support or be used to justify or support relocation by the custodial parent out of the immediate area or the State. Electronic communication between the minor child and the parent may be subject to supervision as ordered by the court. As used in this subsection, "electronic communication" means contact, other than face-to-face contact, facilitated by electronic means, such as by telephone, electronic mail, instant messaging, video teleconferencing, wired or wireless technologies by Internet, or other medium of communication.

(f) In a proceeding for custody of a minor child of a service member, a court may not consider a parent's past deployment or possible future deployment as the only basis in determining the best interest of the child. The court may consider any significant impact on the best interest of the child regarding the parent's past or possible future deployment. (1957, c. 545; 1967, c. 1153, s. 2; 1977, c. 501, s. 2; 1979, c. 967; 1981, c. 735, ss. 1, 2; 1985, c. 575, s. 3; 1987, c. 541, s. 2; c. 776; 1995 (Reg. Sess., 1996), c. 591, s. 5; 2004-186, s. 17.1; 2009-314, s. 1; 2012-146, s. 10; 2013-27, s. 1.)

§ 50-13.2A. Action for visitation of an adopted grandchild.

A biological grandparent may institute an action or proceeding for visitation rights with a child adopted by a stepparent or a relative of the child where a substantial relationship exists between the grandparent and the child. Under no circumstances shall a biological grandparent of a child adopted by adoptive parents, neither of whom is related to the child and where parental rights of both biological parents have been terminated, be entitled to visitation rights. A court may award visitation rights if it determines that visitation is in the best interest of the child. An order awarding visitation rights shall contain findings of fact which support the determination by the judge of the best interest of the child. Procedure, venue, and jurisdiction shall be as in an action for custody. (1985, c. 575, s. 2.)

§ 50-13.3. Enforcement of order for custody.

(a) An order providing for the custody of a minor child is enforceable by proceedings for civil contempt, and its disobedience may be punished by proceedings for criminal contempt, as provided in Chapter 5A, Contempt, of the General Statutes.

Notwithstanding the provisions of G.S. 1-294, an order pertaining to child custody which has been appealed to the appellate division is enforceable in the trial court by proceedings for civil contempt during the pendency of the appeal. Upon motion of an aggrieved party, the court of the appellate division in which the appeal is pending may stay any order for civil contempt entered for child custody until the appeal is decided, if justice requires.

(b) Any court of this State having jurisdiction to make an award of custody of a minor child in an action or proceeding therefor, shall have the power of injunction in such action or proceeding as provided in Article 37 of Chapter 1 of the General Statutes and G.S. 1A-1, Rule 65. (1967, c. 1153, s. 2; 1969, c. 895, s. 16; 1977, c. 711, s. 26; 1983, c. 530, s. 2.)

§ 50-13.4. Action for support of minor child.

(a) Any parent, or any person, agency, organization or institution having custody of a minor child, or bringing an action or proceeding for the custody of such child, or a minor child by his guardian may institute an action for the support of such child as hereinafter provided.

(b) In the absence of pleading and proof that the circumstances otherwise warrant, the father and mother shall be primarily liable for the support of a minor child. In the absence of pleading and proof that the circumstances otherwise warrant, parents of a minor, unemancipated child who is the custodial or noncustodial parent of a child shall share this primary liability for their grandchild's support with the minor parent, the court determining the proper share, until the minor parent reaches the age of 18 or becomes emancipated. If both the parents of the child requiring support were unemancipated minors at the time of the child's conception, the parents of both minor parents share primary liability for their grandchild's support until both minor parents reach the age of 18 or become emancipated. If only one parent of the child requiring support was an unemancipated minor at the time of the child's conception, the parents of both parents are liable for any arrearages in child support owed by the adult or emancipated parent until the other parent reaches the age of 18 or becomes emancipated. In the absence of pleading and proof that the circumstances otherwise warrant, any other person, agency, organization or institution standing in loco parentis shall be secondarily liable for such support. Such other circumstances may include, but shall not be limited to, the relative ability of all the above-mentioned parties to provide support or the inability of one or more of them to provide support, and the needs and estate of the child. The judge may enter an order requiring any one or more of the above-mentioned parties to provide for the support of the child as may be appropriate in the particular case, and if appropriate the court may authorize the application of any separate estate of the child to his support. However, the judge may not order support to be paid by a person who is not the child's parent or an agency, organization or institution standing in loco parentis absent evidence and a finding that such person, agency, organization or institution has voluntarily assumed the obligation of support in writing. The preceding sentence shall not be construed to prevent any court from ordering the support of a child by an agency of the State or county which agency may be responsible under law for such support.

The judge may order responsible parents in a IV-D establishment case to perform a job search, if the responsible parent is not incapacitated. This includes IV-D cases in which the responsible parent is a noncustodial mother or a noncustodial father whose affidavit of parentage has been filed with the court or when paternity is not at issue for the child. The court may further order the responsible parent to participate in work activities, as defined in 42 U.S.C. § 607, as the court deems appropriate.

(c) Payments ordered for the support of a minor child shall be in such amount as to meet the reasonable needs of the child for health, education, and maintenance, having due regard to the estates, earnings, conditions, accustomed standard of living of the child and the parties, the child care and homemaker contributions of each party, and other facts of the particular case. Payments ordered for the support of a minor child shall be on a monthly basis, due and payable on the first day of each month. The requirement that orders be established on a monthly basis does not affect the availability of garnishment of disposable earnings based on an obligor's pay period.

The court shall determine the amount of child support payments by applying the presumptive guidelines established pursuant to subsection (c1) of this section. However, upon request of any party, the Court shall hear evidence, and from the evidence, find the facts relating to the reasonable needs of the child for support and the relative ability of each parent to provide support. If, after considering the evidence, the Court finds by the greater weight of the evidence that the application of the guidelines would not meet or would exceed the reasonable needs of the child considering the relative ability of each parent to provide support or would be otherwise unjust or inappropriate the Court may vary from the guidelines. If the court orders an amount other than the amount determined by application of the presumptive guidelines, the court shall make findings of fact as to the criteria that justify varying from the guidelines and the basis for the amount ordered.

Payments ordered for the support of a child shall terminate when the child reaches the age of 18 except:

(1) If the child is otherwise emancipated, payments shall terminate at that time;

(2) If the child is still in primary or secondary school when the child reaches age 18, support payments shall continue until the child graduates, otherwise ceases to attend school on a regular basis, fails to make satisfactory academic progress towards graduation, or reaches age 20, whichever comes first, unless the court in its discretion orders that payments cease at age 18 or prior to high school graduation.

(3) (See Editor's note for applicability) If the child is enrolled in a cooperative innovative high school program authorized under Part 9 of Article 16 of Chapter 115C of the General Statutes, then payments shall terminate when the child completes his or her fourth year of enrollment or when the child reaches the age of 18, whichever occurs later.

In the case of graduation, or attaining age 20, payments shall terminate without order by the court, subject to the right of the party receiving support to show, upon motion and with notice to the opposing party, that the child has not graduated or attained the age of 20.

If an arrearage for child support or fees due exists at the time that a child support obligation terminates, payments shall continue in the same total amount that was due under the terms of the previous court order or income withholding in effect at the time of the support obligation. The total amount of these payments is to be applied to the arrearage until all arrearages and fees are satisfied or until further order of the court.

(c1) Effective July 1, 1990, the Conference of Chief District Judges shall prescribe uniform statewide presumptive guidelines for the computation of child support obligations of each parent as provided in Chapter 50 or elsewhere in the General Statutes and shall develop criteria for determining when, in a particular case, application of the guidelines would be unjust or inappropriate. Prior to May 1, 1990 these guidelines and criteria shall be reported to the General Assembly by the Administrative Office of the Courts by delivering copies to the President Pro Tempore of the Senate and the Speaker of the House of Representatives. The purpose of the guidelines and criteria shall be to ensure that payments ordered for the support of a minor child are in such amount as to meet the reasonable needs of the child for health, education, and maintenance, having due regard to the estates, earnings, conditions, accustomed standard of living of the child and the parties, the child care and homemaker contributions of each party, and other facts of the particular case. The guidelines shall include a procedure for setting child support, if any, in a joint or shared custody arrangement which shall reflect the other statutory requirements herein.

Periodically, but at least once every four years, the Conference of Chief District Judges shall review the guidelines to determine whether their application results in appropriate child support award amounts. The Conference may modify the guidelines accordingly. The Conference shall give the Department of Health and Human Services, the Administrative Office of the Courts, and the general public an opportunity to provide the Conference with information relevant to the development and review of the guidelines. Any modifications of the guidelines or criteria shall be reported to the General Assembly by the Administrative Office of the Courts before they become effective by delivering copies to the President Pro Tempore of the Senate and the Speaker of the House of Representatives. The guidelines, when adopted or modified, shall be provided to the Department of Health and Human Services and the Administrative Office of the Courts, which shall disseminate them to the public through local IV-D offices, clerks of court, and the media.

Until July 1, 1990, the advisory guidelines adopted by the Conference of Chief District Judges pursuant to this subsection as formerly written shall operate as presumptive guidelines and the factors adopted by the Conference of Chief District Judges pursuant to this subsection as formerly written shall constitute criteria for varying from the amount of support determined by the guidelines.

(d)   In non-IV-D cases, payments for the support of a minor child shall be ordered to be paid to the person having custody of the child or any other proper person, agency, organization or institution, or to the State Child Support Collection and Disbursement Unit, for the benefit of the child. In IV-D cases, payments for the support of a minor child shall be ordered to be paid to the State Child Support Collection and Disbursement Unit for the benefit of the child.

(d1)   For child support orders initially entered on or after January 1, 1994, the immediate income withholding provisions of G.S. 110-136.5(c1) shall apply.

(e)   Payment for the support of a minor child shall be paid by lump sum payment, periodic payments, or by transfer of title or possession of personal property of any interest therein, or a security interest in or possession of real property, as the court may order. The court may order the transfer of title to real property solely owned by the obligor in payment of arrearages of child support so long as the net value of the interest in the property being transferred does not exceed the amount of the arrearage being satisfied. In every case in which payment for the support of a minor child is ordered and alimony or postseparation support is also ordered, the order shall separately state and identify each allowance.

(e1)   In IV-D cases, the order for child support shall provide that the clerk shall transfer the case to another jurisdiction in this State if the IV-D agency requests the transfer on the basis that the obligor, the custodian of the child, and the child do not reside in the jurisdiction in which the order was issued. The IV-D agency shall provide notice of the transfer to the obligor by delivery of written notice in accordance with the notice requirements of Chapter 1A-1, Rule 5(b) of the Rules of Civil Procedure. The clerk shall transfer the case to the jurisdiction requested by the IV-D agency, which shall be a jurisdiction in which the obligor, the custodian of the child, or the child resides. Nothing in this subsection shall be construed to prevent a party from contesting the transfer.

(f) Remedies for enforcement of support of minor children shall be available as herein provided.

(1) The court may require the person ordered to make payments for the support of a minor child to secure the same by means of a bond, mortgage or deed of trust, or any other means ordinarily used to secure an obligation to pay money or transfer property, or by requiring the execution of an assignment of wages, salary or other income due or to become due.

(2) If the court requires the transfer of real or personal property or an interest therein as provided in subsection (e) as a part of an order for payment of support for a minor child, or for the securing thereof, the court may also enter an order which shall transfer title as provided in G.S. 1A-1, Rule 70 and G.S. 1-228.

(3) The remedy of arrest and bail, as provided in Article 34 of Chapter 1 of the General Statutes, shall be available in actions for child-support payments as in other cases.

(4) The remedies of attachment and garnishment, as provided in Article 35 of Chapter 1 of the General Statutes, shall be available in an action for child-support payments as in other cases, and for such purposes the child or person bringing an action for child support shall be deemed a creditor of the defendant. Additionally, in accordance with the provisions of G.S. 110-136, a continuing wage garnishment proceeding for wages due or to become due may be instituted by motion in the original child support proceeding or by independent action through the filing of a petition.

(5) The remedy of injunction, as provided in Article 37 of Chapter 1 of the General Statutes and G.S. 1A-1, Rule 65, shall be available in actions for child support as in other cases.

(6) Receivers, as provided in Article 38 of Chapter 1 of the General Statutes, may be appointed in action for child support as in other cases.

(7) A minor child or other person for whose benefit an order for the payment of child support has been entered shall be a creditor within the meaning of Article 3A of Chapter 39 of the General Statutes pertaining to fraudulent conveyances.

(8) Except as provided in Article 15 of Chapter 44 of the General Statutes, a judgment for child support shall not be a lien against real property unless the judgment expressly so provides, sets out the amount of the lien in a sum certain, and adequately describes the real property affected; but past due periodic payments may by motion in the cause or by a separate action be reduced to judgment which shall be a lien as other judgments and may include provisions for periodic payments.

(9) An order for the periodic payments of child support or a child support judgment that provides for periodic payments is enforceable by proceedings for civil contempt, and disobedience may be punished by proceedings for criminal contempt, as provided in Chapter 5A of the General Statutes.

Notwithstanding the provisions of G.S. 1-294, an order for the payment of child support which has been appealed to the appellate division is enforceable in the trial court by proceedings for civil contempt during the pendency of the appeal. Upon motion of an aggrieved party, the court of the appellate division in which the appeal is pending may stay any order for civil contempt entered for child support until the appeal is decided, if justice requires.

(10) The remedies provided by Chapter 1 of the General Statutes, Article 28, Execution; Article 29B, Execution Sales; and Article 31, Supplemental Proceedings, shall be available for the enforcement of judgments for child support as in other cases, but amounts so payable shall not constitute a debt as to which property is exempt from execution as provided in Article 16 of Chapter 1C of the General Statutes.

(11) The specific enumeration of remedies in this section shall not constitute a bar to remedies otherwise available.

(g) An individual who brings an action or motion in the cause for the support of a minor child, and the individual who defends the action, shall provide to the clerk of the court in which the action is brought or the order is issued, the individual's social security number.

(h) Child support orders initially entered or modified on and after October 1, 1998, shall contain the name of each of the parties, the date of birth of each party, and the court docket number. The Administrative Office of the Courts shall transmit to the Department of Health and Human Services, Child Support Enforcement Program, on a timely basis, the information required to be included on orders under this subsection and the social security number of each party as required under subsection (g) of this section. (1967, c. 1153, s. 2; 1969, c. 895, s. 17; 1975, c. 814; 1977, c. 711, s. 26; 1979, c. 386, s. 10; 1981, c. 472; c. 613, ss. 1, 3; 1983, c. 54; c. 530, s. 1; 1985, c. 689, s. 17; 1985 (Reg. Sess., 1986), c. 1016; 1989, c. 529, ss. 1, 2; 1989 (Reg. Sess., 1990), c. 1067, s. 2; 1993, c. 335, s. 1; c. 517, s. 5; 1995, c. 319, s. 9; c. 518, s. 1; 1997-433, ss. 2.1(a), 2.2, 4.4, 7.1; 1997-443, ss. 11A.118(a), 11A.122; 1998-17, s. 1; 1998-176, s. 1; 1999-293, ss. 3, 4; 1999-456, s. 13; 2001-237, s. 1; 2003-288, s. 1; 2008-12, s. 1; 2012-20, s. 2.)

§ 50-13.5. Procedure in actions for custody or support of minor children.

(a) Procedure. - The procedure in actions for custody and support of minor children shall be as in civil actions, except as provided in this section and in G.S. 50-19. In this G.S. 50-13.5 the words "custody and support" shall be deemed to include custody or support, or both.

(b) Type of Action. - An action brought under the provisions of this section may be maintained as follows:

(1) As a civil action.

(2) Repealed by Session Laws 1979, c. 110, s. 12.

(3) Joined with an action for annulment, or an action for divorce, either absolute or from bed and board, or an action for alimony without divorce.

(4) As a cross action in an action for annulment, or an action for divorce, either absolute or from bed and board, or an action for alimony without divorce.

(5) By motion in the cause in an action for annulment, or an action for divorce, either absolute or from bed and board, or an action for alimony without divorce.

(6) Upon the court's own motion in an action for annulment, or an action for divorce, either absolute or from bed and board, or an action for alimony without divorce.

(7) In any of the foregoing the judge may issue an order requiring that the body of the minor child be brought before him.

(c) Jurisdiction in Actions or Proceedings for Child Support and Child Custody. -

(1) The jurisdiction of the courts of this State to enter orders providing for the support of a minor child shall be as in actions or proceedings for the payment of money or the transfer of property.

(2) The courts of this State shall have jurisdiction to enter orders providing for the custody of a minor child under the provisions of G.S. 50A-201, 50A-202, and 50A-204.

(3) through (6) Repealed by Session Laws 1979, c. 110, s. 12.

(d) Service of Process; Notice; Interlocutory Orders. -

(1) Service of process in civil actions for the custody of minor children shall be as in other civil actions. Motions for support of a minor child in a pending action may be made on 10 days notice to the other parties and compliance with G.S. 50-13.5(e). Motions for custody of a minor child in a pending action may be made on 10 days notice to the other parties and after compliance with G.S. 50A-205.

(2) If the circumstances of the case render it appropriate, upon gaining jurisdiction of the minor child the court may enter orders for the temporary custody and support of the child, pending the service of process or notice as herein provided.

(3) A temporary order for custody which changes the living arrangements of a child or changes custody shall not be entered ex parte and prior to service of process or notice, unless the court finds that the child is exposed to a

substantial risk of bodily injury or sexual abuse or that there is a substantial risk that the child may be abducted or removed from the State of North Carolina for the purpose of evading the jurisdiction of North Carolina courts.

(e) Notice to Additional Persons in Support Actions and Proceedings; Intervention. -

(1) The parents of the minor child whose addresses are reasonably ascertainable; any person, agency, organization or institution having actual care, control, or custody of a minor child; and any person, agency, organization or institution required by court order to provide for the support of a minor child, either in whole or in part, not named as parties and served with process in an action or proceeding for the support of such child, shall be given notice by the party raising the issue of support.

(2) The notice herein required shall be in the manner provided by the Rules of Civil Procedure for the service of notices in actions. Such notice shall advise the person to be notified of the name of the child, the names of the parties to the action or proceeding, the court in which the action or proceeding was instituted, and the date thereof.

(3) In the discretion of the court, failure of such service of notice shall not affect the validity of any order or judgment entered in such action or proceeding.

(4) Any person required to be given notice as herein provided may intervene in an action or proceeding for support of a minor child by filing in apt time notice of appearance or other appropriate pleadings.

(f) Venue. - An action or proceeding in the courts of this State for custody and support of a minor child may be maintained in the county where the child resides or is physically present or in a county where a parent resides, except as hereinafter provided. If an action for annulment, for divorce, either absolute or from bed and board, or for alimony without divorce has been previously instituted in this State, until there has been a final judgment in such case, any action or proceeding for custody and support of the minor children of the marriage shall be joined with such action or be by motion in the cause in such action. If an action or proceeding for the custody and support of a minor child has been instituted and an action for annulment or for divorce, either absolute or from bed and board, or for alimony without divorce is subsequently instituted in the same or another county, the court having jurisdiction of the prior action or proceeding may, in its discretion direct that the action or proceeding for custody and support of a minor child be consolidated with such subsequent action, and in the event consolidation is ordered, shall determine in which court such consolidated action or proceeding shall be heard.

(g) Custody and Support Irrespective of Parents' Rights Inter Partes. - Orders for custody and support of minor children may be entered when the matter is before the court as provided by this section, irrespective of the rights of the wife and the husband as between themselves in an action for annulment or an action for divorce, either absolute or from bed and board, or an action for alimony without divorce.

(h) Court Having Jurisdiction. - When a district court having jurisdiction of the matter shall have been established, actions or proceedings for custody and support of minor children shall be heard without a jury by the judge of such district court, and may be heard at any time.

(i) District Court; Denial of Parental Visitation Right; Written Finding of Fact. - In any case in which an award of child custody is made in a district court, the trial judge, prior to denying a parent the right of reasonable visitation, shall make a written finding of fact that the parent being denied visitation rights is an unfit person to visit the child or that such visitation rights are not in the best interest of the child.

(j) Custody and Visitation Rights of Grandparents. - In any action in which the custody of a minor child has been determined, upon a motion in the cause and a showing of changed circumstances pursuant to G.S. 50-13.7, the grandparents of the child are entitled to such custody or visitation rights as the court, in its discretion, deems appropriate. As used in this subsection, "grandparent" includes a biological grandparent of a child adopted by a stepparent or a relative of the child where a substantial relationship exists between the grandparent and the child. Under no circumstances shall a biological grandparent of a child adopted by adoptive parents, neither of whom is related to the child and where parental rights of both biological parents have been terminated, be entitled to visitation rights. (1858-9, c. 53, s. 2; 1871-2, c. 193, ss. 39, 46; Code, ss. 1292, 1296, 1570, 1662; Rev., ss. 1567, 1570, 1854; 1919, c. 24; C.S., ss. 1664, 1667, 2242; 1921, c. 13; 1923, c. 52; 1939, c. 115; 1941, c. 120; 1943, c. 194; 1949, c. 1010; 1951, c. 893, s. 3; 1953, cc. 813, 925; 1955, cc. 814, 1189; 1957, c. 545; 1965, c. 310, s. 2; 1967, c. 1153, s. 2; 1971, c. 1185, s. 24; 1973, c. 751; 1979, c. 110, s. 12; c. 563; c. 709, s. 3; 1981, c. 735, s. 3; 1983, c. 587; 1985, c. 575, s. 4; 1987 (Reg. Sess., 1988), c. 893, s. 3.1; 1999-223, ss. 11, 12.)

§ 50-13.6. Counsel fees in actions for custody and support of minor children.

In an action or proceeding for the custody or support, or both, of a minor child, including a motion in the cause for the modification or revocation of an existing order for custody or support, or both, the court may in its discretion order payment of reasonable attorney's fees to an interested party acting in good faith who has insufficient means to defray the expense of the suit. Before ordering payment of a fee in a support action, the court must find as a fact that the party ordered to furnish support has refused to provide support which is adequate under the circumstances existing at the time of the institution of the action or proceeding; provided however, should the court find as a fact that the supporting party has initiated a frivolous action or proceeding the court may order payment of reasonable attorney's fees to an interested party as deemed appropriate under the circumstances. (1967, c. 1153, s. 2; 1973, c. 323.)

§ 50-13.7. Modification of order for child support or custody.

(a) Except as otherwise provided in G.S. 50-13.7A, an order of a court of this State for support of a minor child may be modified or vacated at any time, upon motion in the cause and a showing of changed circumstances by either party or anyone interested subject to the limitations of G.S. 50-13.10. Subject to the provisions of G.S. 50A-201, 50A-202, and 50A-204, an order of a court of this State for custody of a minor child may be modified or vacated at any time, upon motion in the cause and a showing of changed circumstances by either party or anyone interested.

(b) When an order for support of a minor child has been entered by a court of another state, a court of this State may, upon gaining jurisdiction, and upon a showing of changed circumstances, enter a new order for support which modifies or supersedes such order for support, subject to the limitations of G.S. 50-13.10. Subject to the provisions of G.S. 50A-201, 50A-202, and 50A-204, when an order for custody of a minor child has been entered by a court of another state, a court of this State may, upon gaining jurisdiction, and a showing of changed circumstances, enter a new order for custody which modifies or supersedes such order for custody. (1858-9, c. 53; 1868-9, c. 116, s. 36; 1871-2, c. 193, s. 46; Code, ss. 1296, 1570, 1661; Rev., ss. 1570, 1853; C.S., ss. 1664, 2241; 1929, c. 270, s. 1; 1939, c. 115; 1941, c. 120; 1943, c. 194; 1949, c. 1010; 1953, c. 813; 1957, c. 545; 1965, c. 310, s. 2; 1967, c. 1153, s. 2; 1979, c.

110, s. 13; 1981, c. 682, s. 12; 1987, c. 739, s. 3; 1999-223, s. 13; 2007-175, s. 1.)

§ 50-13.7A: Repealed by Session Laws 2013-27, s. 2, effective October 1, 2013.

§ 50-13.8. Custody of persons incapable of self-support upon reaching majority.

For the purposes of custody, the rights of a person who is mentally or physically incapable of self-support upon reaching his majority shall be the same as a minor child for so long as he remains mentally or physically incapable of self-support. (1967, c. 1153, s. 2; 1971, c. 218, s. 3; 1973, c. 476, s. 133; 1979, c. 838, s. 29; 1989, c. 210.)

§ 50-13.9. Procedure to insure payment of child support.

(a) Upon its own motion or upon motion of either party, the court may order at any time that support payments be made to the State Child Support Collection and Disbursement Unit for remittance to the party entitled to receive the payments. For child support orders initially entered on or after January 1, 1994, the immediate income withholding provisions of G.S. 110-136.5(c1) apply.

(b) After entry of an order by the court under subsection (a) of this section, the State Child Support Collection and Disbursement Unit shall transmit child support payments that are made to it to the custodial parent or other party entitled to receive them, unless a court order requires otherwise.

(b1) In a IV-D case:

(1) The designated child support enforcement agency shall have the sole responsibility and authority for monitoring the obligor's compliance with all child support orders in the case and for initiating any enforcement procedures that it considers appropriate.

(2) The clerk of court shall maintain all official records in the case.

(3) The designated child support enforcement agency shall maintain any other records needed to monitor the obligor's compliance with or to enforce the child support orders in the case, including records showing the amount of each payment of child support received from or on behalf of the obligor, along with the dates on which each payment was received. In any action establishing, enforcing, or modifying a child support order, the payment records maintained by the designated child support agency shall be admissible evidence, and the court shall permit the designated representative to authenticate those records.

(b2) In a non-IV-D case:

(1) Repealed by Session Laws 2005, ch. 389, s. 1.

(2) The clerk of court shall maintain all official records and all case data concerning child support matters previously enforced by the clerk of court.

(3) Repealed by Session Laws 2005, ch. 389, s. 1.

(c) In a IV-D case, the parties affected by the order shall inform the designated child support enforcement agency of any change of address or other condition that may affect the administration of the order. The court may provide in the order that a party failing to inform the court or, as appropriate, the designated child support enforcement agency, of a change of address within a reasonable period of time may be held in civil contempt.

(d) Upon affidavit of an obligee, the clerk or a district court judge may order the obligor to appear and show cause why the obligor should not be subjected to income withholding or adjudged in contempt of court, or both. The order shall require the obligor to appear and show cause why the obligor should not be subjected to income withholding or adjudged in contempt of court, or both, and shall order the obligor to bring to the hearing records and information relating to the obligor's employment, the obligor's licensing privileges, and the amount and sources of the obligor's disposable income. The order shall state:

(1) That the obligor is under a court order to provide child support, the name of each child for whose benefit support is due, and information sufficient to identify the order;

(2) That the obligor is delinquent and the amount of overdue support;

(2a) That the court may order the revocation of some or all of the obligor's licensing privileges if the obligor is delinquent in an amount equal to the support due for one month;

(3) That the court may order income withholding if the obligor is delinquent in an amount equal to the support due for one month;

(4) That income withholding, if implemented, will apply to the obligor's current payors and all subsequent payors and will be continued until terminated pursuant to G.S. 110-136.10;

(5) That failure to bring to the hearing records and information relating to his employment and the amount and sources of his disposable income will be grounds for contempt;

(6) That if income withholding is not an available or appropriate remedy, the court may determine whether the obligor is in contempt or whether any other enforcement remedy is appropriate.

The order may be signed by the clerk or a district court judge, and shall be served on the obligor pursuant to G.S. 1A-1, Rule 4, Rules of Civil Procedure. On motion of the person to whom support is owed in a non-IV-D case, with the approval of the district court judge, if the district court judge finds it is in the best interest of the child, no order shall be issued.

(e) Repealed by Session Laws 2005, ch. 389, s. 1.

(f) Repealed by Session Laws 2005, ch. 389, s. 1.

(g) Nothing in this section shall preclude the independent initiation by a party of proceedings for civil contempt or for income withholding. (1983, c. 677, s. 1; 1985 (Reg. Sess., 1986), c. 949, ss. 3-6; 1989, c. 479; 1993, c. 517, s. 6; c. 553, s. 67.1; 1995, c. 444, s. 1; c. 538, s. 1.2; 1997-443, s. 11A.118(a); 1999-293, ss. 11-14; 2001-237, s. 7; 2005-389, s. 1; 2006-264, s. 97.)

§ 50-13.10. Past due child support vested; not subject to retroactive modification; entitled to full faith and credit.

(a) Each past due child support payment is vested when it accrues and may not thereafter be vacated, reduced, or otherwise modified in any way for any reason, in this State or any other state, except that a child support obligation may be modified as otherwise provided by law, and a vested past due payment is to that extent subject to divestment, if, but only if, a written motion is filed, and due notice is given to all parties either:

(1) Before the payment is due or

(2) If the moving party is precluded by physical disability, mental incapacity, indigency, misrepresentation of another party, or other compelling reason from filing a motion before the payment is due, then promptly after the moving party is no longer so precluded.

(b) A past due child support payment which is vested pursuant to G.S. 50-13.10(a) is entitled, as a judgment, to full faith and credit in this State and any other state, with the full force, effect, and attributes of a judgment of this State, except that no arrearage shall be entered on the judgment docket of the clerk of superior court or become a lien on real estate, nor shall execution issue thereon, except as provided in G.S. 50-13.4(f)(8) and (10).

(c) As used in this section, "child support payment" includes all payments required by court or administrative order in civil actions and expedited process proceedings under this Chapter, by court order in proceedings under Chapter 49 of the General Statutes, and by agreements entered into and approved by the court under G.S. 110-132 or G.S. 110-133.

(d) For purposes of this section, a child support payment or the relevant portion thereof, is not past due, and no arrearage accrues:

(1) From and after the date of the death of the minor child for whose support the payment, or relevant portion, is made;

(2) From and after the date of the death of the supporting party;

(3) During any period when the child is living with the supporting party pursuant to a valid court order or to an express or implied written or oral agreement transferring primary custody to the supporting party;

(4) During any period when the supporting party is incarcerated, is not on work release, and has no resources with which to make the payment.

(e) When a child support payment that is to be made to the State Child Support Collection and Disbursement Unit is not received by the Unit when due, the payment is not a past due child support payment for purposes of this section, and no arrearage accrues, if the payment is actually made to and received on time by the party entitled to receive it and that receipt is evidenced by a canceled check, money order, or contemporaneously executed and dated written receipt. Nothing in this section shall affect the duties of the clerks or the IV-D agency under this Chapter or Chapter 110 of the General Statutes with respect to payments not received by the Unit on time, but the court, in any action to enforce such a payment, may enter an order directing the clerk or the IV-D agency to enter the payment on the clerk's or IV-D agency's records as having been made on time, if the court finds that the payment was in fact received by the party entitled to receive it as provided in this subsection. (1987, c. 739, s. 4; 1999-293, s. 15.)

§ 50-13.11. Orders and agreements regarding medical support and health insurance coverage for minor children.

(a) The court may order a parent of a minor child or other responsible party to provide medical support for the child, or the parties may enter into a written agreement regarding medical support for the child. An order or agreement for medical support for the child may require one or both parties to pay the medical, hospital, dental, or other health care related expenses.

(a1) The court shall order the parent of a minor child or other responsible party to maintain health insurance for the benefit of the child when health insurance is available at a reasonable cost. If health insurance is not presently available at a reasonable cost, the court shall order the parent of a minor child or other responsible party to maintain health insurance for the benefit of the child when health insurance becomes available at a reasonable cost. As used in this subsection, health insurance is considered reasonable in cost if it is employment related or other group health insurance, regardless of service delivery mechanism. The court may require one or both parties to maintain dental insurance.

(b) The party ordered or under agreement to provide health insurance shall provide written notice of any change in the applicable insurance coverage to the other party.

(c) The employer or insurer of the party required to provide health, hospital, and dental insurance shall release to the other party, upon written request, any information on a minor child's insurance coverage that the employer or insurer may release to the party required to provide health, hospital, and dental insurance.

(d) When a court order or agreement for health insurance is in effect, the signature of either party shall be valid authorization to the insurer to process an insurance claim on behalf of a minor child.

(e) If the party who is required to provide health insurance fails to maintain the insurance coverage for the minor child, the party shall be liable for any health, hospital, or dental expenses incurred from the date of the court order or agreement that would have been covered by insurance if it had been in force.

(f) When a noncustodial parent ordered to provide health insurance changes employment and health insurance coverage is available through the new employer, the obligee shall notify the new employer of the noncustodial parent's obligation to provide health insurance for the child. Upon receipt of notice from the obligee, the new employer shall enroll the child in the employer's health insurance plan. (1989 (Reg. Sess., 1990), c. 1067, s. 1; 1991, c. 419, s. 2; c. 761, s. 42; 1997-433, s. 3.1; 1998-17, s. 1; 2003-288, s. 3.2.)

§ 50-13.12. Forfeiture of licensing privileges for failure to pay child support or for failure to comply with subpoena issued pursuant to child support or paternity establishment proceedings.

(a) As used in this section, the term:

(1) "Licensing board" means a department, division, agency, officer, board, or other unit of state government that issues hunting, fishing, trapping, drivers, or occupational licenses or licensing privileges.

(2) "Licensing privilege" means the privilege of an individual to be authorized to engage in an activity as evidenced by hunting, fishing, or trapping licenses, regular and commercial drivers licenses, and occupational, professional, and business licenses.

(3) "Obligee" means the individual or agency to whom a duty of support is owed or the individual's legal representative.

(4) "Obligor" means the individual who owes a duty to make child support payments under a court order.

(5) "Occupational license" means a license, certificate, permit, registration, or any other authorization issued by a licensing board that allows an obligor to engage in an occupation or profession.

(b) Upon a finding by the district court judge that the obligor is willfully delinquent in child support payments equal to at least one month's child support, or upon a finding that a person has willfully failed to comply with a subpoena issued pursuant to a child support or paternity establishment proceeding, and upon findings as to any specific licensing privileges held by the obligor or held by the person subject to the subpoena, the court may revoke some or all of such privileges until the obligor shall have paid the delinquent amount in full, or, as applicable, until the person subject to the subpoena has complied with the subpoena. The court may stay any such revocation pertaining to the obligor upon conditions requiring the obligor to make full payment of the delinquency over time. Any such stay shall further be conditioned upon the obligor's maintenance of current child support. The court may stay the revocation pertaining to the person subject to the subpoena upon a finding that the person has complied with or is no longer subject to the subpoena. Upon an order revoking such privileges of an obligor that does not stay the revocation, the clerk of superior court shall notify the appropriate licensing board that the obligor is delinquent in child support payments and that the obligor's licensing privileges are revoked until such time as the licensing board receives proof of certification by the clerk that the obligor is no longer delinquent in child support payments. Upon an order revoking such privileges of a person subject to the subpoena that does not stay the revocation, the clerk of superior court shall notify the appropriate licensing board that the person has failed to comply with the subpoena issued pursuant to a child support or paternity establishment proceeding and that the person's licensing privileges are revoked until such time as the licensing board receives proof of certification by the clerk that the person is in compliance with or no longer subject to the subpoena.

(c) An obligor may file a request with the clerk of superior court for certification that the obligor is no longer delinquent in child support payments upon submission of proof satisfactory to the clerk that the obligor has paid the delinquent amount in full. A person whose licensing privileges have been revoked under subsection (b) of this section because of a willful failure to comply with a subpoena may file a request with the clerk of superior court for certification that the person has met the requirements of or is no longer subject to the subpoena. The clerk shall provide a form to be used for a request for certification. If the clerk finds that the obligor has met the requirements for reinstatement under this subsection, then the clerk shall certify that the obligor is no longer delinquent and shall provide a copy of the certification to the obligor. Upon request of the obligor, the clerk shall mail a copy of the certification to the appropriate licensing board. If the clerk finds that the person whose licensing privileges have been revoked under subsection (b) of this section for failure to comply with a subpoena has complied with or is no longer subject to the subpoena, then the clerk shall certify that the person has met the requirements of or is no longer subject to the subpoena and shall provide a copy of the certification to the person. Upon request of the person, the clerk shall mail a copy of the certification to the appropriate licensing board.

(d) If licensing privileges are revoked under this section, the obligor may petition the district court for a reinstatement of such privileges. The court may order the privileges reinstated conditioned upon full payment of the delinquency over time. Any order allowing license reinstatement shall additionally require the obligor's maintenance of current child support. If the licensing privileges of a person other than the obligor are revoked under this section for failure to comply with a subpoena, the person may petition the district court for reinstatement of the privileges. The court may order the privileges reinstated if the person has complied with or is no longer subject to the subpoena that was the basis for revocation. Upon reinstatement under this subsection, the clerk of superior court shall certify that the obligor is no longer delinquent and provide a copy of the certification to the obligor. Upon request of the obligor, the clerk shall mail a copy of the certification to the appropriate licensing board. Upon reinstatement of the person whose licensing privileges were revoked based on failure to comply with a subpoena, the clerk of superior court shall certify that the person has complied with or is no longer subject to the subpoena. Upon request of the person whose licensing privileges are reinstated, the clerk shall mail a copy of the certification to the appropriate licensing board.

(e) An obligor or other person whose licensing privileges are reinstated under this section may provide a copy of the certification set forth in either subsection (c) or (d) to each licensing agency to which the obligor or other person applies for reinstatement of licensing privileges. Upon request of the obligor or other person, the clerk shall mail a copy of the certification to the appropriate licensing board. Upon receipt of a copy of the certification, the licensing board shall reinstate the license.

(f)   Upon receipt of notification by the clerk that an obligor's or other person's licensing privileges are revoked pursuant to this section, the board shall note the revocation on its records and take all necessary steps to implement and enforce the revocation. These steps shall not include the board's independent revocation process pursuant to Chapter 150B of the General Statutes, the Administrative Procedure Act, which process is replaced by the court process prescribed by this section. The revocation pertaining to an obligor shall remain in full force and effect until the board receives certification under this section that the obligor is no longer delinquent in child support payments. The revocation pertaining to the person whose licensing privileges were revoked on the basis of failure to comply with a subpoena shall remain in full force and effect until the board receives certification of reinstatement under subsection (d) of this section. (1995, c. 538, ss. 1, 1.1; 1997-433, s. 5.3; 1998-17, s. 1.)

§ 50-13.13. Motion or claim for relief from child support order based on finding of nonpaternity.

(a)   Notwithstanding G.S. 1A-1, Rule 60 of the North Carolina Rules of Civil Procedure, or any other provision of law, an individual who, as the father of a child, is required to pay child support under an order that was entered by a North Carolina court pursuant to Chapter 49, 50, 52C, or 110 of the General Statutes, or under an agreement between the parties pursuant to G.S. 52-10.1 or otherwise, and that is subject to modification by a North Carolina court under applicable law may file a motion or claim seeking relief from a child support order as provided in this section.

(b)   A motion or claim for relief under this section shall be filed as a motion or claim in the cause in the pending child support action, or as an independent civil action, and shall be filed within one year of the date the moving party knew or reasonably should have known that he was not the father of the child. The motion or claim shall be verified by the moving party and shall state all of the following:

(1)   The basis, with particularity, on which the moving party believes that he is not the child's father.

(2) The moving party has not acknowledged paternity of the child or acknowledged paternity without knowing that he was not the child's biological father.

(3) The moving party has not adopted the child, has not legitimated the child pursuant to G.S. 49-10, 49-12, or 49-12.1, or is not the child's legal father pursuant to G.S. 49A-1.

(4) The moving party did not act to prevent the child's biological father from asserting his paternal rights regarding the child.

(c) The court may appoint a guardian ad litem pursuant to G.S. 1A-1, Rule 17, to represent the interest of the child in connection with a proceeding under this section.

(d) Notwithstanding G.S. 8-50.1(b1), the court shall, upon motion or claim of a party in a proceeding under this section, order the moving party, the child's mother, and the child to submit to genetic paternity testing if the court finds that there is good cause to believe that the moving party is not the child's father and that the moving party may be entitled to relief under this section. If genetic paternity testing is ordered, the provisions of G.S. 8-50.1(b1) shall govern the admissibility and weight of the genetic test results. The moving party shall pay the costs of genetic testing. If a party fails to comply with an order for genetic testing without good cause, the court may hold the party in civil or criminal contempt or impose appropriate sanctions under G.S. 1A-1, Rule 37, of the North Carolina Rules of Civil Procedure, or both. Nothing in this subsection shall be construed to require additional genetic paternity testing if paternity has been set aside pursuant to G.S. 49-14 or G.S. 110-132.

(e) The moving party's child support obligation shall be suspended while the motion or claim is pending before the court if the support is being paid on behalf of the child to the State, or any other assignee of child support, where the child is in the custody of the State or other assignee, or where the moving party is an obligor in a IV-D case as defined in G.S. 110-129(7).

The moving party's child support obligation shall not be suspended while the motion or claim is pending before the court if the support is being paid to the mother of the child.

(f) The court may grant relief from a child support order under this section if paternity has been set aside pursuant to G.S. 49-14 or G.S. 110-132, or if the moving party proves by clear and convincing evidence, and the court, sitting without a jury, finds both of the following:

(1) The results of a valid genetic test establish that the moving party is not the child's biological father.

(2) The moving party either (i) has not acknowledged paternity of the child or (ii) acknowledged paternity without knowing that he was not the child's biological father. For purposes of this section, "acknowledging paternity" means that the moving party has done any of the following:

a. Publicly acknowledged the child as his own and supported the child while married to the child's mother.

b. Acknowledged paternity in a sworn written statement, including an affidavit of parentage executed under G.S. 110-132(a) or G.S. 130A-101(f).

c. Executed a consent order, a voluntary support agreement under G.S. 110-132 or G.S. 110-133, or any other legal agreement to pay child support as the child's father.

d. Admitted paternity in open court or in any pleading.

(g) If the court determines that the moving party has not satisfied the requirements of this section, the court shall deny the motion or claim, and all orders regarding the child's paternity, support, or custody shall remain enforceable and in effect until modified as otherwise provided by law. If the court finds that the moving party did not act in good faith in filing a motion or claim pursuant to this section, the court shall award reasonable attorneys' fees to the prevailing party. The court shall make findings of fact and conclusions of law to support its award of attorneys' fees under this subsection.

(h) If the court determines that the moving party has satisfied the requirements of this section, the court shall enter an order, including written findings of fact and conclusions of law, terminating the moving party's child support obligation regarding the child. The court may tax as costs to the mother of the child the expenses of genetic testing.

Any unpaid support due prior to the filing of the motion or claim is due and owing. If the court finds that the mother of the child used fraud, duress, or misrepresentation, resulting in the belief on the part of the moving party that he was the father of the child, the court may order the mother of the child to reimburse any child support amounts paid and received by the mother after the filing of the motion or claim. The moving party has no right to reimbursement of past child support paid on behalf of the child to the State, or any other assignee of child support, where the child is in the custody of the State or other assignee, or where the moving party is an obligor in a IV-D case as defined in G.S. 110-129(7).

If the child was born in North Carolina and the moving party is named as the father on the child's birth certificate, the court shall order the clerk of superior court to notify the State Registrar of the court's order pursuant to G.S. 130A-118(b)(2). If relief is granted under this subsection, a party may, to the extent otherwise provided by law, apply for modification of or relief from any judgment or order involving the moving party's paternity of the child.

(i) Any servicemember who is deployed on military orders, and is subject to the protections of the Servicemembers Civil Relief Act, shall have the period for filing a motion pursuant to subsection (b) of this section tolled during the servicemember's deployment. If the period remaining allowed for the filing of the motion following the servicemember's redeployment is less than 30 days, then the servicemember shall have 30 days for filing the motion. (2011-328, s. 3.)

§§ 50-14 through 50-15. Repealed by Session Laws 1967, c. 1152, s. 1.

§ 50-16. Repealed by Session Laws 1967, c. 1152, s. 1; c. 1153. s. 1.

§ 50-16.1: Repealed by Session Laws 1995, c. 319, s. 1.

§ 50-16.1A. Definitions.

As used in this Chapter, unless the context clearly requires otherwise, the following definitions apply:

(1) "Alimony" means an order for payment for the support and maintenance of a spouse or former spouse, periodically or in a lump sum, for a specified or for an indefinite term, ordered in an action for divorce, whether absolute or from bed and board, or in an action for alimony without divorce.

(2) "Dependent spouse" means a spouse, whether husband or wife, who is actually substantially dependent upon the other spouse for his or her maintenance and support or is substantially in need of maintenance and support from the other spouse.

(3) "Marital misconduct" means any of the following acts that occur during the marriage and prior to or on the date of separation:

a. Illicit sexual behavior. For the purpose of this section, illicit sexual behavior means acts of sexual or deviate sexual intercourse, deviate sexual acts, or sexual acts defined in G.S. 14-27.1(4), voluntarily engaged in by a spouse with someone other than the other spouse;

b. Involuntary separation of the spouses in consequence of a criminal act committed prior to the proceeding in which alimony is sought;

c. Abandonment of the other spouse;

d. Malicious turning out-of-doors of the other spouse;

e. Cruel or barbarous treatment endangering the life of the other spouse;

f. Indignities rendering the condition of the other spouse intolerable and life burdensome;

g. Reckless spending of the income of either party, or the destruction, waste, diversion, or concealment of assets;

h. Excessive use of alcohol or drugs so as to render the condition of the other spouse intolerable and life burdensome;

i. Willful failure to provide necessary subsistence according to one's means and condition so as to render the condition of the other spouse intolerable and life burdensome.

(3a) through (3d) Reserved for future codification purposes.

(3e) "Payor" means any payor, including any federal, State, or local governmental unit, of disposable income to an obligor. When the payor is an employer, payor means employer as defined under 20 U.S.C. § 203(d) of the Fair Labor Standards Act.

(4) "Postseparation support" means spousal support to be paid until the earlier of any of the following:

a. The date specified in the order for postseparation support.

b. The entry of an order awarding or denying alimony.

c. The dismissal of the alimony claim.

d. The entry of a judgment of absolute divorce if no claim of alimony is pending at the time of entry of the judgment of absolute divorce.

e. Termination of postseparation support as provided in G.S. 50-16.9(b).

Postseparation support may be ordered in an action for divorce, whether absolute or from bed and board, for annulment, or for alimony without divorce. However, if postseparation support is ordered at the time of the entry of a judgment of absolute divorce, a claim for alimony must be pending at the time of the entry of the judgment of divorce.

(5) "Supporting spouse" means a spouse, whether husband or wife, upon whom the other spouse is actually substantially dependent for maintenance and support or from whom such spouse is substantially in need of maintenance and support. (1995, c. 319, s. 2; 1998-176, s. 8; 2005-177, s. 1.)

§ 50-16.2: Repealed by Session Laws 1995, c. 319, s. 1.

§ 50-16.2A. Postseparation support.

(a) In an action brought pursuant to Chapter 50 of the General Statutes, either party may move for postseparation support. The verified pleading, verified motion, or affidavit of the moving party shall set forth the factual basis for the relief requested.

(b) In ordering postseparation support, the court shall base its award on the financial needs of the parties, considering the parties' accustomed standard of living, the present employment income and other recurring earnings of each party from any source, their income-earning abilities, the separate and marital debt service obligations, those expenses reasonably necessary to support each of the parties, and each party's respective legal obligations to support any other persons.

(c)   Except when subsection (d) of this section applies, a dependent spouse is entitled to an award of postseparation support if, based on consideration of the factors specified in subsection (b) of this section, the court finds that the resources of the dependent spouse are not adequate to meet his or her reasonable needs and the supporting spouse has the ability to pay.

(d)   At a hearing on postseparation support, the judge shall consider marital misconduct by the dependent spouse occurring prior to or on the date of separation in deciding whether to award postseparation support and in deciding the amount of postseparation support. When the judge considers these acts by the dependent spouse, the judge shall also consider any marital misconduct by the supporting spouse in deciding whether to award postseparation support and in deciding the amount of postseparation support.

(e)   Nothing herein shall prevent a court from considering incidents of post date-of-separation marital misconduct as corroborating evidence supporting other evidence that marital misconduct occurred during the marriage and prior to date of separation. (1995, c. 319, s. 2.)

§ 50-16.3: Repealed by Session Laws 1995, c. 319, s. 1.

§ 50-16.3A. Alimony.

(a)   Entitlement. - In an action brought pursuant to Chapter 50 of the General Statutes, either party may move for alimony. The court shall award alimony to the dependent spouse upon a finding that one spouse is a dependent spouse, that the other spouse is a supporting spouse, and that an award of alimony is equitable after considering all relevant factors, including those set out in subsection (b) of this section. If the court finds that the dependent spouse participated in an act of illicit sexual behavior, as defined in G.S. 50-16.1A(3)a., during the marriage and prior to or on the date of separation, the court shall not award alimony. If the court finds that the supporting spouse participated in an act of illicit sexual behavior, as defined in G.S. 50-16.1A(3)a., during the marriage and prior to or on the date of separation, then the court shall order that alimony be paid to a dependent spouse. If the court finds that the dependent and the supporting spouse each participated in an act of illicit sexual behavior during the marriage and prior to or on the date of separation, then alimony shall be denied or awarded in the discretion of the court after consideration of all of the circumstances. Any act of illicit sexual behavior by either party that has been condoned by the other party shall not be considered by the court.

The claim for alimony may be heard on the merits prior to the entry of a judgment for equitable distribution, and if awarded, the issues of amount and of whether a spouse is a dependent or supporting spouse may be reviewed by the court after the conclusion of the equitable distribution claim.

(b) Amount and Duration. - The court shall exercise its discretion in determining the amount, duration, and manner of payment of alimony. The duration of the award may be for a specified or for an indefinite term. In determining the amount, duration, and manner of payment of alimony, the court shall consider all relevant factors, including:

(1) The marital misconduct of either of the spouses. Nothing herein shall prevent a court from considering incidents of post date-of-separation marital misconduct as corroborating evidence supporting other evidence that marital misconduct occurred during the marriage and prior to date of separation;

(2) The relative earnings and earning capacities of the spouses;

(3) The ages and the physical, mental, and emotional conditions of the spouses;

(4) The amount and sources of earned and unearned income of both spouses, including, but not limited to, earnings, dividends, and benefits such as medical, retirement, insurance, social security, or others;

(5) The duration of the marriage;

(6) The contribution by one spouse to the education, training, or increased earning power of the other spouse;

(7) The extent to which the earning power, expenses, or financial obligations of a spouse will be affected by reason of serving as the custodian of a minor child;

(8) The standard of living of the spouses established during the marriage;

(9) The relative education of the spouses and the time necessary to acquire sufficient education or training to enable the spouse seeking alimony to find employment to meet his or her reasonable economic needs;

(10) The relative assets and liabilities of the spouses and the relative debt service requirements of the spouses, including legal obligations of support;

(11) The property brought to the marriage by either spouse;

(12) The contribution of a spouse as homemaker;

(13) The relative needs of the spouses;

(14) The federal, State, and local tax ramifications of the alimony award;

(15) Any other factor relating to the economic circumstances of the parties that the court finds to be just and proper.

(16) The fact that income received by either party was previously considered by the court in determining the value of a marital or divisible asset in an equitable distribution of the parties' marital or divisible property.

(c) Findings of Fact. - The court shall set forth the reasons for its award or denial of alimony and, if making an award, the reasons for its amount, duration, and manner of payment. Except where there is a motion before the court for summary judgment, judgment on the pleadings, or other motion for which the Rules of Civil Procedure do not require special findings of fact, the court shall make a specific finding of fact on each of the factors in subsection (b) of this section if evidence is offered on that factor.

(d) In the claim for alimony, either spouse may request a jury trial on the issue of marital misconduct as defined in G.S. 50-16.1A. If a jury trial is requested, the jury will decide whether either spouse or both have established marital misconduct. (1995, c. 319, s. 2; c. 509, s. 135.2(b); 1998-176, s. 11.)

§ 50-16.4. Counsel fees in actions for alimony, postseparation support.

At any time that a dependent spouse would be entitled to alimony pursuant to G.S. 50-16.3A, or postseparation support pursuant to G.S. 50-16.2A, the court may, upon application of such spouse, enter an order for reasonable counsel fees, to be paid and secured by the supporting spouse in the same manner as alimony. (1967, c. 1152, s. 2; 1995, c. 319, s. 3; 2010-14, s. 1.)

§ 50-16.5: Repealed by Session Laws 1995, c. 319, s. 1.

§ 50-16.6. When alimony, postseparation support, counsel fees not payable.

(a)   Repealed by Session Laws 1995, c. 319, s. 4.

(b)   Alimony, postseparation support, and counsel fees may be barred by an express provision of a valid separation agreement, premarital agreement, or marital contract made pursuant to G.S. 52-10(a1) so long as the agreement is performed. (1871-2, c. 193, s. 39; Code, s. 1292; Rev., s. 1567; 1919, c. 24; C.S., s. 1667; 1921, c. 123; 1923, c. 52; 1951, c. 893, s. 3; 1953, c. 925; 1955, cc. 814, 1189; 1967, c. 1152, s. 2; 1995, c. 319, s. 4; c. 509, s. 135.3(f); 2013-140, s. 2.)

§ 50-16.7. How alimony and postseparation support paid; enforcement of decree.

(a)   Alimony or postseparation support shall be paid by lump sum payment, periodic payments, income withholding, or by transfer of title or possession of personal property or any interest therein, or a security interest in or possession of real property, as the court may order. The court may order the transfer of title to real property solely owned by the obligor in payment of lump-sum payments of alimony or postseparation support or in payment of arrearages of alimony or postseparation support so long as the net value of the interest in the property being transferred does not exceed the amount of the arrearage being satisfied. In every case in which either alimony or postseparation support is allowed and provision is also made for support of minor children, the order shall separately state and identify each allowance.

(b)   The court may require the supporting spouse to secure the payment of alimony or postseparation support so ordered by means of a bond, mortgage, or deed of trust, or any other means ordinarily used to secure an obligation to pay money or transfer property, or by requiring the supporting spouse to execute an assignment of wages, salary, or other income due or to become due.

(c) If the court requires the transfer of real or personal property or an interest therein as a part of an order for alimony or postseparation support as provided in subsection (a) or for the securing thereof, the court may also enter an order which shall transfer title, as provided in G.S. 1A-1, Rule 70 and G.S. 1-228.

(d) The remedy of arrest and bail, as provided in Article 34 of Chapter 1 of the General Statutes, shall be available in actions for alimony or postseparation support as in other cases.

(e) The remedies of attachment and garnishment, as provided in Article 35 of Chapter 1 and Article 9 of Chapter 110 of the General Statutes, shall be available in actions for alimony or postseparation support as in other cases, and for such purposes the dependent spouse shall be deemed a creditor of the supporting spouse.

(f) The remedy of injunction, as provided in Article 37 of Chapter 1 of the General Statutes and G.S. 1A-1, Rule 65, shall be available in actions for alimony or postseparation support as in other cases.

(g) Receivers, as provided in Article 38 of Chapter 1 of the General Statutes, may be appointed in actions for alimony or postseparation support as in other cases.

(h) A dependent spouse for whose benefit an order for the payment of alimony or postseparation support has been entered shall be a creditor within the meaning of Article 3A of Chapter 39 of the General Statutes pertaining to fraudulent conveyances.

(i) A judgment for alimony or postseparation support obtained in an action therefor shall not be a lien against real property unless the judgment expressly so provides, sets out the amount of the lien in a sum certain, and adequately describes the real property affected; but past-due periodic payments may by motion in the cause or by a separate action be reduced to judgment which shall be a lien as other judgments.

(j) Any order for the payment of alimony or postseparation support is enforceable by proceedings for civil contempt, and its disobedience may be punished by proceedings for criminal contempt, as provided in Chapter 5A of the General Statutes.

Notwithstanding the provisions of G.S. 1-294 or G.S. 1-289, an order for the periodic payment of alimony that has been appealed to the appellate division is enforceable in the trial court by proceedings for civil contempt during the pendency of the appeal. Upon motion of an aggrieved party, the court of the appellate division in which the appeal is pending may stay any order for civil contempt entered for alimony until the appeal is decided if justice requires.

(k) The remedies provided by Chapter 1 of the General Statutes Article 28, Execution; Article 29B, Execution Sales; and Article 31, Supplemental Proceedings, shall be available for the enforcement of judgments for alimony and postseparation support as in other cases, but amounts so payable shall not constitute a debt as to which property is exempt from execution as provided in Article 16 of Chapter 1C of the General Statutes.

(l) The specific enumeration of remedies in this section shall not constitute a bar to remedies otherwise available.

(l1) The dependent spouse may apply to the court for an order of income withholding for current or delinquent payments of alimony or postseparation support or for any portion of the payments. If the court orders income withholding, a notice of obligation to withhold shall be served on the payor as required by G.S. 1A-1, Rule 4, Rules of Civil Procedure. Copies of the notice shall be filed with the clerk of court and served upon the supporting spouse by first-class mail. (1967, c. 1152, s. 2; 1969, c. 541, s. 5; c. 895, s. 18; 1977, c. 711, s. 26; 1985, c. 482, s. 1; c. 689, s. 18; 1995 c. 319, s. 5; 1998-176, ss. 2, 3; 1999-456, s. 14.)

§ 50-16.8. Procedure in actions for postseparation support.

When an application is made for postseparation support, the court may base its award on a verified pleading, affidavit, or other competent evidence. The court shall set forth the reasons for its award or denial of postseparation support, and if making an award, the reasons for its amount, duration, and manner of payment. (1871-2, c. 193, ss. 37, 38, 39; 1883, c. 67; Code, ss. 1290, 1291, 1292; Rev., ss. 1565, 1566, 1567; 1919, c. 24; C.S., ss. 1665, 1666, 1667; 1921, c. 123; 1923, c. 52; 1951, c. 893, s. 3; 1953, c. 925; 1955, cc. 814, 1189; 1961, c. 80; 1967, c. 1152, s. 2; 1971, c. 1185, s. 25; 1979, c. 709, s. 4; 1995, c. 319, s. 6.)

§ 50-16.9. Modification of order.

(a)   An order of a court of this State for alimony or postseparation support, whether contested or entered by consent, may be modified or vacated at any time, upon motion in the cause and a showing of changed circumstances by either party or anyone interested. This section shall not apply to orders entered by consent before October 1, 1967.

Any motion to modify or terminate alimony or postseparation support based on a resumption of marital relations between parties who remain married to each other shall be determined pursuant to G.S. 52-10.2.

(b)   If a dependent spouse who is receiving postseparation support or alimony from a supporting spouse under a judgment or order of a court of this State remarries or engages in cohabitation, the postseparation support or alimony shall terminate. Postseparation support or alimony shall terminate upon the death of either the supporting or the dependent spouse.

As used in this subsection, cohabitation means the act of two adults dwelling together continuously and habitually in a private heterosexual relationship, even if this relationship is not solemnized by marriage, or a private homosexual relationship. Cohabitation is evidenced by the voluntary mutual assumption of those marital rights, duties, and obligations which are usually manifested by married people, and which include, but are not necessarily dependent on, sexual relations. Nothing in this section shall be construed to make lawful conduct which is made unlawful by other statutes.

(c)   When an order for alimony has been entered by a court of another jurisdiction, a court of this State may, upon gaining jurisdiction over the person of both parties in a civil action instituted for that purpose, and upon a showing of changed circumstances, enter a new order for alimony which modifies or supersedes such order for alimony to the extent that it could have been so modified in the jurisdiction where granted. (1871-2, c. 193, ss. 38, 39; 1883, c. 67; Code, ss. 1291, 1292; Rev., ss. 1566, 1567; 1919, c. 24; C.S., ss. 1666, 1667; 1921, c. 123; 1923, c. 52; 1951, c. 893, s. 3; 1953, c. 925; 1955, cc. 814, 1189; 1961, c. 80; 1967, c. 1152, s. 2; 1987, c. 664, s. 3; 1995, c. 319, s. 7.)

§ 50-16.10. Alimony without action.

Alimony without action may be allowed by confession of judgment under G.S. 1A-1, Rule 68.1. (1967, c. 1152, s. 2; 1985, c. 689, s. 19.)

§ 50-16.11: Repealed by Session Laws 1995, c. 319, s. 1.

§ 50-17. Alimony in real estate, writ of possession issued.

In all cases in which the court grants alimony by the assignment of real estate, the court has power to issue a writ of possession when necessary in the judgment of the court to do so. (1868-9, c. 123, s. 1; Code, s. 1293; Rev., s. 1568; C.S., s. 1668.)

§ 50-18. Residence of military personnel; payment of defendant's travel expenses by plaintiff.

In any action instituted and prosecuted under this Chapter, allegation and proof that the plaintiff or the defendant has resided or been stationed at a United States Army, Navy, Marine Corps, Coast Guard, or Air Force installation or reservation or any other location pursuant to military duty within this State for a period of six months next preceding the institution of the action shall constitute compliance with the residence requirements set forth in this Chapter; provided that personal service is had upon the defendant or service is accepted by the defendant, within or without the State as by law provided.

Upon request of the defendant or attorney for the defendant, the court may order the plaintiff to pay necessary travel expenses from defendant's home to the site of the court in order that the defendant may appear in person to defend said action. (1959, c. 1058; 2011-183, s. 39.)

§ 50-19. Maintenance of certain actions as independent actions permissible.

(a) Notwithstanding the provisions of G.S. 1A-1, Rule 13(a), any action for divorce under the provisions of G.S. 50-5.1 or G.S. 50-6 that is filed as an independent, separate action may be prosecuted during the pendency of an action for:

(1) Alimony;

(2) Postseparation support;

(3) Custody and support of minor children;

(4) Custody and support of a person incapable of self-support upon reaching majority; or

(5) Divorce pursuant to G.S. 50-5.1 or G.S. 50-6.

(b) Notwithstanding the provisions of G.S. 1A-1, Rule 13(a), any action described in subdivision (a)(1) through (a)(5) of this section that is filed as an independent, separate action may be prosecuted during the pendency of an action for divorce under G.S. 50-5.1 or G.S. 50-6.

(c) Repealed by Session Laws 1991, c. 569, s. 1. (1979, c. 709, s. 2; 1985, c. 689, s. 20; 1991, c. 569, s. 1; 1995, c. 319, s. 10.)

§ 50-19.1. Maintenance of certain appeals allowed.

Notwithstanding any other pending claims filed in the same action, a party may appeal from an order or judgment adjudicating a claim for absolute divorce, divorce from bed and board, child custody, child support, alimony, or equitable distribution if the order or judgment would otherwise be a final order or judgment within the meaning of G.S. 1A-1, Rule 54(b), but for the other pending claims in the same action. A party does not forfeit the right to appeal under this section if the party fails to immediately appeal from an order or judgment described in this section. An appeal from an order or judgment under this section shall not deprive the trial court of jurisdiction over any other claims pending in the same action. (2013-411, s. 2.)

§ 50-20. Distribution by court of marital and divisible property.

(a) Upon application of a party, the court shall determine what is the marital property and divisible property and shall provide for an equitable distribution of the marital property and divisible property between the parties in accordance with the provisions of this section.

(b) For purposes of this section:

(1) "Marital property" means all real and personal property acquired by either spouse or both spouses during the course of the marriage and before the date of the separation of the parties, and presently owned, except property determined to be separate property or divisible property in accordance with subdivision (2) or (4) of this subsection. Marital property includes all vested and nonvested pension, retirement, and other deferred compensation rights, and vested and nonvested military pensions eligible under the federal Uniformed Services Former Spouses' Protection Act. It is presumed that all property acquired after the date of marriage and before the date of separation is marital property except property which is separate property under subdivision (2) of this subsection. It is presumed that all real property creating a tenancy by the entirety acquired after the date of marriage and before the date of separation is marital property. Either presumption may be rebutted by the greater weight of the evidence.

(2) "Separate property" means all real and personal property acquired by a spouse before marriage or acquired by a spouse by devise, descent, or gift during the course of the marriage. However, property acquired by gift from the other spouse during the course of the marriage shall be considered separate property only if such an intention is stated in the conveyance. Property acquired in exchange for separate property shall remain separate property regardless of whether the title is in the name of the husband or wife or both and shall not be considered to be marital property unless a contrary intention is expressly stated in the conveyance. The increase in value of separate property and the income derived from separate property shall be considered separate property. All professional licenses and business licenses which would terminate on transfer shall be considered separate property.

(3) "Distributive award" means payments that are payable either in a lump sum or over a period of time in fixed amounts, but shall not include alimony payments or other similar payments for support and maintenance which are treated as ordinary income to the recipient under the Internal Revenue Code.

(4) "Divisible property" means all real and personal property as set forth below:

a. All appreciation and diminution in value of marital property and divisible property of the parties occurring after the date of separation and prior to the date of distribution, except that appreciation or diminution in value which is the result of postseparation actions or activities of a spouse shall not be treated as divisible property.

b. All property, property rights, or any portion thereof received after the date of separation but before the date of distribution that was acquired as a result of the efforts of either spouse during the marriage and before the date of separation, including, but not limited to, commissions, bonuses, and contractual rights.

c. Passive income from marital property received after the date of separation, including, but not limited to, interest and dividends.

d. Passive increases and passive decreases in marital debt and financing charges and interest related to marital debt.

(c) There shall be an equal division by using net value of marital property and net value of divisible property unless the court determines that an equal division is not equitable. If the court determines that an equal division is not equitable, the court shall divide the marital property and divisible property equitably. The court shall consider all of the following factors under this subsection:

(1) The income, property, and liabilities of each party at the time the division of property is to become effective.

(2) Any obligation for support arising out of a prior marriage.

(3) The duration of the marriage and the age and physical and mental health of both parties.

(4) The need of a parent with custody of a child or children of the marriage to occupy or own the marital residence and to use or own its household effects.

(5) The expectation of pension, retirement, or other deferred compensation rights that are not marital property.

(6) Any equitable claim to, interest in, or direct or indirect contribution made to the acquisition of such marital property by the party not having title, including joint efforts or expenditures and contributions and services, or lack thereof, as a spouse, parent, wage earner or homemaker.

(7) Any direct or indirect contribution made by one spouse to help educate or develop the career potential of the other spouse.

(8) Any direct contribution to an increase in value of separate property which occurs during the course of the marriage.

(9) The liquid or nonliquid character of all marital property and divisible property.

(10) The difficulty of evaluating any component asset or any interest in a business, corporation or profession, and the economic desirability of retaining such asset or interest, intact and free from any claim or interference by the other party.

(11) The tax consequences to each party, including those federal and State tax consequences that would have been incurred if the marital and divisible property had been sold or liquidated on the date of valuation. The trial court may, however, in its discretion, consider whether or when such tax consequences are reasonably likely to occur in determining the equitable value deemed appropriate for this factor.

(11a) Acts of either party to maintain, preserve, develop, or expand; or to waste, neglect, devalue or convert the marital property or divisible property, or both, during the period after separation of the parties and before the time of distribution.

(11b) In the event of the death of either party prior to the entry of any order for the distribution of property made pursuant to this subsection:

a. Property passing to the surviving spouse by will or through intestacy due to the death of a spouse.

    b.   Property held as tenants by the entirety or as joint tenants with rights of survivorship passing to the surviving spouse due to the death of a spouse.

    c.   Property passing to the surviving spouse from life insurance, individual retirement accounts, pension or profit-sharing plans, any private or governmental retirement plan or annuity of which the decedent controlled the designation of beneficiary (excluding any benefits under the federal social security system), or any other retirement accounts or contracts, due to the death of a spouse.

    d.   The surviving spouse's right to claim an "elective share" pursuant to G.S. 30-3.1 through G.S. 30-33, unless otherwise waived.

(12)   Any other factor which the court finds to be just and proper.

(c1)   Notwithstanding any other provision of law, a second or subsequent spouse acquires no interest in the marital property and divisible property of his or her spouse from a former marriage until a final determination of equitable distribution is made in the marital property and divisible property of the spouse's former marriage.

(d)   Before, during or after marriage the parties may by written agreement, duly executed and acknowledged in accordance with the provisions of G.S. 52-10 and 52-10.1, or by a written agreement valid in the jurisdiction where executed, provide for distribution of the marital property or divisible property, or both, in a manner deemed by the parties to be equitable and the agreement shall be binding on the parties.

(e)   Subject to the presumption of subsection (c) of this section that an equal division is equitable, it shall be presumed in every action that an in-kind distribution of marital or divisible property is equitable. This presumption may be rebutted by the greater weight of the evidence, or by evidence that the property is a closely held business entity or is otherwise not susceptible of division in-kind. In any action in which the presumption is rebutted, the court in lieu of in-kind distribution shall provide for a distributive award in order to achieve equity between the parties. The court may provide for a distributive award to facilitate, effectuate or supplement a distribution of marital or divisible property. The court may provide that any distributive award payable over a period of time be secured by a lien on specific property.

(f) The court shall provide for an equitable distribution without regard to alimony for either party or support of the children of both parties. After the determination of an equitable distribution, the court, upon request of either party, shall consider whether an order for alimony or child support should be modified or vacated pursuant to G.S. 50-16.9 or 50-13.7.

(g) If the court orders the transfer of real or personal property or an interest therein, the court may also enter an order which shall transfer title, as provided in G.S. 1A-1, Rule 70 and G.S. 1-228.

(h) If either party claims that any real property is marital property or divisible property, that party may cause a notice of lis pendens to be recorded pursuant to Article 11 of Chapter 1 of the General Statutes. Any person whose conveyance or encumbrance is recorded or whose interest is obtained by descent, prior to the filing of the lis pendens, shall take the real property free of any claim resulting from the equitable distribution proceeding. The court may cancel the notice of lis pendens upon substitution of a bond with surety in an amount determined by the court to be sufficient provided the court finds that the claim of the spouse against property subject to the notice of lis pendens can be satisfied by money damages.

(i) Upon filing an action or motion in the cause requesting an equitable distribution or alleging that an equitable distribution will be requested when it is timely to do so, a party may seek injunctive relief pursuant to G.S. 1A-1, Rule 65 and Chapter 1, Article 37, to prevent the disappearance, waste or conversion of property alleged to be marital property, divisible property, or separate property of the party seeking relief. The court, in lieu of granting an injunction, may require a bond or other assurance of sufficient amount to protect the interest of the other spouse in the property. Upon application by the owner of separate property which was removed from the marital home or possession of its owner by the other spouse, the court may enter an order for reasonable counsel fees and costs of court incurred to regain its possession, but such fees shall not exceed the fair market value of the separate property at the time it was removed.

(i1) Unless good cause is shown that there should not be an interim distribution, the court may, at any time after an action for equitable distribution has been filed and prior to the final judgment of equitable distribution, enter orders declaring what is separate property and may also enter orders dividing part of the marital property, divisible property or debt, or marital debt between the parties. The partial distribution may provide for a distributive award and may also provide for a distribution of marital property, marital debt, divisible property, or divisible debt. Any such orders entered shall be taken into consideration at trial and proper credit given.

Hearings held pursuant to this subsection may be held at sessions arranged by the chief district court judge pursuant to G.S. 7A-146 and, if held at such sessions, shall not be subject to the reporting requirements of G.S. 7A-198.

(j)   In any order for the distribution of property made pursuant to this section, the court shall make written findings of fact that support the determination that the marital property and divisible property has been equitably divided.

(k)   The rights of the parties to an equitable distribution of marital property and divisible property are a species of common ownership, the rights of the respective parties vesting at the time of the parties' separation.

(l)   (1)   A claim for equitable distribution, whether an action is filed or not, survives the death of a spouse so long as the parties are living separate and apart at the time of death.

(2)   The provisions of Article 19 of Chapter 28A of the General Statutes shall be applicable to a claim for equitable distribution against the estate of the deceased spouse.

(3)   Any claim for equitable distribution against the surviving spouse made by the estate of the deceased spouse must be filed with the district court within one year of the date of death of the deceased spouse or be forever barred. (1981, c. 815, s. 1; 1983, c. 309; c. 640, ss. 1, 2; c. 758, ss. 1-4; 1985, c. 31, ss. 1-3; c. 143; c. 660, ss. 1-3; 1987, c. 663; c. 844, s. 2; 1991, c. 635, ss. 1, 1.1; 1991 (Reg. Sess., 1992), c. 960, s. 1; 1995, c. 240, s. 1; c. 245, s. 2; 1997-212, ss. 2-5; 1997-302, s. 1; 1998-217, s. 7(c); 2001-364, ss. 2, 3; 2002-159, s. 33; 2003-168, ss. 1, 2; 2005-353, s. 1; 2011-284, s. 51; 2013-103, s. 1.)

§ 50-20.1. Pension and retirement benefits.

(a)   The award of vested pension, retirement, or other deferred compensation benefits may be made payable:

(1) As a lump sum by agreement;

(2) Over a period of time in fixed amounts by agreement;

(3) By appropriate domestic relations order as a prorated portion of the benefits made to the designated recipient at the time the party against whom the award is made actually begins to receive the benefits; or

(4) By awarding a larger portion of other assets to the party not receiving the benefits and a smaller share of other assets to the party entitled to receive the benefits.

(b) The award of nonvested pension, retirement, or other deferred compensation benefits may be made payable:

(1) As a lump sum by agreement;

(2) Over a period of time in fixed amounts by agreement; or

(3) By appropriate domestic relations order as a prorated portion of the benefits made to the designated recipient at the time the party against whom the award is made actually begins to receive the benefits.

(c) Notwithstanding the provisions of subsections (a) and (b) of this section, the court shall not require the administrator of the fund or plan involved to make any payments until the party against whom the award is made actually begins to receive the benefits unless the plan permits an earlier distribution.

(d) The award shall be determined using the proportion of time the marriage existed (up to the date of separation of the parties), simultaneously with the employment which earned the vested and nonvested pension, retirement, or deferred compensation benefit, to the total amount of time of employment. The award shall be based on the vested and nonvested accrued benefit, as provided by the plan or fund, calculated as of the date of separation, and shall not include contributions, years of service, or compensation which may accrue after the date of separation. The award shall include gains and losses on the prorated portion of the benefit vested at the date of separation.

(e) No award shall exceed fifty percent (50%) of the benefits the person against whom the award is made is entitled to receive as vested and nonvested pension, retirement, or other deferred compensation benefits, except that an award may exceed fifty percent (50%) if (i) other assets subject to equitable distribution are insufficient; or (ii) there is difficulty in distributing any asset or any interest in a business, corporation, or profession; or (iii) it is economically desirable for one party to retain an asset or interest that is intact and free from any claim or interference by the other party; or (iv) more than one pension or retirement system or deferred compensation plan or fund is involved, but the benefits award may not exceed fifty percent (50%) of the total benefits of all the plans added together; or (v) both parties consent. In no event shall an award exceed fifty percent (50%) if a plan prohibits an award in excess of fifty percent (50%).

(f) In the event the person receiving the award dies, the unpaid balance, if any, of the award shall pass to the beneficiaries of the recipient by will, if any, or by intestate succession, or by beneficiary designation with the plan consistent with the terms of the plan unless the plan prohibits such designation. In the event the person against whom the award is made dies, the award to the recipient shall remain payable to the extent permitted by the pension or retirement system or deferred compensation plan or fund involved.

(g) The court may require distribution of the award by means of a qualified domestic relations order, or as defined in section 414(p) of the Internal Revenue Code of 1986, or by other appropriate order. To facilitate the calculating and payment of distributive awards, the administrator of the system, plan, or fund may be ordered to certify the total contributions, years of service, and pension, retirement, or other deferred compensation benefits payable.

(h) This section and G.S. 50-21 shall apply to all pension, retirement, and other deferred compensation plans and funds, including vested and nonvested military pensions eligible under the federal Uniform Services Former Spouses Protection Act, and including funds administered by the State pursuant to Articles 84 through 88 of Chapter 58 and Chapters 120, 127A, 128, 135, 143, 143B, and 147 of the General Statutes, to the extent of a member's accrued benefit at the date of separation, as determined by the court. (1997-212, s. 1.)

§ 50-21. Procedures in actions for equitable distribution of property; sanctions for purposeful and prejudicial delay.

(a) At any time after a husband and wife begin to live separate and apart from each other, a claim for equitable distribution may be filed and adjudicated, either as a separate civil action, or together with any other action brought pursuant to Chapter 50 of the General Statutes, or as a motion in the cause as provided by G.S. 50-11(e) or (f). Within 90 days after service of a claim for equitable distribution, the party who first asserts the claim shall prepare and serve upon the opposing party an equitable distribution inventory affidavit listing all property claimed by the party to be marital property and all property claimed by the party to be separate property, and the estimated date-of-separation fair market value of each item of marital and separate property. Within 30 days after service of the inventory affidavit, the party upon whom service is made shall prepare and serve an inventory affidavit upon the other party. The inventory affidavits prepared and served pursuant to this subsection shall be subject to amendment and shall not be binding at trial as to completeness or value. The court may extend the time limits in this subsection for good cause shown. The affidavits are subject to the requirements of G.S. 1A-1, Rule 11, and are deemed to be in the nature of answers to interrogatories propounded to the parties. Any party failing to supply the information required by this subsection in the affidavit is subject to G.S. 1A-1, Rules 26, 33, and 37. During the pendency of the action for equitable distribution, discovery may proceed, and the court shall enter temporary orders as appropriate and necessary for the purpose of preventing the disappearance, waste, or destruction of marital or separate property or to secure the possession thereof.

Real or personal property located outside of North Carolina is subject to equitable distribution in accordance with the provisions of G.S. 50-20, and the court may include in its order appropriate provisions to ensure compliance with the order of equitable distribution.

(b)   For purposes of equitable distribution, marital property shall be valued as of the date of the separation of the parties, and evidence of preseparation and postseparation occurrences or values is competent as corroborative evidence of the value of marital property as of the date of the separation of the parties. Divisible property and divisible debt shall be valued as of the date of distribution.

(c)   Nothing in G.S. 50-20 or this section shall restrict or extend the right to trial by jury as provided by the Constitution of North Carolina.

(d)   Within 120 days after the filing of the initial pleading or motion in the cause for equitable distribution, the party first serving the pleading or application shall apply to the court to conduct a scheduling and discovery conference. If that party fails to make application, then the other party may do so. At the conference the court shall determine a schedule of discovery as well as consider and rule upon any motions for appointment of expert witnesses, or other applications, including applications to determine the date of separation, and shall set a date for the disclosure of expert witnesses and a date on or before which an initial pretrial conference shall be held.

At the initial pretrial conference the court shall make inquiry as to the status of the case and shall enter a date for the completion of discovery, the completion of a mediated settlement conference, if applicable, and the filing and service of motions, and shall determine a date on or after which a final pretrial conference shall be held and a date on or after which the case shall proceed to trial.

The final pretrial conference shall be conducted pursuant to the Rules of Civil Procedure and the General Rules of Practice in the applicable district or superior court, adopted pursuant to G.S. 7A-34. The court shall rule upon any matters reasonably necessary to effect a fair and prompt disposition of the case in the interests of justice.

(e) Upon motion of either party or upon the court's own initiative, the court shall impose an appropriate sanction on a party when the court finds that:

(1) The party has willfully obstructed or unreasonably delayed, or has attempted to obstruct or unreasonably delay, discovery proceedings, including failure to make discovery pursuant to G.S. 1A-1, Rule 37, or has willfully obstructed or unreasonably delayed or attempted to obstruct or unreasonably delay any pending equitable distribution proceeding, and

(2) The willful obstruction or unreasonable delay of the proceedings is or would be prejudicial to the interests of the opposing party.

Delay consented to by the parties is not grounds for sanctions. The sanction may include an order to pay the other party the amount of the reasonable expenses and damages incurred because of the willful obstruction or unreasonable delay, including a reasonable attorneys' fee, and including appointment by the court, at the offending party's expense, of an accountant, appraiser, or other expert whose services the court finds are necessary to secure in order for the discovery or other equitable distribution proceeding to be timely conducted. (1981, c. 815, s. 6; 1983, c. 671, s. 1; 1985, c. 689, s. 21; 1987, c. 844, s. 1; 1991, c. 610, s. 2; 1991 (Reg. Sess., 1992), c. 910, s. 1; 1993, c. 209, s. 1; 1995, c. 244, s. 1; c. 245, s. 1; 1997-302, s. 2; 2001-364, s. 1.)

§ 50-22. Action on behalf of an incompetent.

A duly appointed attorney-in-fact who has the power to sue and defend civil actions on behalf of an incompetent spouse and who has been appointed pursuant to a durable power of attorney executed in accordance with Chapter 32A of the General Statutes, a guardian appointed in accordance with Chapter 35A of the General Statutes, or a guardian ad litem appointed in accordance with G.S. 1A-1, Rules 17 and 25(b), may commence, defend, maintain, arbitrate, mediate, or settle any action authorized by this Chapter on behalf of an incompetent spouse. However, only a competent spouse may commence an action for absolute divorce. (1991, c. 610, s. 1; 2009-224, s. 1.)

§§ 50-23 through 50-29. Reserved for future codification purposes.

Article 2.

Expedited Process for Child Support Cases.

§ 50-30. Findings; policy; and purpose.

(a) Findings. - The General Assembly makes the following findings:

(1) There is a strong public interest in providing fair, efficient, and swift judicial processes for establishing and enforcing child support obligations. Children are entitled to support from their parents, and court assistance is often required for the establishment and enforcement of parental support obligations. Children who do not receive support from their parents often become financially dependent on the State.

(2) The State shall have laws that meet the federal requirements on expedited processes for obtaining and enforcing child support orders for purposes of federal reimbursement under Title IV-D of the Social Security Act, 42 U.S.C. § 66(a)(2). The Secretary of the United States Department of Health and Human Services may waive the expedited process requirement with respect to one or more district court district as defined in G.S. 7A-133 on the basis of the effectiveness and timeliness of support order issuance and enforcement within the district.

(3) The State has a strong financial interest in complying with the expedited process requirement, and other requirements, of Title IV-D of the Social Security Act, but the State would incur substantial expense in creating statewide an expedited child support process as defined by federal law.

(4) The State's judicial system is largely capable of processing child support cases in a timely and efficient manner and has a strong commitment to an expeditious system.

(5) The substantial expense the State would incur in creating a new system for obtaining and enforcing child support orders would be reduced and better spent by improving the present system.

(b) Purpose and Policy. - It is the policy of this State to ensure, to the maximum extent possible, that child support obligations are established and enforced fairly, efficiently, and swiftly through the judicial system by means that make the best use of the State's resources. It is the purpose of this Article to facilitate this policy. The Administrative Office of the Courts and judicial officials in each district court district as defined in G.S. 7A-133 shall make a diligent effort to ensure that child support cases, from the time of filing to the time of disposition, are handled fairly, efficiently, and swiftly. The Administrative Office of the Courts and the State Department of Health and Human Services shall work together to improve procedures for the handling of child support cases in which the State or county has an interest, including all cases that qualify in any respect for federal reimbursement under Title IV-D of the Social Security Act. (1985 (Reg. Sess., 1986), c. 993, s. 1; 1987 (Reg. Sess., 1988), c. 1037, s. 86; 1997-443, s. 11A.18.)

§ 50-31. Definitions.

As used in this Article, unless the context clearly requires otherwise:

(1) "Child support case" means the part of any civil or criminal action or proceeding, whether intrastate or interstate, that involves a claim for the establishment or enforcement of a child support obligation.

(2) "Dispose" or "disposition" of a child support case means the entry of an order in a child support case that:

a. Dismisses the claim for establishment or enforcement of the child support obligation; or

b. Establishes a child support obligation, either temporary or permanent, and directs how that obligation is to be satisfied; or

c. Orders a particular child support enforcement remedy.

(3) "Expedited process" means a procedure for having child support orders established and enforced by a magistrate or clerk who has been designated as a child support hearing officer pursuant to this Article.

(4) "Federal expedited process requirement" means the provision in Title IV, Part D of the Social Security Act, 42 U.S.C. § 666(a)(2), that requires as a condition of the receipt of federal funds that a state have laws that require the use of federally defined expedited processes for obtaining and enforcing child support orders.

(5) "Filing" means the date the defendant is served with a pleading that seeks establishment or enforcement of a child support obligation, or the date written notice or a pleading is sent to a party seeking establishment or enforcement of a child support obligation.

(6) "Hearing officer" or "child support hearing officer" means a clerk or assistant clerk of superior court or a magistrate who has been designated pursuant to this Article to hear and enter orders in child support cases.

(7) "Initiating party" means the party, the attorney for a party, a child support enforcement agency established pursuant to Title IV, Part D of the Social Security Act, or the clerk of superior court who initiates an action, proceeding, or procedure as allowed or required by law for the establishment or enforcement of a child support obligation. (1985 (Reg. Sess., 1986), c. 993, s. 1; 1987, c. 346.)

§ 50-32. Disposition of cases within 60 days; extension.

Except where paternity is at issue, in all child support cases the district court judge shall dispose of the case from filing to disposition within 60 days, except that this period may be extended for a maximum of 30 days by order of the court if:

(1) Either party or his attorney cannot be present for the hearing; or

(2) The parties have consented to an extension. (1985 (Reg. Sess., 1986), c. 993, s. 1.)

§ 50-33. Waiver of expedited process requirement.

(a) State to Seek Waiver. - The State Department of Health and Human Services, with the assistance of the Administrative Office of the Courts, shall vigorously pursue application to the United States Department of Health and Human Services for waivers of the federal expedited process requirement.

(b) Districts That Do Not Qualify. - In any district court district as defined in G.S. 7A-133 that does not qualify for a waiver of the federal expedited process requirement, an expedited process shall be established as provided in G.S. 50-34. (1985 (Reg. Sess., 1986), c. 993, s. 1; 1987 (Reg. Sess., 1988), c. 1037, s. 87; 1997-443, s. 11A.19.)

§ 50-34. Establishment of an expedited process.

(a) Districts Required to Have Expedited Process. - In any district court district as defined in G.S. 7A-133 that is required by G.S. 50-33(b) to establish an expedited child support process, the Director of the Administrative Office of the Courts shall notify the chief district court judge and the clerk or clerks of superior court in the district in writing of the requirement. The Director of the Administrative Office of the Courts, the chief district court judge, and the clerk or clerks of superior court in the district shall implement an expedited child support process as provided in this section.

(b) Procedure for Establishing Expedited Process. - When a district court district as defined in G.S. 7A-133 is required to implement an expedited process, the Director of the Administrative Office of the Courts, the chief district judge, and the clerk of superior court in an affected county shall determine by agreement whether the child support hearing officer or officers for that county shall be one or more clerks or one or more magistrates. If such agreement has not been reached within 15 days after the notice required by subsection (a) when implementation is required, the Director of the Administrative Office of the Courts shall make the decision. If it is decided that the hearing officer or officers for a county shall be magistrates, the chief district judge, the clerk of superior court, and the Director of the Administrative Office of the Courts shall ensure his or their qualification for the position. If it is decided that the hearing officer or officers for a county shall be the clerk or assistant clerks, the clerk of superior court in the county shall designate the person or persons to serve as hearing officer, and the chief district judge, the clerk of superior court, and the Director of the Administrative Office of the Courts shall ensure his or their qualification for the position.

(c) Public To Be Informed. - When an expedited process is to be implemented in a county or district court district as defined in G.S. 7A-133, the chief district court judge, the clerk or clerks of superior court in affected counties in the district, and the Administrative Office of the Courts shall take steps to ensure that attorneys, the general public, and parties to pending child support cases in the county or district are informed of the change in procedures and helped to understand and use the new system effectively. (1985 (Reg. Sess., 1986), c. 993, s. 1; 1987 (Reg. Sess., 1988), c. 1037, s. 88.)

§ 50-35. Authority and duties of a child support hearing officer.

A child support hearing officer who is properly qualified and designated under this Article has the following authority and responsibilities in all child support cases:

(1) To conduct hearings and to ensure that the parties' due process rights are protected;

(2) To take testimony and establish a record;

(3) To evaluate evidence and make decisions regarding the establishment or enforcement of child support orders;

(4) To accept and approve voluntary acknowledgements of support liability and stipulated agreements setting the amount of support obligations;

(5) To accept and approve voluntary acknowledgements and affirmations of paternity;

(6) Except as otherwise provided in this Article, to enter child support orders that have the same force and effect as orders entered by a district court judge;

(7) To enter temporary child support orders pending the resolution of unusual or complicated issues by a district court judge;

(8) To enter default orders; and

(9) To subpoena witnesses and documents. (1985 (Reg. Sess., 1986), c. 993, s. 1.)

§ 50-36. Child support procedures in districts with expedited process.

(a) Scheduling of Cases. - The procedures of this section shall apply to all child support cases in any district court district as defined in G.S. 7A-133 or county in which an expedited process has been established. All claims for the establishment or enforcement of a child support obligation, whether the claim is made in a separate action or as part of a divorce or any other action, shall be scheduled for hearing before the child support hearing officer. The initiating party shall send a notice of the date, time, and place of the hearing to all other parties. Service of process shall be made and notices given as provided by G.S. 1A-1, Rules of Civil Procedure.

(b) Place of Hearing. - The hearing before the child support hearing officer need not take place in a courtroom, but shall be conducted in an appropriate judicial setting.

(c) Hearing Procedures. - The hearing of a case before a child support officer is without a jury. The rules of evidence applicable in the trial of civil actions generally are observed; however, the hearing officer may require the parties to produce and may consider financial affidavits, State and federal tax returns, and other financial or employment records. Except as otherwise provided in this Article, the hearing officer shall determine the parties' child support rights and obligations and enter an appropriate order based on the evidence and the child support laws of the State. All parties shall be provided with a copy of the order.

(d) Record of Proceeding. - The record of a proceeding before a child support hearing officer shall consist of the pleadings filed in the child support case, documentation of proper service or notice or waiver, and a copy of the hearing officer's order. No verbatim recording or transcript shall be required or provided at State expense.

(e) Transfer to District Court Judge. - Upon his own motion or upon motion of any party, the hearing officer shall transfer a case for hearing before a district court judge when the case involves:

(1) A contested paternity action;

(2) A custody dispute;

(3) Contested visitation rights;

(4) The ownership, possession, or transfer of an interest in property to satisfy a child support obligation; or

(5) Other complex issues.

Upon ordering such a transfer, except in cases of contested paternity, the hearing officer shall also enter a temporary order that provides for the payment of a money amount or otherwise addresses the child's need for support pending the resolution of the case by the district court judge. The chief district court judge shall establish a procedure for such transferred cases to be given priority for hearing before a district court judge. (1985 (Reg. Sess., 1986), c. 993, s. 1; 1987 (Reg. Sess., 1988), c. 1037, s. 89.)

§ 50-37. Enforcement authority of child support hearing officer; contempt.

When a child support case is before a child support hearing officer for enforcement of a child support order, the hearing officer has the same authority that a district court judge would have, except in cases of contempt. Orders that commit a party to jail for civil or criminal contempt for the nonpayment of child support, or for otherwise failing to comply with a child support order, may be entered only by a district court judge. When it appears to a hearing officer that there is probable cause for finding such contempt in a case before the child support hearing officer and that no other enforcement remedy would be effective or sufficient, the hearing officer shall enter an order finding probable cause and referring the case for hearing before a district court judge. The order may indicate the amount of payment the responsible parent may make, or other action he may take, or both, to comply with the child support order. If proof of compliance is made to the hearing officer within a time specified in the order, the hearing officer may cancel the referral of the contempt case to district court. Except as specifically limited by this section, a clerk or magistrate acting as a child support hearing officer retains all of the contempt powers he or she otherwise has by virtue of being a clerk or magistrate. (1985 (Reg. Sess., 1986), c. 993, s. 1.)

§ 50-38. Appeal from orders of the child support hearing officer.

(a) Appeal; Hearing De Novo. - Any party may appeal an order of a child support hearing officer for a hearing de novo before a district court judge by giving notice of appeal at the hearing or in writing within 10 days after entry of judgment. Upon appeal noted, the clerk of superior court shall place the case on the civil issue docket of the district court. The chief district court judge shall establish a procedure for such transferred cases to be given priority for hearing before a district court judge. Unless appealed from, the order of the hearing officer is final.

(b) Order Not Stayed Pending Appeal. - Appeal from an order of a child support hearing officer does not stay the execution or enforcement of the order unless, on application of the appellant, a district court judge orders such a stay. (1985 (Reg. Sess., 1986), c. 993, s. 1.)

§ 50-39. Qualifications of child support hearing officer.

(a) Qualifications. - A clerk or assistant clerk of superior court or a magistrate, to be designated and serve as a child support hearing officer, shall satisfy each of the following qualifications:

(1) Be at least 21 years of age and not older than 70 years of age, and have a high school degree or its equivalent.

(2) Be qualified by training and temperament to be effective in relating to parties in child support cases and in conducting hearings fairly and efficiently.

(3) Be certified by the Administrative Office of the Courts as having completed the training required by subsection (b).

(4) Establish that he has one of the following qualifications;

a. Election or appointment as the clerk of superior court; or

b. Three years experience as an assistant clerk of superior court working in child support or related matters; or

c. Six years experience as an assistant clerk of superior court; or

d. Four years experience as a magistrate whose duties have included, in substantial part, the disposition of civil matters; or

e. Pursuant to G.S. 7A-171.1, five to seven years eligibility for pay as a magistrate; or

f. Three years experience working in the field of child support enforcement or a related field.

(b) Training Required. - Before a clerk or assistant clerk or a magistrate may conduct hearings as a child support hearing officer he must satisfactorily complete a course of instruction in the conduct of such hearings established by the Administrative Office of the Courts. The Administrative Office of the Courts shall establish a course in the conduct of such hearings. The Administrative Office of the Courts may contract with qualified educational organizations to conduct the course of instruction and must reimburse the clerks or magistrates attending for travel and subsistence incurred in taking such training. (1985 (Reg. Sess., 1986), c. 993, s. 1.)

§ 50-40. Reserved for future codification purposes.

Article 3.

Family Law Arbitration Act.

§ 50-41. Purpose; short title.

(a) It is the policy of this State to allow, by agreement of all parties, the arbitration of all issues arising from a marital separation or divorce, except for the divorce itself, while preserving a right of modification based on substantial change of circumstances related to alimony, child custody, and child support. Pursuant to this policy, the purpose of this Article is to provide for arbitration as an efficient and speedy means of resolving these disputes, consistent with Chapters 50, 50A, 50B, 51, 52, 52B, and 52C of the General Statutes and similar legislation, to provide default rules for the conduct of arbitration proceedings, and to assure access to the courts of this State for proceedings ancillary to this arbitration.

(b) This Article may be cited as the North Carolina Family Law Arbitration Act. (1999-185, s. 1.)

§ 50-42. Arbitration agreements made valid, irrevocable, and enforceable.

(a) During, or after marriage, parties may agree in writing to submit to arbitration any controversy, except for the divorce itself, arising out of the marital relationship. Before marriage, parties may agree in writing to submit to arbitration any controversy, except for child support, child custody, or the divorce itself, arising out of the marital relationship. This agreement is valid, enforceable, and irrevocable except with both parties' consent, without regard to the justiciable character of the controversy and without regard to whether litigation is pending as to the controversy.

(b) This Article does not apply to an agreement to arbitrate in which a provision stipulates that this Article does not apply or to any arbitration or award under an agreement in which a provision stipulates that this Article does not apply. (1999-185, s. 1.)

§ 50-42.1. Nonwaivable provisions.

(a) Except as otherwise provided in subsections (b) and (c) of this section or in this Article, a party to an agreement to arbitrate or an arbitration proceeding may waive, or the parties may vary the effect of, the requirements of this Article to the extent provided by law. Any waiver or agreement must be in writing.

(b) Before a controversy arises that is subject to an agreement to arbitrate, a party to the agreement may not:

(1) Waive or agree to vary the effect of the requirements of G.S. 50-42, 50-49(a), (b), or (c), 50-58, or 50-59.

(2) Agree to unreasonably restrict the right to notice of the initiation of an arbitration proceeding under G.S. 50-42.2(a) or (b).

(3) Agree to unreasonably restrict the right to disclosure of any facts by a neutral arbitrator under G.S. 50-45.1.

(c) Except as otherwise provided in this Article, a party to an agreement to arbitrate or an arbitration proceeding may not waive, or the parties shall not vary the effect of, the requirements of this section or G.S. 50-43, 50-45(f), 50-52 through 50-57, or 50-60 through 50-62.

(d) Any waiver contrary to this section shall not be effective but shall not have the effect of voiding the agreement to arbitrate. (2005-187, s. 1.)

§ 50-42.2. Notice.

(a) A person initiates an arbitration proceeding by giving written notice to the other parties to the agreement to arbitrate in the manner in which the parties have agreed or, in the absence of agreement, by certified or registered mail, return receipt requested, or by service as authorized for the commencement of a civil action under the North Carolina Rules of Civil Procedure.

(b) Unless a person objects to the lack or insufficiency of notice not later than the beginning of the hearing, the person's appearance at the hearing waives the objection.

(c) Except as otherwise provided in this Article, a person gives notice to another person by taking action that is reasonably necessary to inform the other person in the ordinary course of business, regardless of whether the person acquires knowledge of the notice.

(d) A person has notice if the person has knowledge of the notice or has received notice.

(e) A person receives notice when it comes to the person's attention or the notice is delivered at the person's place of residence or place of business or at another location held out by the person as a place of delivery of communications. (2005-187, s. 1.)

§ 50-43. Proceedings to compel or stay arbitration.

(a) On a party's application showing an agreement under G.S. 50-42 and an opposing party's refusal to arbitrate, the court shall order the parties to proceed with the arbitration. If an opposing party denies existence of an agreement to arbitrate, the court shall proceed summarily to determine whether a valid agreement exists and shall order arbitration if it finds for the moving party; otherwise, the application shall be denied.

(b) Upon the application of a party, the court may stay an arbitration proceeding commenced or threatened on a showing that there is no agreement to arbitrate. This issue, when in substantial and bona fide dispute, shall be immediately and summarily tried and the court shall order a stay if it finds for the moving party. If the court finds for the opposing party, the court shall order the parties to go to arbitration. An arbitrator shall decide whether a condition precedent to arbitrability has been fulfilled and whether a contract containing a valid agreement to arbitrate is enforceable. If a party to a judicial proceeding challenges the existence of, or claims that a controversy is not subject to, an agreement to arbitrate, the arbitration proceeding may continue pending final resolution of the issue by the court unless the court otherwise orders.

(c) If an issue referable to arbitration under an alleged agreement is involved in an action or proceeding pending in a court of competent jurisdiction, the application shall be made in that court. Otherwise, the application may be made in any court of competent jurisdiction.

(d) The court shall order a stay in any action or proceeding involving an issue subject to arbitration if an order or an application for arbitration has been made under this section. If the issue is severable, the stay may be with respect to that specific issue only. When the application is made in an action or proceeding, the order compelling arbitration shall include a stay of the court action or proceeding.

(e) An order for arbitration shall not be refused and a stay of arbitration shall not be granted on the ground that the claim in issue lacks merit or because grounds for the claim have not been shown. (1999-185, s. 1; 2005-187, s. 2.)

§ 50-44. Interim relief and interim measures.

(a) In the case of an arbitration where arbitrators have not yet been appointed, or where the arbitrators are unavailable, a party may seek interim relief directly from a court as provided in subsection (c) of this section. Enforcement shall be granted as provided by the law applicable to the type of interim relief sought.

(b) In all other cases a party shall seek interim measures as described in subsection (d) of this section from the arbitrators. A party has no right to seek interim relief from a court, except that a party to an arbitration governed by this Article may request from the court enforcement of the arbitrators' order granting interim measures and review or modification of any interim measures governing child support or child custody.

(c) In connection with an agreement to arbitrate or a pending arbitration, the court may grant under subsection (a) of this section any of the following:

(1) An order of attachment or garnishment;

(2) A temporary restraining order or preliminary injunction;

(3) An order for claim and delivery;

(4) Appointment of a receiver;

(5) Delivery of money or other property into court;

(6) Notice of lis pendens;

(7) Any relief permitted by G.S. 7B-502, 7B-1902, 50-13.5(d), 50-16.2A, 50-20(h), 50-20(i), or 50-20(i1); or Chapter 50A, Chapter 50B, or Chapter 52C of the General Statutes;

(8) Any relief permitted by federal law or treaties to which the United States is a party; or

(9) Any other order necessary to ensure preservation or availability of assets or documents, the destruction or absence of which would likely prejudice the conduct or effectiveness of the arbitration.

(d) The arbitrators may, at a party's request, order any party to take any interim measures of protection that the arbitrators consider necessary in respect to the subject matter of the dispute, including interim measures analogous to interim relief specified in subsection (c) of this section. The arbitrators may require any party to provide appropriate security, including security for costs as provided in G.S. 50-51, in connection with interim measures.

(e) In considering a request for interim relief or enforcement of interim relief, any finding of fact of the arbitrators in the proceeding shall be binding on the court, including any finding regarding the probable validity of the claim that is the subject of the interim relief sought or granted, except that the court may review any findings of fact or modify any interim measures governing child support or child custody.

(f) Where the arbitrators have not ruled on an objection to their jurisdiction, the findings of the arbitrators shall not be binding on the court until the court has made an independent finding as to the arbitrators' jurisdiction. If the court rules that the arbitrators do not have jurisdiction, the application for interim relief shall be denied.

(g) Availability of interim relief or interim measures under this section may be limited by the parties' prior written agreement, except for relief pursuant to G.S. 7B-502, 7B-1902, 50-13.5(d), 50-20(h), 50B-3, Chapter 52C of the General Statutes; federal law; or treaties to which the United States is a party, whose purpose is to provide immediate, emergency relief or protection.

(h) Arbitrators who have cause to suspect that any child is abused or neglected shall report the case of that child to the director of the department of social services of the county where the child resides or, if the child resides out-of-state, of the county where the arbitration is conducted.

(i) A party seeking interim measures, or any other proceeding before the arbitrators, shall proceed in accordance with the agreement to arbitrate. If the agreement to arbitrate does not provide for a method of seeking interim measures, or for other proceedings before the arbitrators, the party shall request interim measures or a hearing by notifying the arbitrators and all other parties of the request. The arbitrators shall notify the parties of the date, time, and place of the hearing.

(j)   A party does not waive the right to arbitrate by proceeding under this section. (1999-185, s. 1; 2005-187, s. 3.)

§ 50-45. Appointment of arbitrators; rules for conducting the arbitration.

(a)   Unless the parties otherwise agree in writing, a single arbitrator shall be chosen by the parties to arbitrate all matters in dispute.

(b)   If the arbitration agreement provides a method of appointment of arbitrators, this method shall be followed. The agreement may provide for appointing one or more arbitrators. Upon the application of a party, the court shall appoint arbitrators in any of the following situations:

(1)   The method agreed upon by the parties in the arbitration agreement fails or for any reason cannot be followed.

(2)   An arbitrator who has already been appointed fails or is unable to act, and a successor has not been chosen by the parties.

(3)   The parties cannot agree on an arbitrator.

(c)   Arbitrators appointed by the court have all the powers of those arbitrators specifically named in the agreement. In appointing arbitrators, a court shall consult with prospective arbitrators as to their availability and shall refer to each of the following:

(1)   The positions and desires of the parties.

(2)   The issues in dispute.

(3)   The skill, substantive training, and experience of prospective arbitrators in those issues, including their skill, substantive training, and experience in family law issues.

(4)   The availability of prospective arbitrators.

(d) The parties may agree in writing to employ an established arbitration institution to conduct the arbitration. If the agreement does not provide a method for appointment of arbitrators and the parties cannot agree on an arbitrator, the court may appoint an established arbitration institution the court considers qualified in family law arbitration to conduct the arbitration.

(e) The parties may agree in writing on rules for conducting the arbitration. If the parties cannot agree on rules for conducting the arbitration, the arbitrators shall select the rules for conducting the arbitration after hearing all parties and taking particular reference to model rules developed by arbitration institutions or similar sources. If the arbitrators cannot decide on rules for conducting the arbitration, upon application by a party, the court may order use of rules for conducting the arbitration, taking particular reference to model rules developed by arbitration institutions or similar sources.

(f) Arbitrators and established arbitration institutions, whether chosen by the parties or appointed by the court, have the same immunity as judges from civil liability for their conduct in the arbitration.

(g) "Arbitration institution" means any neutral, independent organization, association, agency, board, or commission that initiates, sponsors, or administers arbitration proceedings, including involvement in appointment of arbitrators.

(h) The court may award costs under G.S. 50-51(f) in connection with applications and other proceedings under this section. (1999-185, s. 1; 2005-187, s. 4.)

§ 50-45.1. Disclosure by arbitrator.

(a) Before accepting appointment, an individual who is requested to serve as an arbitrator, after making a reasonable inquiry, shall disclose to all parties to the agreement to arbitrate and to the arbitration proceeding and to any other arbitrators any known facts that a reasonable person would consider likely to affect the impartiality of the arbitrator in the arbitration proceeding, including:

(1) A financial or personal interest in the outcome of the arbitration proceeding.

(2) An existing or past relationship with any of the parties to the agreement to arbitrate or to the arbitration proceeding, their counsel or representatives, a witness, or other arbitrators.

(b) An arbitrator has a continuing obligation to disclose to all parties to the agreement to arbitrate and to the arbitration proceeding and to any other arbitrators any facts that the arbitrator learns after accepting appointment that a reasonable person would consider likely to affect the impartiality of the arbitrator.

(c) If an arbitrator discloses a fact required by subsection (a) or (b) of this section to be disclosed and a party timely objects to the appointment or continued service of the arbitrator based upon the fact disclosed, the objection may be grounds for vacating an award made by the arbitrator under G.S. 50-54(a)(2).

(d) If the arbitrator did not disclose a fact as required by subsection (a) or (b) of this section, upon timely objection by a party, the court may vacate an award pursuant to G.S. 50-54(a)(2).

(e) An arbitrator appointed as a neutral arbitrator who does not disclose a known, direct, and material interest in the outcome of the arbitration proceeding or a known, existing, and substantial relationship with a party is presumed to act with evident partiality under G.S. 50-54(a)(2).

(f) If the parties to an arbitration proceeding agree to the procedures of an arbitration institution or any other procedures for challenges to arbitrators before an award is made, substantial compliance with those procedures is a condition precedent to a motion to vacate an award on those grounds pursuant to G.S. 50-54(a)(2). (2005-187, s. 5.)

§ 50-46. Majority action by arbitrators.

The arbitrators' powers shall be exercised by a majority unless otherwise provided by the parties' written arbitration agreement or this Article. (1999-185, s. 1; 2005-187, s. 6.)

§ 50-47. Hearing.

Unless otherwise provided by the parties' written agreement:

(1) The arbitrators shall appoint a time and place for the hearing and notify the parties or their counsel by personal service or by registered or certified mail, return receipt requested, not less than five days before the hearing. Appearance of a party at the hearing waives any claim of deficiency of notice. The arbitrators may adjourn the hearing from time to time as necessary and, on request of a party and for good cause shown, or upon their own motion, may postpone the hearing to a time not later than the date fixed by the written agreement for making the award unless the parties consent to a later date. The arbitrators may hear and determine the controversy upon the evidence produced notwithstanding the failure of a party duly notified to appear. Upon application of a party, the court may direct the arbitrators to proceed promptly with the hearing and determination of the controversy.

(2) The parties are entitled to be heard, to present evidence material to the controversy, and to cross-examine witnesses appearing at the hearing.

(3) All the arbitrators shall conduct the hearing, but a majority may determine any question and may render a final award. If, during the course of the hearing, an arbitrator for any reason ceases to act, the remaining arbitrators appointed to act as neutrals may continue with the hearing and determination of the controversy.

(4) Upon request of any party or at the election of any arbitrator, the arbitrators shall cause to be made a record of testimony and evidence introduced at the hearing. The arbitrators shall decide how the cost of the record will be apportioned. (1999-185, s. 1; 2005-187, s. 7.)

§ 50-48. Representation by attorney.

A party has the right to be represented by counsel at any proceeding or hearing under this Article. A waiver of representation prior to a proceeding or hearing is ineffective. (1999-185, s. 1.)

§ 50-49. Witnesses; subpoenas; depositions; court assistance.

(a) The arbitrators have the power to administer oaths and may issue subpoenas for attendance of witnesses and for production of books, records, documents, and other evidence. Subpoenas issued by the arbitrators shall be served and, upon application to the court by a party or the arbitrators, enforced in the manner provided by law for service and enforcement of subpoenas in a civil action.

(b) On the application of a party and for use as evidence, the arbitrators may permit depositions to be taken in the manner and upon the terms the arbitrators designate.

(c) All provisions of law compelling a person under subpoena to testify apply.

(d) The arbitrators or a party with the approval of the arbitrators may request assistance from the court in obtaining discovery and taking evidence, in which event the Rules of Civil Procedure under Chapter 1A of the General Statutes and Chapters 50, 50A, 52B, and 52C of the General Statutes apply. The court may execute the request within its competence and according to its rules on discovery and evidence and may impose sanctions for failure to comply with its orders.

(e) A subpoena may be issued as provided by G.S. 8-59, in which case the witness compensation provisions of G.S. 6-51, 6-53, and 7A-314 shall apply. (1999-185, s. 1.)

§ 50-50: Repealed by Session Laws 2005-187, s. 8, effective October 1, 2005.

§ 50-50.1. Consolidation.

(a) Except as otherwise provided in subsection (c) of this section, upon motion of a party to an agreement or arbitration proceeding, the court may order consolidation of separate arbitration proceedings as to all or some of the claims if all of the following apply:

(1) There are separate agreements to arbitrate or separate arbitration proceedings between the same parties or one of them is a party to a separate agreement to arbitrate or a separate arbitration with a third party.

(2) The claims subject to the agreements to arbitrate arise in substantial part from the same transaction or series of related transactions.

(3) The existence of a common issue of law or fact creates the possibility of conflicting decisions in the separate arbitration proceedings.

(4) Prejudice resulting from a failure to consolidate is not outweighed by the risk of undue delay or prejudice to the rights of or hardship to parties opposing consolidation.

(b) The court may order consolidation of separate arbitration proceedings as to some claims and allow other claims to be resolved in separate arbitration proceedings.

(c) The court shall not order consolidation of the claims of a party to an agreement to arbitrate if the agreement prohibits consolidation. (2005-187, s. 9.)

§ 50-51. Award; costs.

(a) The award shall be in writing, dated and signed by the arbitrators joining in the award, with a statement of the place where the arbitration was conducted and the place where the award was made. Where there is more than one arbitrator, the signatures of a majority of the arbitrators suffice, but the reason for any omitted signature shall be stated. The arbitrators shall deliver a copy of the award to each party personally or by registered or certified mail, return receipt requested, or as provided in the parties' written agreement. Time of delivery shall be computed from the date of personal delivery or date of mailing.

(b) Unless the parties otherwise agree in writing, the award shall state the reasons upon which it is based.

(c) Unless the parties otherwise agree in writing, the arbitrators may award interest as provided by law.

(d) The arbitrators in their discretion may award specific performance to a party requesting an award of specific performance when that would be an appropriate remedy.

(e) Unless the parties otherwise agree in writing, the arbitrators may not award punitive damages. If arbitrators award punitive damages, they shall state the award in a record and shall specify facts justifying the award and the amount of the award attributable to punitive damages.

(f) Costs:

(1) Unless the parties otherwise agree in writing, awarding of costs of an arbitration shall be in the arbitrators' discretion.

(2) In making an award of costs, the arbitrators may include any or all of the following as costs:

a. Fees and expenses of the arbitrators, expert witnesses, and translators;

b. Fees and expenses of counsel, to the extent allowed by law unless the parties otherwise agree in writing, and of an institution supervising the arbitration, if any;

c. Any other expenses incurred in connection with the arbitration proceedings;

d. Sanctions awarded by the arbitrators or the court, including those provided by N.C.R. Civ. P. 11 and 37; and

e. Costs allowed by Chapters 6 and 7A of the General Statutes.

(3) In making an award of costs, the arbitrators shall specify each of the following:

a. The party entitled to costs;

b. The party who shall pay costs;

c. The amount of costs or method of determining that amount; and

d. The manner in which costs shall be paid.

(g) An award shall be made within the time fixed by the agreement. If no time is fixed by the agreement, the award shall be made within the time the court orders on a party's application. The parties may extend the time in writing either before or after the expiration of this time. A party waives objection that an award was not made within the time required unless that party notifies the arbitrators of his or her objection prior to delivery of the award to that party. (1999-185, s. 1; 2005-187, s. 10.)

§ 50-52. Change of award by arbitrators.

(a) On a party's application to the arbitrators or, if an application to the court is pending under G.S. 50-53 through G.S. 50-56, on submission to the arbitrators by the court under the conditions ordered by the court, the arbitrators may modify or correct the award for any of the following reasons:

(1) Upon grounds stated in G.S. 50-55(a)(1) and (a)(3).

(2) If the arbitrators have not made a final and definite award upon a claim submitted by the parties to the arbitration proceeding.

(3) To clarify the award.

(b) The application shall be made within 20 days after delivery of the award to the opposing party. The application must include a statement that the opposing party must serve any objections to the application within 10 days from notice. An award modified or corrected under this section is subject to the provisions of G.S. 50-51(a) through G.S. 50-51(f) and G.S. 50-53 through G.S. 50-56. (1999-185, s. 1; 2005-187, s. 11.)

§ 50-53. Confirmation of award.

(a) Unless the parties otherwise agree in writing that part or all of an award shall not be confirmed by the court, upon a party's application, the court shall confirm an award, except when within time limits imposed under G.S. 50-54 through G.S. 50-56 grounds are urged for vacating or modifying or correcting the award, in which case the court shall proceed as provided in G.S. 50-54 through G.S. 50-56.

(b)   The court may award costs, as provided in G.S. 50-51(f), of the application and subsequent proceedings. (1999-185, s. 1; 2003-61, s. 1; 2005-187, s. 12.)

§ 50-54. Vacating an award.

(a)   Upon a party's application, the court shall vacate an award for any of the following reasons:

(1)   The award was procured by corruption, fraud, or other undue means;

(2)   There was evident partiality by an arbitrator appointed as a neutral, corruption of an arbitrator, or misconduct prejudicing the rights of a party;

(3)   The arbitrators exceeded their powers;

(4)   The arbitrators refused to postpone the hearing upon a showing of sufficient cause for the postponement, refused to hear evidence material to the controversy, or otherwise conducted the hearing contrary to the provisions of G.S. 50-47;

(5)   There was no arbitration agreement, the issue was not adversely determined in proceedings under G.S. 50-43, and the party did not participate in the arbitration hearing without raising the objection. The fact that the relief awarded either could not or would not be granted by a court is not a ground for vacating or refusing to confirm the award;

(6)   The court determines that the award for child support or child custody is not in the best interest of the child. The burden of proof at a hearing under this subdivision is on the party seeking to vacate the arbitrator's award;

(7)   The award included punitive damages, and the court determines that the award for punitive damages is clearly erroneous; or

(8)   If the parties contract in an arbitration agreement for judicial review of errors of law in the award, the court shall vacate the award if the arbitrators have committed an error of law prejudicing a party's rights.

(b)   An application under this section shall be made within 90 days after delivery of a copy of the award to the applicant. If the application is predicated on corruption, fraud, or other undue means, it shall be made within 90 days after these grounds are known or should have been known.

(c)   In vacating an award on grounds other than stated in subdivision (5) of subsection (a) of this section, the court may order a rehearing before arbitrators chosen as provided in the agreement, or in the absence of a provision regarding the appointment of arbitrators, by the court in accordance with G.S. 50-45, except in the case of a vacated award for child support or child custody in which case the court may proceed to hear and determine all such issues. The time within which the agreement requires an award to be made applies to the rehearing and commences from the date of the order.

(d)   The court shall confirm the award and may award costs of the application and subsequent proceedings under G.S. 50-51(f) if an application to vacate is denied, no motion to modify or correct the award is pending, and the parties have not agreed in writing that the award shall not be confirmed under G.S. 50-53. (1999-185, s. 1; 2005-187, s. 13.)

§ 50-55. Modification or correction of award.

(a)   Upon application made within 90 days after delivery of a copy of an award to an applicant, the court shall modify or correct the award where at least one of the following occurs:

(1)   There is an evident miscalculation of figures or an evident mistake in the description of a person, thing, or property referred to in the award;

(2)   The arbitrators have awarded upon a matter not submitted to them, and the award may be corrected without affecting the merits of the decision upon the issues submitted; or

(3)   The award is imperfect in a matter of form, not affecting the merits of the controversy.

(b)   If the application is granted, the court shall modify or correct the award to effect its intent and shall confirm the award as modified or corrected. Otherwise, the court shall confirm the award as made.

(c) An application to modify or correct an award may be joined in the alternative with an application to vacate the award.

(d) The court may award costs, as provided in G.S. 50-51(f), of the application and subsequent proceedings. (1999-185, s. 1.)

§ 50-56. Modification of award for alimony, postseparation support, child support, or child custody based on substantial change of circumstances.

(a) A court or the arbitrators may modify an award for postseparation support, alimony, child support, or child custody under conditions stated in G.S. 50-13.7 and G.S. 50-16.9 as provided in subsections (b) through (f) of this section.

(b) Unless the parties have agreed in writing that an award for postseparation support or alimony shall be nonmodifiable, an award by arbitrators for postseparation support or alimony under G.S. 50-16.2A, 50-16.3A, 50-16.4, or 50-16.7 may be modified if a court order for alimony or postseparation support could be modified under G.S. 50-16.9.

(c) An award by arbitrators for child support or child custody may be modified if a court order for child support or child custody could be modified under G.S. 50-13.7.

(d) If an award for modifiable postseparation support or alimony, or an award for child support or child custody, has not been confirmed under G.S. 50-53, upon the parties' written agreement these matters may be submitted to arbitrators chosen by the parties under G.S. 50-45. G.S. 50-52 through G.S. 50-56 shall apply to this modified award.

(e) If an award for modifiable postseparation support or alimony, or an award for child support or child custody has been confirmed pursuant to G.S. 50-53, upon the parties' agreement in writing and joint motion, the court may remit these matters to arbitrators chosen by the parties as provided in G.S. 50-45, in which case G.S. 50-52 through G.S. 50-56 apply to this modified award.

(f) Except as otherwise provided in this section, the provisions of G.S. 50-55 apply to modifications or corrections of awards for postseparation support, alimony, child support, or child custody. (1999-185, s. 1; 2005-187, s. 14.)

§ 50-57. Orders or judgments on award.

(a) Upon granting an order confirming, modifying, or correcting an award, an order or judgment shall be entered in conformity with the order and docketed and enforced as any other order or judgment. The court may award costs, as provided in G.S. 50-51(f), of the application and of proceedings subsequent to the application and disbursements.

(b) Notwithstanding G.S. 7A-109, 7A-276.1, or 132-1 or similar law, the court, in its discretion, may order that any arbitration award or order or any judgment or court order entered as a court order or judgment under this Article, or any part of the arbitration award or order or judgment or court order, be sealed, to be opened only upon order of the court upon good cause shown. Upon good cause shown, the court may order resealing of the opened arbitration awards or orders or judgments or court orders. The court, in its discretion, may order that any arbitration award or order or any judgment or court order entered as a court order or judgment under this Article, or any part of the arbitration award or order or judgment or court order, be redacted, the redactions to be opened only upon order of the court upon good cause shown. Upon good cause shown, the court may order redaction of the previously redacted arbitration awards or orders or judgments or court orders opened under the court's order. (1999-185, s. 1; 2005-187, s. 15.)

§ 50-58. Applications to the court.

Except as otherwise provided, an application to a court under this Article shall be by motion and shall be heard in the manner and upon notice provided by law or rule of court for making and hearing motions in civil actions. Unless the parties otherwise agree in writing, notice of an initial application for an order shall be served in the manner provided by law for service of summons in civil actions. (1999-185, s. 1; 2005-187, s. 16.)

§ 50-59. Court; jurisdiction; other definitions.

(a) The term "court" means a court of competent jurisdiction of this State. Making an agreement in this State described in G.S. 50-42 or any agreement providing for arbitration in this State or under its laws confers jurisdiction on the court to enforce the agreement under this Article and to enter judgment on an award under the agreement.

(b) The term "person" means an individual, corporation, business trust, estate, trust, partnership, limited liability company, association, joint venture, government, governmental subdivision, agency or instrumentality, public corporation, or any other legal or commercial entity. (1999-185, s. 1; 2005-187, s. 17.)

§ 50-60. Appeals.

(a) An appeal may be based on failure to comply with the procedural aspects of this Article. An appeal may be taken from any of the following:

(1) An order denying an application to compel arbitration made under G.S. 50-43;

(2) An order granting an application to stay arbitration made under G.S. 50-43(b);

(3) An order confirming or denying confirmation of an award;

(4) An order modifying or correcting an award;

(5) An order vacating an award without directing a rehearing; or

(6) A judgment entered pursuant to provisions of this Article.

(b) Unless the parties contract in an arbitration agreement for judicial review of errors of law as provided in G.S. 50-54(a), a party may not appeal on the basis that the arbitrator failed to apply correctly the law under Chapters 50, 50A, 52B, or 52C of the General Statutes.

(c) The appeal shall be taken in the manner and to the same extent as from orders or judgments in a civil action. (1999-185, s. 1.)

§ 50-61. Article not retroactive.

This Article applies to agreements made on or after October 1, 1999, unless parties by separate written agreement after that date state that this Article shall apply to agreements dated before October 1, 1999. (1999-185, s. 1; 2005-187, s. 18.)

§ 50-62. Construction; uniformity of interpretation.

(a) Certain provisions of this Article have been adapted from the Uniform Arbitration Act formerly in force in this State, the Revised Uniform Arbitration Act in force in this State, the North Carolina International Commercial Arbitration and Conciliation Act, and Chapters 50, 50A, 50B, 51, 52, and 52C of the General Statutes. This Article shall be construed to effect its general purpose to make uniform provisions of these Acts and Chapters 50, 50A, 50B, 51, 52, 52B, and 52C of the General Statutes.

(b) The provisions of this Article governing the legal effect, validity, or enforceability of electronic records or electronic signatures, or of contracts performed with the use of these records or signatures, conform to the requirements of section 102 of the Electronic Signatures in Global and National Commerce Act, 15 U.S.C. § 7001, et seq., or as otherwise authorized by federal or State law governing these electronic records or electronic signatures. (1999-185, s. 1; 2005-187, s. 19.)

§§ 50-63 through 50-69: Reserved for future codification purposes. (2003-371, s. 1.)

Article 4.

Collaborative Law Proceedings.

§ 50-70. Collaborative law.

As an alternative to judicial disposition of issues arising in a civil action under this Article, except for a claim for absolute divorce, on a written agreement of the parties and their attorneys, a civil action may be conducted under collaborative law procedures as set forth in this Article. (2003-371, s. 1.)

§ 50-71. Definitions.

As used in this article, the following terms mean:

(1) Collaborative law. - A procedure in which a husband and wife who are separated and are seeking a divorce, or are contemplating separation and divorce, and their attorneys agree to use their best efforts and make a good faith attempt to resolve their disputes arising from the marital relationship on an agreed basis. The procedure shall include an agreement by the parties to attempt to resolve their disputes without having to resort to judicial intervention, except to have the court approve the settlement agreement and sign the orders required by law to effectuate the agreement of the parties as the court deems appropriate. The procedure shall also include an agreement where the parties' attorneys agree not to serve as litigation counsel, except to ask the court to approve the settlement agreement.

(2) Collaborative law agreement. - A written agreement, signed by a husband and wife and their attorneys, that contains an acknowledgement by the parties to attempt to resolve the disputes arising from their marriage in accordance with collaborative law procedures.

(3) Collaborative law procedures. - The process for attempting to resolve disputes arising from a marriage as set forth in this Article.

(4) Collaborative law settlement agreement. - An agreement entered into between a husband and wife as a result of collaborative law procedures that resolves the disputes arising from the marriage of the husband and wife.

(5) Third-party expert. - A person, other than the parties to a collaborative law agreement, hired pursuant to a collaborative law agreement to assist the parties in the resolution of their disputes. (2003-371, s. 1.)

§ 50-72. Agreement requirements.

A collaborative law agreement must be in writing, signed by all the parties to the agreement and their attorneys, and must include provisions for the withdrawal of all attorneys involved in the collaborative law procedure if the collaborative law procedure does not result in settlement of the dispute. (2003-371, s. 1.)

§ 50-73. Tolling of time periods.

A validly executed collaborative law agreement shall toll all legal time periods applicable to legal rights and issues under law between the parties for the amount of time the collaborative law agreement remains in effect. This section applies to any applicable statutes of limitations, filing deadlines, or other time limitations imposed by law or court rule, including setting a hearing or trial in the case, imposing discovery deadlines, and requiring compliance with scheduling orders. (2003-371, s. 1.)

§ 50-74. Notice of collaborative law agreement.

(a)   No notice shall be given to the court of any collaborative law agreement entered into prior to the filing of a civil action under this Article.

(b)   If a civil action is pending, a notice of a collaborative law agreement, signed by the parties and their attorneys, shall be filed with the court. After the filing of a notice of a collaborative law agreement, the court shall take no action in the case, including dismissal, unless the court is notified in writing that the parties have done one of the following:

(1)   Failed to reach a collaborative law settlement agreement.

(2)   Both voluntarily dismissed the action.

(3)   Asked the court to enter a judgment or order to make the collaborative law settlement agreement an act of the court in accordance with G.S. 50-75. (2003-371, s. 1.)

§ 50-75. Judgment on collaborative law settlement agreement.

A party is entitled to an entry of judgment or order to effectuate the terms of a collaborative law settlement agreement if the agreement is signed by each party to the agreement. (2003-371, s. 1.)

§ 50-76. Failure to reach settlement; disposition by court; duty of attorney to withdraw.

(a) If the parties fail to reach a settlement and no civil action has been filed, either party may file a civil action, unless the collaborative law agreement first provides for the use of arbitration or alternative dispute resolution.

(b) If a civil action is pending and the collaborative law procedures do not result in a collaborative law settlement agreement, upon notice to the court, the court may enter orders as appropriate, free of the restrictions of G.S. 50-74(b).

(c) If a civil action is filed or set for trial pursuant to subsection (a) or (b) of this section, the attorneys representing the parties in the collaborative law proceedings may not represent either party in any further civil proceedings and shall withdraw as attorney for either party. (2003-371, s. 1.)

§ 50-77. Privileged and inadmissible evidence.

(a) All statements, communications, and work product made or arising from a collaborative law procedure are confidential and are inadmissible in any court proceeding. Work product includes any written or verbal communications or analysis of any third-party experts used in the collaborative law procedure.

(b) All communications and work product of any attorney or third-party expert hired for purposes of participating in a collaborative law procedure shall be privileged and inadmissible in any court proceeding, except by agreement of the parties. (2003-371, s. 1.)

§ 50-78. Alternate dispute resolution permitted.

Nothing in this Article shall be construed to prohibit the parties from using, by mutual agreement, other forms of alternate dispute resolution, including mediation or binding arbitration, to reach a settlement on any of the issues included in the collaborative law agreement. The parties' attorneys for the collaborative law proceeding may also serve as counsel for any form of alternate dispute resolution pursued as part of the collaborative law agreement. (2003-371, s. 1.)

§ 50-79. Collaborative law procedures surviving death.

Consistent with G.S. 50-20(l), the personal representative of the estate of a deceased spouse may continue a collaborative law procedure with respect to equitable distribution that has been initiated by a collaborative law agreement prior to death, notwithstanding the death of one of the spouses. The provisions of G.S. 50-73 shall apply to time limits applicable under G.S. 50-20(l) for collaborative law procedures continued pursuant to this section. (2003-371, s. 1.)

§ 50-80: Reserved for future codification purposes.

§ 50-81: Reserved for future codification purposes.

§ 50-82: Reserved for future codification purposes.

§ 50-83: Reserved for future codification purposes.

§ 50-84: Reserved for future codification purposes.

§ 50-85: Reserved for future codification purposes.

§ 50-86: Reserved for future codification purposes.

§ 50-87: Reserved for future codification purposes.

§ 50-88: Reserved for future codification purposes.

§ 50-89: Reserved for future codification purposes.

Article 5.

Parenting Coordinator.

§ 50-90. Definitions.

As used in this Article, the following terms mean:

(1) High-conflict case. - A child custody action involving minor children brought under Article 1 of this Chapter where the parties demonstrate an ongoing pattern of any of the following:

a. Excessive litigation.

b. Anger and distrust.

c. Verbal abuse.

d. Physical aggression or threats of physical aggression.

e. Difficulty communicating about and cooperating in the care of the minor children.

f. Conditions that in the discretion of the court warrant the appointment of a parenting coordinator.

(2) Minor child. - A person who is less than 18 years of age and who is not married or legally emancipated.

(3) Parenting coordinator. - An impartial person who meets the qualifications of G.S. 50-93. (2005-228, s. 1.)

§ 50-91. Appointment of parenting coordinator.

(a) The court may appoint a parenting coordinator at any time during the proceedings of a child custody action involving minor children brought under Article 1 of this Chapter if all parties consent to the appointment. The parties may agree to limit the parenting coordinator's decision-making authority to specific issues or areas.

(b) The court may appoint a parenting coordinator without the consent of the parties upon entry of a custody order other than an ex parte order, or upon entry of a parenting plan only if the court also makes specific findings that the action is a high-conflict case, that the appointment of the parenting coordinator is in the best interests of any minor child in the case, and that the parties are able to pay for the cost of the parenting coordinator.

(c) The order appointing a parenting coordinator shall specify the issues the parenting coordinator is directed to assist the parties in resolving and deciding. The order may also incorporate any agreement regarding the role of the parenting coordinator made by the parties under subsection (a) of this section. The court shall give a copy of the appointment order to the parties prior to the appointment conference. Notwithstanding the appointment of a parenting coordinator, the court shall retain exclusive jurisdiction to determine fundamental issues of custody, visitation, and support, and the authority to exercise management and control of the case.

(d) The court shall select a parenting coordinator from a list maintained by the district court. Prior to the appointment conference, the court must complete and give to the parenting coordinator a referral form listing contact information for the parties and their attorneys, the court's findings in support of the appointment, and any agreement by the parties. (2005-228, s. 1.)

§ 50-92. Authority of parenting coordinator.

(a) The authority of a parenting coordinator shall be specified in the court order appointing the parenting coordinator and shall be limited to matters that will aid the parties:

(1) Identify disputed issues.

(2) Reduce misunderstandings.

(3) Clarify priorities.

(4) Explore possibilities for compromise.

(5) Develop methods of collaboration in parenting.

(6) Comply with the court's order of custody, visitation, or guardianship.

(b) Notwithstanding subsection (a) of this section, the court may authorize a parenting coordinator to decide issues regarding the implementation of the parenting plan that are not specifically governed by the court order and which the parties are unable to resolve. The parties must comply with the parenting coordinator's decision until the court reviews the decision. The parenting coordinator, any party, or the attorney for any party may request an expedited hearing to review a parenting coordinator's decision. Only the judge presiding over the case may subpoena the parenting coordinator to appear and testify at the hearing.

(c) The parenting coordinator shall not provide any professional services or counseling to either parent or any of the minor children. The parenting coordinator shall refer financial issues to the parties' attorneys. (2005-228, s. 1.)

§ 50-93. Qualifications.

(a) To be eligible to be included on the district court's list of parenting coordinators, a person must meet all of the following requirements:

(1) Hold a masters or doctorate degree in psychology, law, social work, counseling, medicine, or a related subject area.

(2) Have at least five years of related professional post-degree experience.

(3) Hold a current license in the parenting coordinator's area of practice, if applicable.

(4) Participate in 24 hours of training in topics related to the developmental stages of children, the dynamics of high-conflict families, the stages and effects of divorce, problem solving techniques, mediation, and legal issues.

(b) In order to remain eligible as a parenting coordinator, the person must also attend parenting coordinator seminars that provide continuing education, group discussion, and peer review and support. (2005-228, s. 1.)

§ 50-94. Appointment conference.

(a) The parties, their attorneys, and the proposed parenting coordinator must all attend the appointment conference.

(b) At the time of the appointment conference, the court shall do all of the following:

(1) Explain to the parties the parenting coordinator's role, authority, and responsibilities as specified in the appointment order and any agreement entered into by the parties.

(2) Determine the information each party must provide to the parenting coordinator.

(3) Determine financial arrangements for the parenting coordinator's fee to be paid by each party and authorize the parenting coordinator to charge any party separately for individual contacts made necessary by that party's behavior.

(4) Inform the parties, their attorneys, and the parenting coordinator of the rules regarding communications among them and with the court.

(5) Enter the appointment order.

(c) The parenting coordinator and any guardians ad litem shall bring to the appointment conference all necessary releases, contracts, and consents. The parenting coordinator must also schedule the first sessions with the parties. (2005-228, s. 1.)

§ 50-95. Fees.

(a) The parenting coordinator shall be entitled to reasonable compensation from the parties for services rendered and to a reasonable retainer. The parenting coordinator may request a hearing in the event of a fee dispute.

(b) The court may make the appointment of a parenting coordinator contingent upon the parties' payment of a specific fee to the parenting coordinator. The parenting coordinator shall not begin any duties until the fee has been paid. (2005-228, s. 1.)

§ 50-96. Meetings and communications.

Meetings between the parenting coordinator and the parties may be informal and ex parte. Communications between the parties and the parenting coordinator are not confidential. The parenting coordinator and the court shall not engage in any ex parte communications. (2005-228, s. 1.)

§ 50-97. Reports.

(a) The parenting coordinator shall promptly provide written notification to the court, the parties, and attorneys for the parties if the parenting coordinator makes any of the following determinations:

(1) The existing custody order is not in the best interests of the child.

(2) The parenting coordinator is not qualified to address or resolve certain issues in the case.

(b) The court shall schedule a hearing and review the matter no later than two weeks following receipt of the report. The parenting coordinator shall remain involved in the case until the hearing.

(c) If the parties agree to any fundamental change in the child custody order, the parenting coordinator shall send the agreement to the parties' attorneys for preparation of a consent order. (2005-228, s. 1.)

§ 50-98. Parenting coordinator records.

(a) The parenting coordinator shall provide the following to the attorneys for the parties and to the parties:

(1) A written summary of the developments in the case following each meeting with the parties.

(2) Copies of any other written communications.

(b) The parenting coordinator shall maintain records of each meeting. These records may only be subpoenaed by order of the judge presiding over the case. The court must review the records in camera and may release the records to the parties and their attorneys only if the court determines release of the information contained in the records will assist the parties with the presentation of their case at trial. (2005-228, s. 1.)

§ 50-99. Modification or termination of parenting coordinator appointment.

(a) For good cause shown, the court may terminate or modify the parenting coordinator appointment upon motion of either party at the request of the parenting coordinator, upon the agreement of the parties and the parenting coordinator, or by the court on its own motion. Good cause includes any of the following:

(1) Lack of reasonable progress over a significant period of time despite the best efforts of the parties and the parenting coordinator.

(2) A determination that the parties no longer need the assistance of a parenting coordinator.

(3) Impairment on the part of a party that significantly interferes with the party's participation in the process.

(4) The parenting coordinator is unable or unwilling to continue to serve.

(b) If the parties agreed to the appointment of the parenting coordinator under G.S. 50-91(a), the court may terminate or modify the appointment according to that agreement or according to a subsequent agreement by the parties. (2005-228, s. 1.)

§ 50-100. Parenting coordinator immunity.

A parenting coordinator shall not be liable for damages for acts or omissions of ordinary negligence arising out of that person's duties and responsibilities as a parenting coordinator. This section does not apply to actions arising out of the operation of a motor vehicle. (2005-228, s. 1.)

Chapter 50A.

Uniform Child-Custody Jurisdiction and Enforcement Act and Uniform Deployed Parents Custody and Visitation Act.

Article 1.

Uniform Child Custody Jurisdiction Act.

§§ 50A-1 through 50A-25: Repealed by Session Laws 1999-223, s. 1(b), effective October 1, 1999, and applicable to causes of action arising on or after that date.

Article 2.

Uniform Child-Custody Jurisdiction and Enforcement Act.

Part 1. General Provisions.

§ 50A-101. Short title.

This Article may be cited as the Uniform Child-Custody Jurisdiction and Enforcement Act. (1979, c. 110, s. 1; 1999-223, s. 3.)

§ 50A-102. Definitions.

In this Article:

(1) "Abandoned" means left without provision for reasonable and necessary care or supervision.

(2) "Child" means an individual who has not attained 18 years of age.

(3) "Child-custody determination" means a judgment, decree, or other order of a court providing for the legal custody, physical custody, or visitation with respect to a child. The term includes a permanent, temporary, initial, and modification order. The term does not include an order relating to child support or other monetary obligation of an individual.

(4) "Child-custody proceeding" means a proceeding in which legal custody, physical custody, or visitation with respect to a child is an issue. The term includes a proceeding for divorce, separation, neglect, abuse, dependency, guardianship, paternity, termination of parental rights, and protection from domestic violence in which the issue may appear. The term does not include a proceeding involving juvenile delinquency, contractual emancipation, or enforcement under Part 3 of this Article.

(5) "Commencement" means the filing of the first pleading in a proceeding.

(6) "Court" means an entity authorized under the law of a state to establish, enforce, or modify a child-custody determination.

(7) "Home state" means the state in which a child lived with a parent or a person acting as a parent for at least six consecutive months immediately before the commencement of a child-custody proceeding. In the case of a child less than six months of age, the term means the state in which the child lived from birth with any of the persons mentioned. A period of temporary absence of any of the mentioned persons is part of the period.

(8) "Initial determination" means the first child-custody determination concerning a particular child.

(9) "Issuing court" means the court that makes a child-custody determination for which enforcement is sought under this Article.

(10) "Issuing state" means the state in which a child-custody determination is made.

(11) "Modification" means a child-custody determination that changes, replaces, supersedes, or is otherwise made after a previous determination concerning the same child, whether or not it is made by the court that made the previous determination.

(12) "Person" means an individual, corporation, business trust, estate, trust, partnership, limited liability company, association, joint venture, government; governmental subdivision, agency, or instrumentality; public corporation; or any other legal or commercial entity.

(13) "Person acting as a parent" means a person, other than a parent, who:

a. Has physical custody of the child or has had physical custody for a period of six consecutive months, including any temporary absence, within one year immediately before the commencement of a child-custody proceeding; and

b. Has been awarded legal custody by a court or claims a right to legal custody under the law of this State.

(14) "Physical custody" means the physical care and supervision of a child.

(15) "State" means a state of the United States, the District of Columbia, Puerto Rico, the United States Virgin Islands, or any territory or insular possession subject to the jurisdiction of the United States.

(16) "Tribe" means an Indian tribe or band, or Alaskan Native village, which is recognized by federal law or formally acknowledged by a state.

(17) "Warrant" means an order issued by a court authorizing law enforcement officers to take physical custody of a child. (1979, c. 110, s. 1; 1999-223, s. 3.)

§ 50A-103. Proceedings governed by other law.

This Article does not govern an adoption proceeding or a proceeding pertaining to the authorization of emergency medical care for a child. (1999-223, s. 3.)

§ 50A-104. Application to Indian tribes.

(a) A child-custody proceeding that pertains to an Indian child, as defined in the Indian Child Welfare Act, 25 U.S.C. § 1901 et seq., is not subject to this Article to the extent that it is governed by the Indian Child Welfare Act.

(b) A court of this State shall treat a tribe as if it were a state of the United States for the purpose of applying Parts 1 and 2.

(c) A child-custody determination made by a tribe under factual circumstances in substantial conformity with the jurisdictional standards of this Article must be recognized and enforced under Part 3. (1999-223, s. 3.)

§ 50A-105. International application of Article.

(a) A court of this State shall treat a foreign country as if it were a state of the United States for the purpose of applying Parts 1 and 2.

(b) Except as otherwise provided in subsection (c), a child-custody determination made in a foreign country under factual circumstances in substantial conformity with the jurisdictional standards of this Article must be recognized and enforced under Part 3.

(c)   A court of this State need not apply this Article if the child-custody law of a foreign country violates fundamental principles of human rights. (1979, c. 110, s. 1; 1999-223, s. 3.)

§ 50A-106. Effect of child-custody determination.

A child-custody determination made by a court of this State that had jurisdiction under this Article binds all persons who have been served in accordance with the laws of this State or notified in accordance with G.S. 50A-108 or who have submitted to the jurisdiction of the court and who have been given an opportunity to be heard. As to those persons, the determination is conclusive as to all decided issues of law and fact except to the extent the determination is modified. (1979, c. 110, s.1; 1999-223, s. 3.)

§ 50A-107. Priority.

If a question of existence or exercise of jurisdiction under this Article is raised in a child-custody proceeding, the question, upon request of a party, must be given priority on the calendar and handled expeditiously. (1999-223, s. 3.)

§ 50A-108. Notice to persons outside State.

(a)   Notice required for the exercise of jurisdiction when a person is outside this State may be given in a manner prescribed by the law of this State for service of process or by the law of the state in which the service is made. Notice must be given in a manner reasonably calculated to give actual notice but may be by publication if other means are not effective.

(b)   Proof of service may be made in the manner prescribed by the law of this State or by the law of the state in which the service is made.

(c)   Notice is not required for the exercise of jurisdiction with respect to a person who submits to the jurisdiction of the court. (1999-223, s. 3.)

§ 50A-109. Appearance and limited immunity.

(a) A party to a child-custody proceeding, including a modification proceeding, or a petitioner or respondent in a proceeding to enforce or register a child-custody determination, is not subject to personal jurisdiction in this State for another proceeding or purpose solely by reason of having participated, or of having been physically present for the purpose of participating, in the proceeding.

(b) A person who is subject to personal jurisdiction in this State on a basis other than physical presence is not immune from service of process in this State. A party present in this State who is subject to the jurisdiction of another state is not immune from service of process allowable under the laws of that state.

(c) The immunity granted by subsection (a) does not extend to civil litigation based on acts unrelated to the participation in a proceeding under this Article committed by an individual while present in this State. (1999-223, s. 3.)

§ 50A-110. Communication between courts.

(a) A court of this State may communicate with a court in another state concerning a proceeding arising under this Article.

(b) The court may allow the parties to participate in the communication. If the parties are not able to participate in the communication, they must be given the opportunity to present facts and legal arguments before a decision on jurisdiction is made.

(c) Communication between courts on schedules, calendars, court records, and similar matters may occur without informing the parties. A record need not be made of the communication.

(d) Except as otherwise provided in subsection (c), a record must be made of a communication under this section. The parties must be informed promptly of the communication and granted access to the record.

(e) For the purposes of this section, "record" means information that is inscribed on a tangible medium or that is stored in an electronic or other medium and is retrievable in perceivable form. (1999-223, s. 3.)

§ 50A-111. Taking testimony in another state.

(a) In addition to other procedures available to a party, a party to a child-custody proceeding may offer testimony of witnesses who are located in another state, including testimony of the parties and the child, by deposition or other means allowable in this State for testimony taken in another state. The court on its own motion may order that the testimony of a person be taken in another state and may prescribe the manner in which and the terms upon which the testimony is taken.

(b) A court of this State may permit an individual residing in another state to be deposed or to testify by telephone, audiovisual means, or other electronic means before a designated court or at another location in that state. A court of this State shall cooperate with courts of other states in designating an appropriate location for the deposition or testimony.

(c) Documentary evidence transmitted from another state to a court of this State by technological means that do not produce an original writing may not be excluded from evidence on an objection based on the means of transmission. (1979, c. 110, s. 1; 1999-223, s. 3.)

§ 50A-112. Cooperation between courts; preservation of records.

(a) A court of this State may request the appropriate court of another state to:

(1) Hold an evidentiary hearing;

(2) Order a person to produce or give evidence pursuant to procedures of that state;

(3) Order that an evaluation be made with respect to the custody of a child involved in a pending proceeding;

(4) Forward to the court of this State a certified copy of the transcript of the record of the hearing, the evidence otherwise presented, and any evaluation prepared in compliance with the request; and

(5) Order a party to a child-custody proceeding or any person having physical custody of the child to appear in the proceeding with or without the child.

(b) Upon request of a court of another state, a court of this State may hold a hearing or enter an order described in subsection (a).

(c) Travel and other necessary and reasonable expenses incurred under subsections (a) and (b) may be assessed against the parties according to the law of this State.

(d) A court of this State shall preserve the pleadings, orders, decrees, records of hearings, evaluations, and other pertinent records with respect to a child-custody proceeding until the child attains 18 years of age. Upon appropriate request by a court or law enforcement official of another state, the court shall forward a certified copy of those records. (1979, c. 110, s. 1; 1999-223, s. 3.)

Part 2. Jurisdiction.

§ 50A-201. Initial child-custody jurisdiction.

(a) Except as otherwise provided in G.S. 50A-204, a court of this State has jurisdiction to make an initial child-custody determination only if:

(1) This State is the home state of the child on the date of the commencement of the proceeding, or was the home state of the child within six months before the commencement of the proceeding, and the child is absent from this State but a parent or person acting as a parent continues to live in this State;

(2) A court of another state does not have jurisdiction under subdivision (1), or a court of the home state of the child has declined to exercise jurisdiction on the ground that this State is the more appropriate forum under G.S. 50A-207 or G.S. 50A-208, and:

a. The child and the child's parents, or the child and at least one parent or a person acting as a parent, have a significant connection with this State other than mere physical presence; and

b. Substantial evidence is available in this State concerning the child's care, protection, training, and personal relationships;

(3) All courts having jurisdiction under subdivision (1) or (2) have declined to exercise jurisdiction on the ground that a court of this State is the more appropriate forum to determine the custody of the child under G.S. 50A-207 or G.S. 50A-208; or

(4) No court of any other state would have jurisdiction under the criteria specified in subdivision (1), (2), or (3).

(b) Subsection (a) is the exclusive jurisdictional basis for making a child-custody determination by a court of this State.

(c) Physical presence of, or personal jurisdiction over, a party or a child is not necessary or sufficient to make a child-custody determination. (1979, c. 110, s. 1; 1999-223, s. 3.)

§ 50A-202. Exclusive, continuing jurisdiction.

(a) Except as otherwise provided in G.S. 50A-204, a court of this State which has made a child-custody determination consistent with G.S. 50A-201 or G.S. 50A-203 has exclusive, continuing jurisdiction over the determination until:

(1) A court of this State determines that neither the child, the child's parents, and any person acting as a parent do not have a significant connection with this State and that substantial evidence is no longer available in this State concerning the child's care, protection, training, and personal relationships; or

(2) A court of this State or a court of another state determines that the child, the child's parents, and any person acting as a parent do not presently reside in this State.

(b) A court of this State which has made a child-custody determination and does not have exclusive, continuing jurisdiction under this section may modify that determination only if it has jurisdiction to make an initial determination under G.S. 50A-201. (1999-223, s. 3.)

§ 50A-203. Jurisdiction to modify determination.

Except as otherwise provided in G.S. 50A-204, a court of this State may not modify a child-custody determination made by a court of another state unless a court of this State has jurisdiction to make an initial determination under G.S. 50A-201(a)(1) or G.S. 50A-201(a)(2) and:

(1)   The court of the other state determines it no longer has exclusive, continuing jurisdiction under G.S. 50A-202 or that a court of this State would be a more convenient forum under G.S. 50A-207; or

(2)   A court of this State or a court of the other state determines that the child, the child's parents, and any person acting as a parent do not presently reside in the other state. (1979, c. 110, s. 1; 1999-223, s. 3.)

§ 50A-204. Temporary emergency jurisdiction.

(a)   A court of this State has temporary emergency jurisdiction if the child is present in this State and the child has been abandoned or it is necessary in an emergency to protect the child because the child, or a sibling or parent of the child, is subjected to or threatened with mistreatment or abuse.

(b)   If there is no previous child-custody determination that is entitled to be enforced under this Article and a child-custody proceeding has not been commenced in a court of a state having jurisdiction under G.S. 50A-201 through G.S. 50A-203, a child-custody determination made under this section remains in effect until an order is obtained from a court of a state having jurisdiction under G.S. 50A-201 through G.S. 50A-203. If a child-custody proceeding has not been or is not commenced in a court of a state having jurisdiction under G.S. 50A-201 through G.S. 50A-203, a child-custody determination made under this section becomes a final determination if it so provides, and this State becomes the home state of the child.

(c)   If there is a previous child-custody determination that is entitled to be enforced under this Article, or a child-custody proceeding has been commenced in a court of a state having jurisdiction under G.S. 50A-201 through G.S. 50A-203, any order issued by a court of this State under this section must specify in the order a period that the court considers adequate to allow the person seeking an order to obtain an order from the state having jurisdiction under G.S. 50A-201 through G.S. 50A-203. The order issued in this State remains in effect until an order is obtained from the other state within the period specified or the period expires.

(d) A court of this State which has been asked to make a child-custody determination under this section, upon being informed that a child-custody proceeding has been commenced in, or a child-custody determination has been made by, a court of a state having jurisdiction under G.S. 50A-201 through G.S. 50A-203 shall immediately communicate with the other court. A court of this State which is exercising jurisdiction pursuant to G.S. 50A-201 through G.S. 50A-203, upon being informed that a child-custody proceeding has been commenced in, or a child-custody determination has been made by, a court of another state under a statute similar to this section shall immediately communicate with the court of that state to resolve the emergency, protect the safety of the parties and the child, and determine a period for the duration of the temporary order. (1979, c. 110, s. 1; 1999-223, s. 3.)

§ 50A-205. Notice; opportunity to be heard; joinder.

(a) Before a child-custody determination is made under this Article, notice and an opportunity to be heard in accordance with the standards of G.S. 50A-108 must be given to all persons entitled to notice under the law of this State as in child-custody proceedings between residents of this State, any parent whose parental rights have not been previously terminated, and any person having physical custody of the child.

(b) This Article does not govern the enforceability of a child-custody determination made without notice or an opportunity to be heard.

(c) The obligation to join a party and the right to intervene as a party in a child-custody proceeding under this Article are governed by the law of this State as in child-custody proceedings between residents of this State. (1979, c. 110, s. 1; 1999-223, s. 3.)

§ 50A-206. Simultaneous proceedings.

(a) Except as otherwise provided in G.S. 50A-204, a court of this State may not exercise its jurisdiction under this Part if, at the time of the commencement of the proceeding, a proceeding concerning the custody of the child has been commenced in a court of another state having jurisdiction substantially in conformity with this Article, unless the proceeding has been terminated or is stayed by the court of the other state because a court of this State is a more convenient forum under G.S. 50A-207.

(b) Except as otherwise provided in G.S. 50A-204, a court of this State, before hearing a child-custody proceeding, shall examine the court documents and other information supplied by the parties pursuant to G.S. 50A-209. If the court determines that a child-custody proceeding has been commenced in a court in another state having jurisdiction substantially in accordance with this Article, the court of this State shall stay its proceeding and communicate with the court of the other state. If the court of the state having jurisdiction substantially in accordance with this Article does not determine that the court of this State is a more appropriate forum, the court of this State shall dismiss the proceeding.

(c) In a proceeding to modify a child-custody determination, a court of this State shall determine whether a proceeding to enforce the determination has been commenced in another state. If a proceeding to enforce a child-custody determination has been commenced in another state, the court may:

(1) Stay the proceeding for modification pending the entry of an order of a court of the other state enforcing, staying, denying, or dismissing the proceeding for enforcement;

(2) Enjoin the parties from continuing with the proceeding for enforcement; or

(3) Proceed with the modification under conditions it considers appropriate. (1979, c. 110, s. 1; 1999-223, s. 3.)

§ 50A-207. Inconvenient forum.

(a) A court of this State which has jurisdiction under this Article to make a child-custody determination may decline to exercise its jurisdiction at any time if it determines that it is an inconvenient forum under the circumstances, and that a court of another state is a more appropriate forum. The issue of inconvenient forum may be raised upon motion of a party, the court's own motion, or request of another court.

(b) Before determining whether it is an inconvenient forum, a court of this State shall consider whether it is appropriate for a court of another state to exercise jurisdiction. For this purpose, the court shall allow the parties to submit information and shall consider all relevant factors, including:

(1) Whether domestic violence has occurred and is likely to continue in the future and which state could best protect the parties and the child;

(2) The length of time the child has resided outside this State;

(3) The distance between the court in this State and the court in the state that would assume jurisdiction;

(4) The relative financial circumstances of the parties;

(5) Any agreement of the parties as to which state should assume jurisdiction;

(6) The nature and location of the evidence required to resolve the pending litigation, including testimony of the child;

(7) The ability of the court of each state to decide the issue expeditiously and the procedures necessary to present the evidence; and

(8) The familiarity of the court of each state with the facts and issues in the pending litigation.

(c) If a court of this State determines that it is an inconvenient forum and that a court of another state is a more appropriate forum, it shall stay the proceedings upon condition that a child-custody proceeding be promptly commenced in another designated state and may impose any other condition the court considers just and proper.

(d) A court of this State may decline to exercise its jurisdiction under this Article if a child-custody determination is incidental to an action for divorce or another proceeding while still retaining jurisdiction over the divorce or other proceeding. (1979, c. 110, s. 1; 1999-223, s. 3.)

§ 50A-208. Jurisdiction declined by reason of conduct.

(a) Except as otherwise provided in G.S. 50A-204 or by other law of this State, if a court of this State has jurisdiction under this Article because a person seeking to invoke its jurisdiction has engaged in unjustifiable conduct, the court shall decline to exercise its jurisdiction unless:

(1) The parents and all persons acting as parents have acquiesced in the exercise of jurisdiction;

(2) A court of the state otherwise having jurisdiction under G.S. 50A-201 through G.S. 50A-203 determines that this State is a more appropriate forum under G.S. 50A-207; or

(3) No court of any other state would have jurisdiction under the criteria specified in G.S. 50A-201 through G.S. 50A-203.

(b) If a court of this State declines to exercise its jurisdiction pursuant to subsection (a), it may fashion an appropriate remedy to ensure the safety of the child and prevent a repetition of the unjustifiable conduct, including staying the proceeding until a child-custody proceeding is commenced in a court having jurisdiction under G.S. 50A-201 through G.S. 50A-203.

(c) If a court dismisses a petition or stays a proceeding because it declines to exercise its jurisdiction pursuant to subsection (a), it shall assess against the party seeking to invoke its jurisdiction necessary and reasonable expenses including costs, communication expenses, attorneys' fees, investigative fees, expenses for witnesses, travel expenses, and child care during the course of the proceedings, unless the party from whom fees are sought establishes that the assessment would be clearly inappropriate. The court may not assess fees, costs, or expenses against this State unless authorized by law other than this Article. (1979, c. 110, s. 1; 1999-223, s. 3.)

§ 50A-209. Information to be submitted to court.

(a) In a child-custody proceeding, each party, in its first pleading or in an attached affidavit, shall give information, if reasonably ascertainable, under oath as to the child's present address or whereabouts, the places where the child has lived during the last five years, and the names and present addresses of the persons with whom the child has lived during that period. The pleading or affidavit must state whether the party:

(1) Has participated, as a party or witness or in any other capacity, in any other proceeding concerning the custody of or visitation with the child and, if so, the pleading or affidavit shall identify the court, the case number, and the date of the child-custody determination, if any;

(2) Knows of any proceeding that could affect the current proceeding, including proceedings for enforcement and proceedings relating to domestic violence, protective orders, termination of parental rights, and adoptions and, if so, the pleading or affidavit shall identify the court, the case number, and the nature of the proceeding; and

(3) Knows the names and addresses of any person not a party to the proceeding who has physical custody of the child or claims rights of legal custody or physical custody of, or visitation with, the child and, if so, the names and addresses of those persons.

(b) If the information required by subdivisions (a) is not furnished, the court, upon motion of a party or its own motion, may stay the proceeding until the information is furnished.

(c) If the declaration as to any of the items described in subdivisions (a)(1) through (3) is in the affirmative, the declarant shall give additional information under oath as required by the court. The court may examine the parties under oath as to details of the information furnished and other matters pertinent to the court's jurisdiction and the disposition of the case.

(d) Each party has a continuing duty to inform the court of any proceeding in this or any other state that could affect the current proceeding.

(e) If a party alleges in an affidavit or a pleading under oath that the health, safety, or liberty of a party or child would be jeopardized by disclosure of identifying information, the information must be sealed and may not be disclosed to the other party or the public unless the court orders the disclosure to be made after a hearing in which the court takes into consideration the health, safety, or liberty of the party or child and determines that the disclosure is in the interest of justice. (1979, c. 110, s. 1; 1999-223, s. 3.)

§ 50A-210. Appearance of parties and child.

(a) In a child-custody proceeding in this State, the court may order a party to the proceeding who is in this State to appear before the court in person with or without the child. The court may order any person who is in this State and who has physical custody or control of the child to appear in person with the child.

(b) If a party to a child-custody proceeding whose presence is desired by the court is outside this State, the court may order that a notice given pursuant to G.S. 50A-108 include a statement directing the party to appear in person with or without the child and informing the party that failure to appear may result in a decision adverse to the party.

(c) The court may enter any orders necessary to ensure the safety of the child and of any person ordered to appear under this section.

(d) If a party to a child-custody proceeding who is outside this State is directed to appear under subsection (b) or desires to appear personally before the court with or without the child, the court may require another party to pay reasonable and necessary travel and other expenses of the party so appearing and of the child. (1979, c. 110, s. 1; 1999-223, s. 3.)

Part 3. Enforcement.

§ 50A-301. Definitions.

In this Part:

(1) "Petitioner" means a person who seeks enforcement of an order for return of a child under the Hague Convention on the Civil Aspects of International Child Abduction or enforcement of a child-custody determination.

(2) "Respondent" means a person against whom a proceeding has been commenced for enforcement of an order for return of a child under the Hague Convention on the Civil Aspects of International Child Abduction or enforcement of a child-custody determination. (1999-223, s. 3.)

§ 50A-302. Enforcement under Hague Convention.

Under this Part, a court of this State may enforce an order for the return of the child made under the Hague Convention on the Civil Aspects of International Child Abduction as if it were a child-custody determination. (1999-223, s. 3.)

§ 50A-303. Duty to enforce.

(a) A court of this State shall recognize and enforce a child-custody determination of a court of another state if the latter court exercised jurisdiction in substantial conformity with this Article or the determination was made under factual circumstances meeting the jurisdictional standards of this Article, and the determination has not been modified in accordance with this Article.

(b) A court of this State may utilize any remedy available under other law of this State to enforce a child-custody determination made by a court of another state. The remedies provided in this Part are cumulative and do not affect the availability of other remedies to enforce a child-custody determination. (1979, c. 110, s. 1; 1999-223, s. 3.)

§ 50A-304. Temporary visitation.

(a) A court of this State which does not have jurisdiction to modify a child-custody determination may issue a temporary order enforcing:

(1) A visitation schedule made by a court of another state; or

(2) The visitation provisions of a child-custody determination of another state that does not provide for a specific visitation schedule.

(b) If a court of this State makes an order under subdivisions (a)(2) of this section, it shall specify in the order a period that it considers adequate to allow the petitioner to obtain an order from a court having jurisdiction under the criteria specified in Part 2. The order remains in effect until an order is obtained from the other court or the period expires. (1999-223, s. 3.)

§ 50A-305. Registration of child-custody determination.

(a) A child-custody determination issued by a court of another state may be registered in this State, with or without a simultaneous request for enforcement, by sending to the appropriate court in this State:

(1) A letter or other document requesting registration;

(2) Two copies, including one certified copy, of the determination sought to be registered, and a statement under penalty of perjury that to the best of the knowledge and belief of the person seeking registration the order has not been modified; and

(3) Except as otherwise provided in G.S. 50A-209, the name and address of the person seeking registration and any parent or person acting as a parent who has been awarded custody or visitation in the child-custody determination sought to be registered.

(b) On receipt of the documents required by subsection (a), the registering court shall:

(1) Cause the determination to be filed as a foreign judgment, together with one copy of any accompanying documents and information, regardless of their form; and

(2) Direct the petitioner to serve notice upon the persons named pursuant to subdivision (a)(3) of this section, including notice of their opportunity to contest the registration in accordance with this section.

(c) The notice required by subdivision (b)(2) must state that:

(1) A registered determination is enforceable as of the date of the registration in the same manner as a determination issued by a court of this State;

(2) A hearing to contest the validity of the registered determination must be requested within 20 days after service of notice; and

(3) Failure to contest the registration will result in confirmation of the child-custody determination and preclude further contest of that determination with respect to any matter that could have been asserted.

(d) A person seeking to contest the validity of a registered order must request a hearing within 20 days after service of the notice. At that hearing, the court shall confirm the registered order unless the person contesting registration establishes that:

(1) The issuing court did not have jurisdiction under Part 2;

(2) The child-custody determination sought to be registered has been vacated, stayed, or modified by a court having jurisdiction to do so under Part 2; or

(3) The person contesting registration was entitled to notice, but notice was not given in accordance with the standards of G.S. 50A-108 in the proceedings before the court that issued the order for which registration is sought.

(e) If a timely request for a hearing to contest the validity of the registration is not made, the registration is confirmed as a matter of law, and the person requesting registration and all persons served must be notified of the confirmation.

(f) Confirmation of a registered order, whether by operation of law or after notice and hearing, precludes further contest of the order with respect to any matter that could have been asserted at the time of registration. (1979, c. 110, s. 1; 1997-81, s. 1; 1999-223, s. 3; 2007-484, s. 8.)

§ 50A-306. Enforcement of registered determination.

(a) A court of this State may grant any relief normally available under the law of this State to enforce a registered child-custody determination made by a court of another state.

(b) A court of this State shall recognize and enforce, but may not modify, except in accordance with Part 2, a registered child-custody determination of a court of another state. (1999-223, s. 3.)

§ 50A-307. Simultaneous proceedings.

If a proceeding for enforcement under this Part is commenced in a court of this State and the court determines that a proceeding to modify the determination is pending in a court of another state having jurisdiction to modify the determination under Part 2, the enforcing court shall immediately communicate with the modifying court. The proceeding for enforcement continues unless the enforcing court, after consultation with the modifying court, stays or dismisses the proceeding. (1999-223, s. 3.)

§ 50A-308. Expedited enforcement of child-custody determination.

(a) A petition under this Part must be verified. Certified copies of all orders sought to be enforced and of any order confirming registration must be attached to the petition. A copy of a certified copy of an order may be attached instead of the original.

(b) A petition for enforcement of a child-custody determination must state:

(1) Whether the court that issued the determination identified the jurisdictional basis it relied upon in exercising jurisdiction and, if so, what the basis was;

(2) Whether the determination for which enforcement is sought has been vacated, stayed, or modified by a court whose decision must be enforced under this Article and, if so, identify the court, the case number, and the nature of the proceeding;

(3) Whether any proceeding has been commenced that could affect the current proceeding, including proceedings relating to domestic violence, protective orders, termination of parental rights, and adoptions and, if so, identify the court, the case number, and the nature of the proceeding;

(4) The present physical address of a child and the respondent, if known;

(5) Whether relief in addition to the immediate physical custody of the child and attorneys' fees is sought, including a request for assistance from law enforcement officials and, if so, the relief sought; and

(6) If the child-custody determination has been registered and confirmed under G.S. 50A-305, the date and place of registration.

(c) Upon the filing of a petition, the court shall issue an order directing the respondent to appear in person with or without the child at a hearing and may enter any order necessary to ensure the safety of the parties and the child. The hearing must be held on the next judicial day after service of the order unless that date is impossible. In that event, the court shall hold the hearing on the first judicial day possible. The court may extend the date of hearing at the request of the petitioner.

(d) An order issued under subsection (c) must state the time and place of the hearing and advise the respondent that at the hearing the court will order that the petitioner may take immediate physical custody of the child and the payment of fees, costs, and expenses under G.S. 50A-312, and may schedule a hearing to determine whether further relief is appropriate, unless the respondent appears and establishes that:

(1) The child-custody determination has not been registered and confirmed under G.S. 50A-305 and that:

a. The issuing court did not have jurisdiction under Part 2;

b. The child-custody determination for which enforcement is sought has been vacated, stayed, or modified by a court having jurisdiction to do so under Part 2;

c. The respondent was entitled to notice, but notice was not given in accordance with the standards of G.S. 50A-108 in the proceedings before the court that issued the order for which enforcement is sought; or

(2) The child-custody determination for which enforcement is sought was registered and confirmed under G.S. 50A-304, but has been vacated, stayed, or modified by a court of a state having jurisdiction to do so under Part 2. (1999-223, s. 3.)

§ 50A-309. Service of petition and order.

Except as otherwise provided in G.S. 50A-311, the petition and order must be served, by any method authorized by the law of this State, upon respondent and any person who has physical custody of the child. (1999-223, s. 3.)

§ 50A-310. Hearing and order.

(a) Unless the court issues a temporary emergency order pursuant to G.S. 50A-204 upon a finding that a petitioner is entitled to immediate physical custody of the child, the court shall order that the petitioner may take immediate physical custody of the child unless the respondent establishes that:

(1) The child-custody determination has not been registered and confirmed under G.S. 50A-305 and that:

a. The issuing court did not have jurisdiction under Part 2;

b. The child-custody determination for which enforcement is sought has been vacated, stayed, or modified by a court of a state having jurisdiction to do so under Part 2; or

c. The respondent was entitled to notice, but notice was not given in accordance with the standards of G.S. 50A-108 in the proceedings before the court that issued the order for which enforcement is sought; or

(2) The child-custody determination for which enforcement is sought was registered and confirmed under G.S. 50A-305 but has been vacated, stayed, or modified by a court of a state having jurisdiction to do so under Part 2.

(b) The court shall award the fees, costs, and expenses authorized under G.S. 50A-312 and may grant additional relief, including a request for the assistance of law enforcement officials, and set a further hearing to determine whether additional relief is appropriate.

(c) If a party called to testify refuses to answer on the ground that the testimony may be self-incriminating, the court may draw an adverse inference from the refusal.

(d) A privilege against disclosure of communications between spouses and a defense of immunity based on the relationship of husband and wife or parent and child may not be invoked in a proceeding under this Part. (1979, c. 110, s. 1; 1999-223, s. 3.)

§ 50A-311. Warrant to take physical custody of child.

(a) Upon the filing of a petition seeking enforcement of a child-custody determination, the petitioner may file a verified application for the issuance of a warrant to take physical custody of the child if the child is immediately likely to suffer serious physical harm or be removed from this State.

(b) If the court, upon the testimony of the petitioner or other witness, finds that the child is imminently likely to suffer serious physical harm or be removed from this State, it may issue a warrant to take physical custody of the child. The petition must be heard on the next judicial day after the warrant is executed unless that date is impossible. In that event, the court shall hold the hearing on the first judicial day possible. The application for the warrant must include the statements required by G.S. 50A-308(b).

(c) A warrant to take physical custody of a child must:

(1) Recite the facts upon which a conclusion of imminent serious physical harm or removal from the jurisdiction is based;

(2) Direct law enforcement officers to take physical custody of the child immediately; and

(3) Provide for the placement of the child pending final relief.

(d) The respondent must be served with the petition, warrant, and order immediately after the child is taken into physical custody.

(e) A warrant to take physical custody of a child is enforceable throughout this State. If the court finds on the basis of the testimony of the petitioner or other witness that a less intrusive remedy is not effective, it may authorize law enforcement officers to enter private property to take physical custody of the child. If required by exigent circumstances of the case, the court may authorize law enforcement officers to make a forcible entry at any hour.

(f) The court may impose conditions upon placement of a child to ensure the appearance of the child and the child's custodian. (1999-223, s. 3.)

§ 50A-312. Costs, fees, and expenses.

(a) The court shall award the prevailing party, including a state, necessary and reasonable expenses incurred by or on behalf of the party, including costs, communication expenses, attorneys' fees, investigative fees, expenses for witnesses, travel expenses, and child care during the course of the proceedings, unless the party from whom fees or expenses are sought establishes that the award would be clearly inappropriate.

(b) The court may not assess fees, costs, or expenses against a state unless authorized by law other than this Article. (1999-223, s. 3.)

§ 50A-313. Recognition and enforcement.

A court of this State shall accord full faith and credit to an order issued by another state and consistent with this Article which enforces a child-custody determination by a court of another state unless the order has been vacated, stayed, or modified by a court having jurisdiction to do so under Part 2. (1979, c.110, s.1; 1999-223, s. 3.)

§ 50A-314. Appeals.

An appeal may be taken from a final order in a proceeding under this Part in accordance with expedited appellate procedures in other civil cases. Unless the court enters a temporary emergency order under G.S. 50A-204, the enforcing court may not stay an order enforcing a child-custody determination pending appeal. (1999-223, s. 3.)

§ 50A-315. Role of prosecutor or public official.

(a) In a case arising under this Article or involving the Hague Convention on the Civil Aspects of International Child Abduction, the prosecutor or other appropriate public official may take any lawful action, including resort to a proceeding under this Part or any other available civil proceeding to locate a child, obtain the return of a child, or enforce a child-custody determination if there is:

(1) An existing child-custody determination;

(2) A request to do so from a court in a pending child-custody proceeding;

(3) A reasonable belief that a criminal statute has been violated; or

(4) A reasonable belief that the child has been wrongfully removed or retained in violation of the Hague Convention on the Civil Aspects of International Child Abduction.

(b) A prosecutor or appropriate public official acting under this section acts on behalf of the court and may not represent any party. (1999-223, s. 3.)

§ 50A-316. Role of law enforcement.

At the request of a prosecutor or other appropriate public official acting under G.S. 50A-315, a law enforcement officer may take any lawful action reasonably necessary to locate a child or a party and assist a prosecutor or appropriate public official with responsibilities under G.S. 50A-315. (1979, c. 110, s. 1; 1999-223, s. 3.)

§ 50A-317. Costs and expenses.

If the respondent is not the prevailing party, the court may assess against the respondent all direct expenses and costs incurred by the prosecutor or other appropriate public official and law enforcement officers under G.S. 50A-315 or G.S. 50A-316. (1999-223, s. 3.)

§ 50A-318: Reserved for future codification purposes.

§ 50A-319: Reserved for future codification purposes.

§ 50A-320: Reserved for future codification purposes.

§ 50A-321: Reserved for future codification purposes.

§ 50A-322: Reserved for future codification purposes.

§ 50A-323: Reserved for future codification purposes.

§ 50A-324: Reserved for future codification purposes.

§ 50A-325: Reserved for future codification purposes.

§ 50A-326: Reserved for future codification purposes.

§ 50A-327: Reserved for future codification purposes.

§ 50A-328: Reserved for future codification purposes.

§ 50A-329: Reserved for future codification purposes.

§ 50A-330: Reserved for future codification purposes.

§ 50A-331: Reserved for future codification purposes.

§ 50A-332: Reserved for future codification purposes.

§ 50A-333: Reserved for future codification purposes.

§ 50A-334: Reserved for future codification purposes.

§ 50A-335: Reserved for future codification purposes.

§ 50A-336: Reserved for future codification purposes.

§ 50A-337: Reserved for future codification purposes.

§ 50A-338: Reserved for future codification purposes.

§ 50A-339: Reserved for future codification purposes.

§ 50A-340: Reserved for future codification purposes.

§ 50A-341: Reserved for future codification purposes.

§ 50A-342: Reserved for future codification purposes.

§ 50A-343: Reserved for future codification purposes.

§ 50A-344: Reserved for future codification purposes.

§ 50A-345: Reserved for future codification purposes.

§ 50A-346: Reserved for future codification purposes.

§ 50A-347: Reserved for future codification purposes.

§ 50A-348: Reserved for future codification purposes.

§ 50A-349: Reserved for future codification purposes.

Article 3.

Uniform Deployed Parents Custody and Visitation Act.

Part 1. General Provisions.

§ 50A-350. Short title.

This Article may be cited as the "Uniform Deployed Parents Custody and Visitation Act." (2013-27, s. 3.)

§ 50A-351. Definitions.

The following definitions apply in this Article:

(1) Adult. - An individual who is at least 18 years of age or an emancipated minor.

(2) Caretaking authority. - The right to live with and care for a child on a day-to-day basis, including physical custody, parenting time, right to access, and visitation.

(3) Child. - An (i) unemancipated individual who has not attained 18 years of age or (ii) adult son or daughter by birth or adoption who is the subject of an existing court order concerning custodial responsibility.

(4) Close and substantial relationship. - A relationship in which a significant bond exists between a child and a nonparent.

(5) Court. - An entity authorized under the laws of this State to establish, enforce, or modify a decision regarding custodial responsibility.

(6) Custodial responsibility. - A comprehensive term that includes any and all powers and duties relating to caretaking authority and decision-making authority for a child. The term includes custody, physical custody, legal custody, parenting time, right to access, visitation, and the authority to designate limited contact with a child.

(7) Decision-making authority. - The power to make important decisions regarding a child, including decisions regarding the child's education, religious training, health care, extracurricular activities, and travel. The term does not include day-to-day decisions that necessarily accompany a grant of caretaking authority.

(8) Deploying parent. - A service member, who is deployed or has been notified of impending deployment, and is (i) a parent of a child or (ii) an individual other than a parent who has custodial responsibility of a child.

(9) Deployment. - The movement or mobilization of a service member to a location for more than 90 days, but less than 18 months, pursuant to an official order that (i) is designated as unaccompanied; (ii) does not authorize dependent travel; or (iii) otherwise does not permit the movement of family members to that location.

(10) Family member. - A sibling, aunt, uncle, cousin, stepparent, or grandparent of a child, and an individual recognized to be in a familial relationship with a child.

(11) Limited contact. - The opportunity for a nonparent to visit with a child for a limited period of time. The term includes authority to take the child to a place other than the residence of the child.

(12) Nonparent. - An individual other than a deploying parent or other parent.

(13) Other parent. - An individual who, in common with a deploying parent, is (i) the parent of a child or (ii) an individual other than a parent with custodial responsibility of a child.

(14) Record. - Information that is inscribed on a tangible medium or that is stored in an electronic or other medium and is retrievable in perceivable form.

(15) Return from deployment. - The conclusion of a service member's deployment as specified in uniformed service orders.

(16) Service member. - A member of a uniformed service.

(17) State. - A state of the United States, the District of Columbia, Puerto Rico, and the United States Virgin Islands, or any territory or insular possession subject to the jurisdiction of the United States.

(18) Uniformed service. - Service which includes (i) the active and reserve components of the Army, Navy, Air Force, Marine Corps, or Coast Guard of the United States; (ii) the Merchant Marine, the commissioned corps of the Public Health Service, or the commissioned corps of the National Oceanic and Atmospheric Administration of the United States; or (iii) the National Guard. (2013-27, s. 3.)

§ 50A-352. Remedies for noncompliance.

In addition to other relief provided under the laws of this State, if a court finds that a party to a proceeding under this Article has acted in bad faith or intentionally failed to comply with the requirements of this Article or a court order issued under this Article, the court may assess reasonable attorneys' fees and costs against the opposing party and order other appropriate relief. (2013-27, s. 3.)

§ 50A-353. Jurisdiction.

(a) A court may issue an order regarding custodial responsibility under this Article only if the court has jurisdiction pursuant to Uniform Child-Custody Jurisdiction and Enforcement Act (UCCJEA) under Article 2 of this Chapter. If the court has issued a temporary order regarding custodial responsibility pursuant to Part 3 of this Article, for purposes of the UCCJEA, the residence of the deploying parent is not changed by reason of the deployment during the deployment.

(b) If a court has issued a permanent order regarding custodial responsibility before notice of deployment and the parents modify that order temporarily by agreement pursuant to Part 2 of this Article, for purposes of the

UCCJEA, the residence of the deploying parent is not changed by reason of the deployment.

(c) If a court in another state has issued a temporary order regarding custodial responsibility as a result of impending or current deployment, for purposes of the UCCJEA, the residence of the deploying parent is not changed by reason of the deployment.

(d) This section does not prohibit the exercise of temporary emergency jurisdiction by a court under the UCCJEA. (2013-27, s. 3.)

§ 50A-354. Notice required of deploying parent.

(a) Except as provided in subsections (c) and (d) of this section, a deploying parent shall, in a record, notify the other parent of a pending deployment not later than seven days after receiving notice of deployment unless the deploying parent is reasonably prevented from notifying the other parent by the circumstances of service. If the circumstances of service prevent notification within seven days, the notification shall be made as soon as reasonably possible thereafter.

(b) Except as provided in subsections (c) and (d) of this section, each parent shall, in a record, provide the other parent with a plan for fulfilling that parent's share of custodial responsibility during deployment as soon as reasonably possible after receiving notice of deployment under subsection (a) of this section.

(c) If an existing court order prohibits disclosure of the address or contact information of the other parent, a notification of deployment under subsection (a) of this section, or notification of a plan for custodial responsibility during deployment under subsection (b) of this section, may be made only to the issuing court. If the address of the other parent is available to the issuing court, the court shall forward the notification to the other parent. The court shall keep confidential the address or contact information of the other parent.

(d) Notice in a record is not required if the parents are living in the same residence and there is actual notice of the deployment or plan.

(e) In a proceeding regarding custodial responsibility between parents, a court may consider the reasonableness of a parent's efforts to comply with this section. (2013-27, s. 3.)

§ 50A-355. Notification required for change of address.

(a) Except as otherwise provided in subsection (b) of this section, an individual to whom custodial responsibility has been assigned or granted during deployment under Part 2 or Part 3 of this Article shall notify the deploying parent and any other individual with custodial responsibility of any change of mailing address or residence until the assignment or grant is terminated. The individual shall provide the notice to any court that has issued an existing custody or child support order concerning the child.

(b) If an existing court order prohibits disclosure of the address or contact information of an individual to whom custodial responsibility has been assigned or granted, a notification of change of mailing address or residence under subsection (a) of this section may be made only to the court that issued the order. The court shall keep confidential the mailing address or residence of the individual to whom custodial responsibility has been assigned or granted. (2013-27, s. 3.)

§ 50A-356: Reserved for future codification purposes.

§ 50A-357: Reserved for future codification purposes.

§ 50A-358: Reserved for future codification purposes.

§ 50A-359: Reserved for future codification purposes.

Part 2. Agreement Addressing Custodial Responsibility During Deployment.

§ 50A-360. Form of agreement.

(a) The parents of a child may enter into a temporary agreement granting custodial responsibility during deployment.

(b) An agreement under subsection (a) of this section shall be (i) in writing and (ii) signed by both parents or any nonparent to whom custodial responsibility is granted.

(c) An agreement under subsection (a) of this section may include the following:

(1) To the extent feasible, identify the destination, duration, and conditions of the deployment that is the basis for the agreement.

(2) Specify the allocation of caretaking authority among the deploying parent, the other parent, and any nonparent, if applicable.

(3) Specify any decision-making authority that accompanies a grant of caretaking authority.

(4) Specify any grant of limited contact to a nonparent.

(5) If the agreement shares custodial responsibility between the other parent and a nonparent, or between two nonparents, provide a process to resolve any dispute that may arise.

(6) Specify (i) the frequency, duration, and means, including electronic means, by which the deploying parent will have contact with the child; (ii) any role to be played by the other parent in facilitating the contact; and (iii) the allocation of any costs of communications.

(7) Specify the contact between the deploying parent and child during the time the deploying parent is on leave or is otherwise available.

(8) Acknowledge that any party's existing child-support obligation cannot be modified by the agreement, and that changing the terms of the obligation during deployment requires modification in the appropriate court.

(9) Provide that the agreement terminates following the deploying parent's return from deployment according to the procedures under Part 4 of this Article.

(10) If the agreement must be filed pursuant to G.S. 50A-364, specify which parent shall file the agreement. (2013-27, s. 3.)

§ 50A-361. Nature of authority created by agreement.

(a) An agreement under this Part is temporary and terminates pursuant to Part 4 of this Article following the return from deployment of the deployed parent, unless the agreement has been terminated before that time by court order or modification of the agreement under G.S. 50A-362. The agreement derives from the parents' custodial responsibility and does not create an independent, continuing right to caretaking authority, decision-making authority, or limited contact in an individual to whom custodial responsibility is given.

(b) A nonparent given caretaking authority, decision-making authority, or limited contact by an agreement under this Part has standing to enforce the agreement until it has been modified pursuant to an agreement of the parents under G.S. 50A-362 or terminated under Part 4 of this Article or by court order. (2013-27, s. 3.)

§ 50A-362. Modification of agreement.

The parents may by mutual consent modify an agreement regarding custodial responsibility made pursuant to this Part. If an agreement made under this subsection is modified before deployment of a deploying parent, the modification shall be in writing and signed by both parents and any nonparent who will exercise custodial responsibility under the modified agreement. If an agreement made under this section is modified during deployment of a deploying parent, the modification shall be agreed to, in a record, by both parents and any nonparent who will exercise custodial responsibility under the modified agreement. (2013-27, s. 3.)

§ 50A-363. Power of attorney.

If no other parent possesses custodial responsibility or if an existing court order prohibits contact between the child and the other parent, a deploying parent, by power of attorney, may delegate all or part of custodial responsibility to an adult nonparent for the period of deployment. The power of attorney is revocable by the deploying parent through a revocation of the power of attorney signed by the deploying parent. (2013-27, s. 3.)

§ 50A-364. Filing agreement or power of attorney with court.

An agreement or power of attorney created pursuant to this Part shall be filed within a reasonable period of time with any court that has entered an existing order on custodial responsibility or child support concerning the child. The case number and heading of the existing case concerning custodial responsibility or child support shall be provided to the court with the agreement or power of attorney. (2013-27, s. 3.)

§ 50A-365: Reserved for future codification purposes.

§ 50A-366: Reserved for future codification purposes.

§ 50A-367: Reserved for future codification purposes.

§ 50A-368: Reserved for future codification purposes.

§ 50A-369: Reserved for future codification purposes.

Part 3. Judicial Procedure for Granting Custodial Responsibility During Deployment.

§ 50A-370. Proceeding for temporary custody order.

(a) After a deploying parent receives notice of deployment and during the deployment, a court may issue a temporary order granting custodial responsibility unless prohibited by the Servicemembers Civil Relief Act, 50 U.S.C. §§ 521-522. A court may not issue a permanent order granting custodial responsibility in the absence of the deploying parent without the consent of the deploying parent.

(b) At any time after a deploying parent receives notice of deployment, either parent may file a motion regarding custodial responsibility of a child during deployment. The motion shall be filed in an existing proceeding for custodial responsibility of the child with jurisdiction under Part 1 of this Article or, if there is no existing proceeding in a court with jurisdiction under Part 1 of this Article, in a new action for granting custodial responsibility during deployment. (2013-27, s. 3.)

§ 50A-371. Expedited hearing.

The court shall conduct an expedited hearing if a motion to grant custodial responsibility is filed before a deploying parent deploys. (2013-27, s. 3.)

§ 50A-372. Testimony by electronic means.

In a proceeding brought under this Part, a party or witness who is not reasonably available to appear personally may appear and provide testimony and present evidence by electronic means unless the court finds good cause to require a personal appearance. (2013-27, s. 3.)

§ 50A-373. Effect of prior judicial decree or agreement.

In a proceeding for a grant of custodial responsibility pursuant to this Part, the following shall apply:

(1)   A prior judicial order designating custodial responsibility of a child in the event of deployment is binding on the court unless the circumstances require modifying a judicial order regarding custodial responsibility.

(2)   The court shall enforce a prior written agreement between the parents for designating custodial responsibility of a child in the event of deployment, including a prior written agreement executed under Part 2 of this Article, unless the court finds the agreement contrary to the best interest of the child. (2013-27, s. 3.)

§ 50A-374. Grant of caretaking or decision-making authority to nonparent.

(a)   In accordance with the laws of this State and on the motion of a deploying parent, a court may grant caretaking authority of a child to a nonparent who is an adult family member of the child or an adult with whom the child has a close and substantial relationship if it is in the best interest of the child.

(b)   Unless the grant of caretaking authority to a nonparent under subsection (a) of this section is agreed to by the other parent, the grant is limited to an amount of time not greater than (i) the time granted to the deploying parent in an existing permanent custody order, except that the court may add unusual travel time necessary to transport the child or (ii) in the absence of an existing permanent custody order, the amount of time that the deploying parent habitually cared for the child before being notified of deployment, except that the court may add unusual travel time necessary to transport the child.

(c) A court may grant part of the deploying parent's decision-making authority for a child to a nonparent who is an adult family member of the child or an adult with whom the child has a close and substantial relationship if the deploying parent is unable to exercise that authority. When a court grants the authority to a nonparent, the court shall specify the decision-making powers that will and will not be granted, including applicable health, educational, and religious decisions.

(d) Any nonparent to whom caretaking authority or decision-making authority is granted shall be made a party to the action until the grant of caretaking authority or decision-making authority is terminated. (2013-27, s. 3.)

§ 50A-375. Grant of limited contact.

(a) In accordance with laws of this State and on motion of a deploying parent, a court shall grant limited contact with a child to a nonparent who is either a family member of the child or an individual with whom the child has a close and substantial relationship, unless the court finds that the contact would be contrary to the best interest of the child.

(b) Any nonparent who is granted limited contact shall be made a party to the action until the grant of limited contact is terminated. (2013-27, s. 3.)

§ 50A-376. Nature of authority created by order.

(a) A grant made pursuant to this Part is temporary and terminates pursuant to Part 4 of this Article following the return from deployment of the deployed parent, unless the grant has been terminated before that time by court order. The grant does not create an independent, continuing right to caretaking authority, decision-making authority, or limited contact in an individual to whom it is granted.

(b) A nonparent granted caretaking authority, decision-making authority, or limited contact under this Part has standing to enforce the grant until it is terminated under Part 4 of this Article or by court order.

(c) Any nonparent made a party because of a grant of caretaking authority, decision-making authority, or limited contact shall have no continuing right to party status after the grant of caretaking authority, decision-making authority, or limited contact is terminated pursuant to Part 4 of this Article or by court order. (2013-27, s. 3.)

§ 50A-377. Content of temporary custody order.

(a) An order granting custodial responsibility under this Part shall (i) designate the order as temporary and (ii) identify to the extent feasible the destination, duration, and conditions of the deployment.

(b) If applicable, a temporary order for custodial responsibility shall comply with each of the following:

(1) Specify the allocation of caretaking authority, decision-making authority, or limited contact among the deploying parent, the other parent, and any nonparent.

(2) If the order divides caretaking or decision-making authority between individuals, or grants caretaking authority to one individual and limited contact to another, provide a process to resolve any significant dispute that may arise.

(3) Provide for liberal communication between the deploying parent and the child during deployment, including through electronic means, unless contrary to the best interest of the child, and allocate any costs of communications.

(4) Provide for liberal contact between the deploying parent and the child during the time the deploying parent is on leave or is otherwise available, unless contrary to the best interest of the child.

(5) Provide for reasonable contact between the deploying parent and the child following return from deployment until the temporary order is terminated, which may include more time than the deploying parent spent with the child before entry of the temporary order.

(6) Provide that the order will terminate following return from deployment according to the procedures under Part 4 of this Article. (2013-27, s. 3.)

§ 50A-378. Order for child support.

If a court has issued an order providing for grant of caretaking authority under this Part, or an agreement granting caretaking authority has been executed under Part 2 of this Article, the court may enter a temporary order for child support consistent with the laws of this State regarding child support if the court has jurisdiction under the Uniform Interstate Family Support Act under Chapter 52C of the General Statutes. (2013-27, s. 3.)

§ 50A-379. Modifying or terminating assignment or grant of custodial responsibility to nonparent.

(a) Except for an order in accordance with G.S. 50A-373 or as otherwise provided in subsection (b) of this section, and consistent with the Servicemembers Civil Relief Act, 50 U.S.C. §§ 521-522, on motion of a deploying or other parent or any nonparent to whom caretaking authority, decision-making authority, or limited contact has been granted, the court may modify or terminate a grant of caretaking authority, decision-making authority, or limited contact made pursuant to this Article if the modification or termination is consistent with this Part and the court finds it is in the best interest of the child. Any modification shall be temporary and terminates following the conclusion of deployment of the deployed parent according to the procedures under Part 4 of this Article, unless the grant has been terminated before that time by court order.

(b) On motion of a deploying parent, the court shall terminate a grant of limited contact. (2013-27, s. 3.)

§ 50A-380: Reserved for future codification purposes.

§ 50A-381: Reserved for future codification purposes.

§ 50A-382: Reserved for future codification purposes.

§ 50A-383: Reserved for future codification purposes.

§ 50A-384: Reserved for future codification purposes.

Part 4. Return From Deployment.

§ 50A-385. Procedure for terminating temporary grant of custodial responsibility established by agreement.

(a) At any time following return from deployment, a temporary agreement granting custodial responsibility under Part 2 of this Article may be terminated by an agreement to terminate signed by the deploying parent and the other parent.

(b) The temporary agreement granting custodial responsibility terminates if (i) the agreement to terminate specifies a date for termination or (ii) the agreement to terminate does not specify a date, on the date the agreement to terminate is signed by both parents.

(c) In the absence of an agreement to terminate, the temporary agreement granting custodial responsibility terminates 60 days from the date of one of the following:

(1) The date the deploying parent gives notice to the other parent that the deploying parent has returned from deployment.

(2) The date stated in an order terminating the temporary grant of custodial responsibility.

(3) The death of the deploying parent.

(d) If the temporary agreement granting custodial responsibility was filed with a court pursuant to G.S. 50A-364, an agreement to terminate the temporary agreement shall also be filed with that court within a reasonable period of time after the signing of the agreement. The case number and heading of the existing custodial responsibility or child support case shall be provided to the court with the agreement to terminate. (2013-27, s. 3.)

§ 50A-386. Consent procedure for terminating temporary grant of custodial responsibility established by court order.

At any time following return from deployment, the deploying parent and the other parent may file with the court an agreement to terminate a temporary order for custodial responsibility issued under Part 3 of this Article. After an agreement has been filed, the court shall issue an order terminating the temporary order on the date specified in the agreement. If no date is specified, the court shall issue the order immediately. (2013-27, s. 3.)

§ 50A-387. Visitation before termination of temporary grant of custodial responsibility.

After a deploying parent returns from deployment and until a temporary agreement or order for custodial responsibility established under Part 2 or Part 3 of this Article is terminated, the court shall enter a temporary order granting the deploying parent reasonable contact with the child unless it is contrary to the best interest of the child. The court shall enter a temporary order granting contact under this section even if the time exceeds the time the deploying parent spent with the child before deployment. (2013-27, s. 3.)

§ 50A-388. Termination by operation of law of temporary grant of custodial responsibility established by court order.

(a) A temporary order for custodial responsibility issued under Part 3 of this Article shall terminate, if no agreement between the parties to terminate a temporary order for custodial responsibility has been filed, 60 days from (i) the date the deploying parent gives notice of having returned from deployment to the other parent or any nonparent granted custodial responsibility or (ii) the death of the deploying parent.

(b) Any proceedings seeking to terminate or prevent termination of a temporary order for custodial responsibility are governed by laws of this State. (2013-27, s. 3.)

§ 50A-389: Reserved for future codification purposes.

§ 50A-390: Reserved for future codification purposes.

§ 50A-391: Reserved for future codification purposes.

§ 50A-392: Reserved for future codification purposes.

§ 50A-393: Reserved for future codification purposes.

§ 50A-394: Reserved for future codification purposes.

Part 5. Miscellaneous Provisions.

§ 50A-395. Uniformity of application and construction.

In applying and construing this Article, consideration shall be given to the need to promote uniformity of the law with respect to its subject matter among states that enact it. (2013-27, s. 3.)

§ 50A-396. Relation to Electronic Signatures in Global and National Commerce Act.

This Article modifies, limits, and supersedes the federal Electronic Signatures in Global and National Commerce Act, 15 U.S.C. § 7001, et seq., but does not modify, limit, or supersede section 101(c) of that act, 15 U.S.C. § 7001(c), or authorize electronic delivery of any of the notices described in section 103(b) of that act, 15 U.S.C. § 7003(b). (2013-27, s. 3.)

Chapter 50B.

Domestic Violence.

§ 50B-1. Domestic violence; definition.

(a)   Domestic violence means the commission of one or more of the following acts upon an aggrieved party or upon a minor child residing with or in the custody of the aggrieved party by a person with whom the aggrieved party has or has had a personal relationship, but does not include acts of self-defense:

(1) Attempting to cause bodily injury, or intentionally causing bodily injury; or

(2) Placing the aggrieved party or a member of the aggrieved party's family or household in fear of imminent serious bodily injury or continued harassment, as defined in G.S. 14-277.3A, that rises to such a level as to inflict substantial emotional distress; or

(3) Committing any act defined in G.S. 14-27.2 through G.S. 14-27.7.

(b) For purposes of this section, the term "personal relationship" means a relationship wherein the parties involved:

(1) Are current or former spouses;

(2) Are persons of opposite sex who live together or have lived together;

(3) Are related as parents and children, including others acting in loco parentis to a minor child, or as grandparents and grandchildren. For purposes of this subdivision, an aggrieved party may not obtain an order of protection against a child or grandchild under the age of 16;

(4) Have a child in common;

(5) Are current or former household members;

(6) Are persons of the opposite sex who are in a dating relationship or have been in a dating relationship. For purposes of this subdivision, a dating relationship is one wherein the parties are romantically involved over time and on a continuous basis during the course of the relationship. A casual acquaintance or ordinary fraternization between persons in a business or social context is not a dating relationship.

(c) As used in this Chapter, the term "protective order" includes any order entered pursuant to this Chapter upon hearing by the court or consent of the parties. (1979, c. 561, s. 1; 1985, c. 113, s. 1; 1987, c. 828; 1987 (Reg. Sess., 1988), c. 893, ss. 1, 3; 1995 (Reg. Sess., 1996), c. 591, s. 1; 1997-471, s. 1; 2001-518, s. 3; 2003-107, s. 1; 2009-58, s. 5.)

§ 50B-2. Institution of civil action; motion for emergency relief; temporary orders; temporary custody.

(a) Any person residing in this State may seek relief under this Chapter by filing a civil action or by filing a motion in any existing action filed under Chapter 50 of the General Statutes alleging acts of domestic violence against himself or herself or a minor child who resides with or is in the custody of such person. Any aggrieved party entitled to relief under this Chapter may file a civil action and proceed pro se, without the assistance of legal counsel. The district court division of the General Court of Justice shall have original jurisdiction over actions instituted under this Chapter. Any action for a domestic violence protective order requires that a summons be issued and served. The summons issued pursuant to this Chapter shall require the defendant to answer within 10 days of the date of service. Attachments to the summons shall include the complaint, notice of hearing, any temporary or ex parte order that has been issued, and other papers through the appropriate law enforcement agency where the defendant is to be served. In compliance with the federal Violence Against Women Act, no court costs or attorneys' fees shall be assessed for the filing, issuance, registration, or service of a protective order or petition for a protective order or witness subpoena, except as provided in G.S. 1A-1, Rule 11.

(b) Emergency Relief. - A party may move the court for emergency relief if he or she believes there is a danger of serious and immediate injury to himself or herself or a minor child. A hearing on a motion for emergency relief, where no ex parte order is entered, shall be held after five days' notice of the hearing to the other party or after five days from the date of service of process on the other party, whichever occurs first, provided, however, that no hearing shall be required if the service of process is not completed on the other party. If the party is proceeding pro se and does not request an ex parte hearing, the clerk shall set a date for hearing and issue a notice of hearing within the time periods provided in this subsection, and shall effect service of the summons, complaint, notice, and other papers through the appropriate law enforcement agency where the defendant is to be served.

(c) Ex Parte Orders. -

(1) Prior to the hearing, if it clearly appears to the court from specific facts shown, that there is a danger of acts of domestic violence against the aggrieved party or a minor child, the court may enter orders as it deems necessary to protect the aggrieved party or minor children from those acts.

(2) A temporary order for custody ex parte and prior to service of process and notice shall not be entered unless the court finds that the child is exposed to a substantial risk of physical or emotional injury or sexual abuse.

(3) If the court finds that the child is exposed to a substantial risk of physical or emotional injury or sexual abuse, upon request of the aggrieved party, the court shall consider and may order the other party to (i) stay away from a minor child, or (ii) return a minor child to, or not remove a minor child from, the physical care of a parent or person in loco parentis, if the court finds that the order is in the best interest of the minor child and is necessary for the safety of the minor child.

(4) If the court determines that it is in the best interest of the minor child for the other party to have contact with the minor child or children, the court shall issue an order designed to protect the safety and well-being of the minor child and the aggrieved party. The order shall specify the terms of contact between the other party and the minor child and may include a specific schedule of time and location of exchange of the minor child, supervision by a third party or supervised visitation center, and any other conditions that will ensure both the well-being of the minor child and the aggrieved party.

(5) Upon the issuance of an ex parte order under this subsection, a hearing shall be held within 10 days from the date of issuance of the order or within seven days from the date of service of process on the other party, whichever occurs later. A continuance shall be limited to one extension of no more than 10 days unless all parties consent or good cause is shown. The hearing shall have priority on the court calendar.

(6) If an aggrieved party acting pro se requests ex parte relief, the clerk of superior court shall schedule an ex parte hearing with the district court division of the General Court of Justice within 72 hours of the filing for said relief, or by the end of the next day on which the district court is in session in the county in which the action was filed, whichever shall first occur. If the district court is not in session in said county, the aggrieved party may contact the clerk of superior court in any other county within the same judicial district who shall schedule an ex parte hearing with the district court division of the General Court of Justice by the end of the next day on which said court division is in session in that county.

(7) Upon the issuance of an ex parte order under this subsection, if the party is proceeding pro se, the Clerk shall set a date for hearing and issue a notice of hearing within the time periods provided in this subsection, and shall

effect service of the summons, complaint, notice, order and other papers through the appropriate law enforcement agency where the defendant is to be served.

(c1) Ex Parte Orders by Authorized Magistrate. - The chief district court judge may authorize a magistrate or magistrates to hear any motions for emergency relief ex parte. Prior to the hearing, if the magistrate determines that at the time the party is seeking emergency relief ex parte the district court is not in session and a district court judge is not and will not be available to hear the motion for a period of four or more hours, the motion may be heard by the magistrate. If it clearly appears to the magistrate from specific facts shown that there is a danger of acts of domestic violence against the aggrieved party or a minor child, the magistrate may enter orders as it deems necessary to protect the aggrieved party or minor children from those acts, except that a temporary order for custody ex parte and prior to service of process and notice shall not be entered unless the magistrate finds that the child is exposed to a substantial risk of physical or emotional injury or sexual abuse. If the magistrate finds that the child is exposed to a substantial risk of physical or emotional injury or sexual abuse, upon request of the aggrieved party, the magistrate shall consider and may order the other party to stay away from a minor child, or to return a minor child to, or not remove a minor child from, the physical care of a parent or person in loco parentis, if the magistrate finds that the order is in the best interest of the minor child and is necessary for the safety of the minor child. If the magistrate determines that it is in the best interest of the minor child for the other party to have contact with the minor child or children, the magistrate shall issue an order designed to protect the safety and well-being of the minor child and the aggrieved party. The order shall specify the terms of contact between the other party and the minor child and may include a specific schedule of time and location of exchange of the minor child, supervision by a third party or supervised visitation center, and any other conditions that will ensure both the well-being of the minor child and the aggrieved party. An ex parte order entered under this subsection shall expire and the magistrate shall schedule an ex parte hearing before a district court judge by the end of the next day on which the district court is in session in the county in which the action was filed. Ex parte orders entered by the district court judge pursuant to this subsection shall be entered and scheduled in accordance with subsection (c) of this section.

(c2) The authority granted to authorized magistrates to award temporary child custody pursuant to subsection (c1) of this section and pursuant to G.S. 50B-3(a)(4) is granted subject to custody rules to be established by the supervising chief district judge of each judicial district.

(d) Pro Se Forms. - The clerk of superior court of each county shall provide to pro se complainants all forms that are necessary or appropriate to enable them to proceed pro se pursuant to this section. The clerk shall, whenever feasible, provide a private area for complainants to fill out forms and make inquiries. The clerk shall provide a supply of pro se forms to authorized magistrates who shall make the forms available to complainants seeking relief under subsection (c1) of this section. (1979, c. 561, s. 1; 1985, c. 113, ss. 2, 3; 1987 (Reg. Sess., 1988), c. 893, s. 2; 1989, c. 461, s. 1; 1994, Ex. Sess., c. 4, s. 1; 1997-471, s. 2; 2001-518, s. 4; 2002-126, s. 29A.6(a); 2004-186, ss. 17.2, 19.1; 2009-342, s. 2; 2012-20, s. 1; 2013-390, s. 1.)

§ 50B-3. Relief.

(a) If the court, including magistrates as authorized under G.S. 50B-2(c1), finds that an act of domestic violence has occurred, the court shall grant a protective order restraining the defendant from further acts of domestic violence. A protective order may include any of the following types of relief:

(1) Direct a party to refrain from such acts.

(2) Grant to a party possession of the residence or household of the parties and exclude the other party from the residence or household.

(3) Require a party to provide a spouse and his or her children suitable alternate housing.

(4) Award temporary custody of minor children and establish temporary visitation rights pursuant to G.S. 50B-2 if the order is granted ex parte, and pursuant to subsection (a1) of this section if the order is granted after notice or service of process.

(5) Order the eviction of a party from the residence or household and assistance to the victim in returning to it.

(6) Order either party to make payments for the support of a minor child as required by law.

(7) Order either party to make payments for the support of a spouse as required by law.

(8) Provide for possession of personal property of the parties, including the care, custody, and control of any animal owned, possessed, kept, or held as a pet by either party or minor child residing in the household.

(9) Order a party to refrain from doing any or all of the following:

a. Threatening, abusing, or following the other party.

b. Harassing the other party, including by telephone, visiting the home or workplace, or other means.

b1. Cruelly treating or abusing an animal owned, possessed, kept, or held as a pet by either party or minor child residing in the household.

c. Otherwise interfering with the other party.

(10) Award attorney's fees to either party.

(11) Prohibit a party from purchasing a firearm for a time fixed in the order.

(12) Order any party the court finds is responsible for acts of domestic violence to attend and complete an abuser treatment program if the program is approved by the Domestic Violence Commission.

(13) Include any additional prohibitions or requirements the court deems necessary to protect any party or any minor child.

(a1) Upon the request of either party at a hearing after notice or service of process, the court shall consider and may award temporary custody of minor children and establish temporary visitation rights as follows:

(1) In awarding custody or visitation rights, the court shall base its decision on the best interest of the minor child with particular consideration given to the safety of the minor child.

(2) For purposes of determining custody and visitation issues, the court shall consider:

a. Whether the minor child was exposed to a substantial risk of physical or emotional injury or sexual abuse.

b. Whether the minor child was present during acts of domestic violence.

c. Whether a weapon was used or threatened to be used during any act of domestic violence.

d. Whether a party caused or attempted to cause serious bodily injury to the aggrieved party or the minor child.

e. Whether a party placed the aggrieved party or the minor child in reasonable fear of imminent serious bodily injury.

f. Whether a party caused an aggrieved party to engage involuntarily in sexual relations by force, threat, or duress.

g. Whether there is a pattern of abuse against an aggrieved party or the minor child.

h. Whether a party has abused or endangered the minor child during visitation.

i. Whether a party has used visitation as an opportunity to abuse or harass the aggrieved party.

j. Whether a party has improperly concealed or detained the minor child.

k. Whether a party has otherwise acted in a manner that is not in the best interest of the minor child.

(3) If the court awards custody, the court shall also consider whether visitation is in the best interest of the minor child. If ordering visitation, the court shall provide for the safety and well-being of the minor child and the safety of the aggrieved party. The court may consider any of the following:

a. Ordering an exchange of the minor child to occur in a protected setting or in the presence of an appropriate third party.

b. Ordering visitation supervised by an appropriate third party, or at a supervised visitation center or other approved agency.

c. Ordering the noncustodial parent to attend and complete, to the satisfaction of the court, an abuser treatment program as a condition of visitation.

d. Ordering either or both parents to abstain from possession or consumption of alcohol or controlled substances during the visitation or for 24 hours preceding an exchange of the minor child.

e. Ordering the noncustodial parent to pay the costs of supervised visitation.

f. Prohibiting overnight visitation.

g. Requiring a bond from the noncustodial parent for the return and safety of the minor child.

h. Ordering an investigation or appointment of a guardian ad litem or attorney for the minor child.

i. Imposing any other condition that is deemed necessary to provide for the safety and well-being of the minor child and the safety of the aggrieved party.

If the court grants visitation, the order shall specify dates and times for the visitation to take place or other specific parameters or conditions that are appropriate. A person, supervised visitation center, or other agency may be approved to supervise visitation after appearing in court or filing an affidavit accepting that responsibility and acknowledging accountability to the court.

(4) A temporary custody order entered pursuant to this Chapter shall be without prejudice and shall be for a fixed period of time not to exceed one year. Nothing in this section shall be construed to affect the right of the parties to a de novo hearing under Chapter 50 of the General Statutes. Any subsequent custody order entered under Chapter 50 of the General Statutes supersedes a temporary order issued pursuant to this Chapter.

(b) Protective orders entered pursuant to this Chapter shall be for a fixed period of time not to exceed one year. The court may renew a protective order for a fixed period of time not to exceed two years, including an order that previously has been renewed, upon a motion by the aggrieved party filed before the expiration of the current order; provided, however, that a temporary award of custody entered as part of a protective order may not be renewed to extend a temporary award of custody beyond the maximum one-year period. The court may renew a protective order for good cause. The commission of an act as defined in G.S. 50B-1(a) by the defendant after entry of the current order is not required for an order to be renewed. Protective orders entered, including consent orders, shall not be mutual in nature except where both parties file a claim and the court makes detailed findings of fact indicating that both parties acted as aggressors, that neither party acted primarily in self-defense, and that the right of each party to due process is preserved.

(b1) A consent protective order may be entered pursuant to this Chapter without findings of fact and conclusions of law if the parties agree in writing that no findings of fact and conclusions of law will be included in the consent protective order. The consent protective order shall be valid and enforceable and shall have the same force and effect as a protective order entered with findings of fact and conclusions of law.

(c) A copy of any order entered and filed under this Article shall be issued to each party. In addition, a copy of the order shall be issued promptly to and retained by the police department of the city of the victim's residence. If the victim does not reside in a city or resides in a city with no police department, copies shall be issued promptly to and retained by the sheriff, and the county police department, if any, of the county in which the victim resides. If the defendant is ordered to stay away from the child's school, a copy of the order shall be delivered promptly by the sheriff to the principal or, in the principal's absence, the assistant principal or the principal's designee of each school named in the order.

(c1) When a protective order issued under this Chapter is filed with the Clerk of Superior Court, the clerk shall provide to the applicant an informational sheet developed by the Administrative Office of the Courts that includes:

(1) Domestic violence agencies and services.

(2) Sexual assault agencies and services.

(3) Victims' compensation services.

(4) Legal aid services.

(5) Address confidentiality services.

(6) An explanation of the plaintiff's right to apply for a permit under G.S. 14-415.15.

(d) The sheriff of the county where a domestic violence order is entered shall provide for prompt entry of the order into the National Crime Information Center registry and shall provide for access of such orders to magistrates on a 24-hour-a-day basis. Modifications, terminations, renewals, and dismissals of the order shall also be promptly entered. (1979, c. 561, s. 1; 1985, c. 463; 1994, Ex. Sess., c. 4, s. 2; 1995, c. 527, s. 1; 1995 (Reg. Sess., 1996), c. 591, s. 2; c. 742, s. 42.1.; 1999-23, s. 1; 2000-125, s. 9; 2002-105, s. 2; 2002-126, s. 29A.6(b); 2003-107, s. 2; 2004-186, ss. 17.3-17.5; 2005-343, s. 2; 2005-423, s. 1; 2007-116, s. 3; 2009-425, s. 1; 2013-237, s. 1.)

§ 50B-3.1. Surrender and disposal of firearms; violations; exemptions.

(a) Required Surrender of Firearms. - Upon issuance of an emergency or ex parte order pursuant to this Chapter, the court shall order the defendant to surrender to the sheriff all firearms, machine guns, ammunition, permits to purchase firearms, and permits to carry concealed firearms that are in the care, custody, possession, ownership, or control of the defendant if the court finds any of the following factors:

(1) The use or threatened use of a deadly weapon by the defendant or a pattern of prior conduct involving the use or threatened use of violence with a firearm against persons.

(2) Threats to seriously injure or kill the aggrieved party or minor child by the defendant.

(3) Threats to commit suicide by the defendant.

(4) Serious injuries inflicted upon the aggrieved party or minor child by the defendant.

(b) Ex Parte or Emergency Hearing. - The court shall inquire of the plaintiff, at the ex parte or emergency hearing, the presence of, ownership of, or otherwise access to firearms by the defendant, as well as ammunition, permits to purchase firearms, and permits to carry concealed firearms, and include, whenever possible, identifying information regarding the description, number, and location of firearms, ammunition, and permits in the order.

(c) Ten-Day Hearing. - The court, at the 10-day hearing, shall inquire of the defendant the presence of, ownership of, or otherwise access to firearms by the defendant, as well as ammunition, permits to purchase firearms, and permits to carry concealed firearms, and include, whenever possible, identifying information regarding the description, number, and location of firearms, ammunition, and permits in the order.

(d) Surrender. - Upon service of the order, the defendant shall immediately surrender to the sheriff possession of all firearms, machine guns, ammunition, permits to purchase firearms, and permits to carry concealed firearms that are in the care, custody, possession, ownership, or control of the defendant. In the event that weapons cannot be surrendered at the time the order is served, the defendant shall surrender the firearms, ammunitions, and permits to the sheriff within 24 hours of service at a time and place specified by the sheriff. The sheriff shall store the firearms or contract with a licensed firearms dealer to provide storage.

(1) If the court orders the defendant to surrender firearms, ammunition, and permits, the court shall inform the plaintiff and the defendant of the terms of the protective order and include these terms on the face of the order, including that the defendant is prohibited from possessing, purchasing, or receiving or attempting to possess, purchase, or receive a firearm for so long as the protective order or any successive protective order is in effect. The terms of the order shall include instructions as to how the defendant may request retrieval of any firearms, ammunition, and permits surrendered to the sheriff when the protective order is no longer in effect. The terms shall also include notice of the penalty for violation of G.S. 14-269.8.

(2) The sheriff may charge the defendant a reasonable fee for the storage of any firearms and ammunition taken pursuant to a protective order. The fees are payable to the sheriff. The sheriff shall transmit the proceeds of these fees to the county finance officer. The fees shall be used by the sheriff to pay the costs of administering this section and for other law enforcement purposes. The county shall expend the restricted funds for these purposes only. The sheriff shall not release firearms, ammunition, or permits without a court order granting the release. The defendant must remit all fees owed prior to the authorized return of any firearms, ammunition, or permits. The sheriff shall not incur any civil or criminal liability for alleged damage or deterioration due to storage or transportation of any firearms or ammunition held pursuant to this section.

(e) Retrieval. - If the court does not enter a protective order when the ex parte or emergency order expires, the defendant may retrieve any weapons surrendered to the sheriff unless the court finds that the defendant is precluded from owning or possessing a firearm pursuant to State or federal law or final disposition of any pending criminal charges committed against the person that is the subject of the current protective order.

(f) Motion for Return. - The defendant may request the return of any firearms, ammunition, or permits surrendered by filing a motion with the court at the expiration of the current order or final disposition of any pending criminal charges committed against the person that is the subject of the current protective order and not later than 90 days after the expiration of the current order or final disposition of any pending criminal charges committed against the person that is the subject of the current protective order. Upon receipt of the motion, the court shall schedule a hearing and provide written notice to the plaintiff who shall have the right to appear and be heard and to the sheriff who has control of the firearms, ammunition, or permits. The court shall determine whether the defendant is subject to any State or federal law or court order that precludes the defendant from owning or possessing a firearm. The inquiry shall include:

(1) Whether the protective order has been renewed.

(2) Whether the defendant is subject to any other protective orders.

(3) Whether the defendant is disqualified from owning or possessing a firearm pursuant to 18 U.S.C. § 922 or any State law.

(4) Whether the defendant has any pending criminal charges, in either State or federal court, committed against the person that is the subject of the current protective order.

The court shall deny the return of firearms, ammunition, or permits if the court finds that the defendant is precluded from owning or possessing a firearm pursuant to State or federal law or if the defendant has any pending criminal charges, in either State or federal court, committed against the person that is the subject of the current protective order until the final disposition of those charges.

(g) Motion for Return by Third-Party Owner. - A third-party owner of firearms, ammunition, or permits who is otherwise eligible to possess such items may file a motion requesting the return to said third party of any such items in the possession of the sheriff seized as a result of the entry of a domestic violence protective order. The motion must be filed not later than 30 days after the seizure of the items by the sheriff. Upon receipt of the third party's motion, the court shall schedule a hearing and provide written notice to all parties and the sheriff. The court shall order return of the items to the third party unless the court determines that the third party is disqualified from owning or possessing said items pursuant to State or federal law. If the court denies the return of said items to the third party, the items shall be disposed of by the sheriff as provided in subsection (h) of this section.

(h)   Disposal of Firearms. - If the defendant does not file a motion requesting the return of any firearms, ammunition, or permits surrendered within the time period prescribed by this section, if the court determines that the defendant is precluded from regaining possession of any firearms, ammunition, or permits surrendered, or if the defendant or third-party owner fails to remit all fees owed for the storage of the firearms or ammunition within 30 days of the entry of the order granting the return of the firearms, ammunition, or permits, the sheriff who has control of the firearms, ammunition, or permits shall give notice to the defendant, and the sheriff shall apply to the court for an order of disposition of the firearms, ammunition, or permits. The judge, after a hearing, may order the disposition of the firearms, ammunition, or permits in one or more of the ways authorized by law, including subdivision (4), (4b), (5), or (6) of G.S. 14-269.1. If a sale by the sheriff does occur, any proceeds from the sale after deducting any costs associated with the sale, and in accordance with all applicable State and federal law, shall be provided to the defendant, if requested by the defendant by motion made before the hearing or at the hearing and if ordered by the judge.

(i)   It is unlawful for any person subject to a protective order prohibiting the possession or purchase of firearms to:

(1)   Fail to surrender all firearms, ammunition, permits to purchase firearms, and permits to carry concealed firearms to the sheriff as ordered by the court;

(2)   Fail to disclose all information pertaining to the possession of firearms, ammunition, and permits to purchase and permits to carry concealed firearms as requested by the court; or

(3)   Provide false information to the court pertaining to any of these items.

(j) Violations. - In accordance with G.S. 14-269.8, it is unlawful for any person to possess, purchase, or receive or attempt to possess, purchase, or receive a firearm, as defined in G.S. 14-409.39(2), machine gun, ammunition, or permits to purchase or carry concealed firearms if ordered by the court for so long as that protective order or any successive protective order entered against that person pursuant to this Chapter is in effect. Any defendant violating the provisions of this section shall be guilty of a Class H felony.

(k) Official Use Exemption. - This section shall not prohibit law enforcement officers and members of any branch of the Armed Forces of the United States, not otherwise prohibited under federal law, from possessing or using firearms for official use only.

(l) Nothing in this section is intended to limit the discretion of the court in granting additional relief as provided in other sections of this Chapter. (2003-410, s. 1; 2004-203, s. 34(a); 2005-287, s. 4; 2005-423, ss. 2, 3; 2011-183, s. 40; 2011-268, ss. 23, 24.)

§ 50B-4. Enforcement of orders.

(a) A party may file a motion for contempt for violation of any order entered pursuant to this Chapter. This party may file and proceed with that motion pro se, using forms provided by the clerk of superior court or a magistrate authorized under G.S. 50B-2(c1). Upon the filing pro se of a motion for contempt under this subsection, the clerk, or the authorized magistrate, if the facts show clearly that there is danger of acts of domestic violence against the aggrieved party or a minor child and the motion is made at a time when the clerk is not available, shall schedule and issue notice of a show cause hearing with the district court division of the General Court of Justice at the earliest possible date pursuant to G.S. 5A-23. The Clerk, or the magistrate in the case of notice issued by the magistrate pursuant to this subsection, shall effect service of the motion, notice, and other papers through the appropriate law enforcement agency where the defendant is to be served.

(b) Repealed by Session Laws 1999-23, s. 2, effective February 1, 2000.

(c) A valid protective order entered pursuant to this Chapter shall be enforced by all North Carolina law enforcement agencies without further order of the court.

(d) A valid protective order entered by the courts of another state or the courts of an Indian tribe shall be accorded full faith and credit by the courts of North Carolina whether or not the order has been registered and shall be enforced by the courts and the law enforcement agencies of North Carolina as if it were an order issued by a North Carolina court. In determining the validity of an out-of-state order for purposes of enforcement, a law enforcement officer may rely upon a copy of the protective order issued by another state or the courts of an Indian tribe that is provided to the officer and on the statement of a person protected by the order that the order remains in effect. Even though registration is not required, a copy of a protective order may be registered in North Carolina by filing with the clerk of superior court in any county a copy of the order and an affidavit by a person protected by the order that to the best of that person's knowledge the order is presently in effect as written. Notice of the registration shall not be given to the defendant. Upon registration of the order, the clerk shall promptly forward a copy to the sheriff of that county. Unless the issuing state has already entered the order, the sheriff shall provide for prompt entry of the order into the National Crime Information Center registry pursuant to G.S. 50B-3(d).

(e) Upon application or motion by a party to the court, the court shall determine whether an out-of-state order remains in full force and effect.

(f) The term "valid protective order," as used in subsections (c) and (d) of this section, shall include an emergency or ex parte order entered under this Chapter. (1979, c. 561, s. 1; 1985, c. 113, s. 4; 1987, c. 739, s. 6; 1989, c. 461, s. 2; 1994, Ex. Sess., c. 4, s. 3; 1995 (Reg. Sess., 1996), c. 591, s. 3; 1999-23, s. 2; 2002-126, s. 29A.6(c); 2003-107, s. 3; 2009-342, s. 4.)

§ 50B-4.1. Violation of valid protective order.

(a) Except as otherwise provided by law, a person who knowingly violates a valid protective order entered pursuant to this Chapter or who knowingly violates a valid protective order entered by the courts of another state or the courts of an Indian tribe shall be guilty of a Class A1 misdemeanor.

(b) A law enforcement officer shall arrest and take a person into custody, with or without a warrant or other process, if the officer has probable cause to believe that the person knowingly has violated a valid protective order excluding the person from the residence or household occupied by a victim of domestic violence or directing the person to refrain from doing any or all of the acts specified in G.S. 50B-3(a)(9).

(c) When a law enforcement officer makes an arrest under this section without a warrant, and the party arrested contests that the out-of-state order or the order issued by an Indian court remains in full force and effect, the party arrested shall be promptly provided with a copy of the information applicable to the party which appears on the National Crime Information Center registry by the sheriff of the county in which the arrest occurs.

(d) Unless covered under some other provision of law providing greater punishment, a person who commits a felony at a time when the person knows the behavior is prohibited by a valid protective order as provided in subsection (a) of this section shall be guilty of a felony one class higher than the principal felony described in the charging document. This subsection shall not apply to a person who is charged with or convicted of a Class A or B1 felony or to a person charged under subsection (f) or subsection (g) of this section.

(e) An indictment or information that charges a person with committing felonious conduct as described in subsection (d) of this section shall also allege that the person knowingly violated a valid protective order as described in subsection (a) of this section in the course of the conduct constituting the underlying felony. In order for a person to be punished as described in subsection (d) of this section, a finding shall be made that the person knowingly violated the protective order in the course of conduct constituting the underlying felony.

(f) Unless covered under some other provision of law providing greater punishment, any person who knowingly violates a valid protective order as provided in subsection (a) of this section, after having been previously convicted of two offenses under this Chapter, shall be guilty of a Class H felony.

(g) Unless covered under some other provision of law providing greater punishment, any person who, while in possession of a deadly weapon on or about his or her person or within close proximity to his or her person, knowingly violates a valid protective order as provided in subsection (a) of this section by failing to stay away from a place, or a person, as so directed under the terms of the order, shall be guilty of a Class H felony.

(g1) Unless covered under some other provision of law providing greater punishment, any person who is subject to a valid protective order, as provided in subsection (a) of this section, who enters property operated as a safe house or haven for victims of domestic violence, where a person protected under the order is residing, shall be guilty of a Class H felony. A person violates this subsection regardless of whether the person protected under the order is present on the property.

(h)   For the purposes of this section, the term "valid protective order" shall include an emergency or ex parte order entered under this Chapter. (1997-471, s. 3; 1997-456, s. 27; 1999-23, s. 4; 2001-518, s. 5; 2007-190, s. 1; 2008-93, s. 1; 2009-342, s. 5; 2009-389, s. 2; 2010-5, s. 1.)

§ 50B-4.2. False statement regarding protective order a misdemeanor.

A person who knowingly makes a false statement to a law enforcement agency or officer that a protective order entered pursuant to this Chapter or by the courts of another state or Indian tribe remains in effect shall be guilty of a Class 2 misdemeanor. (1999-23, s. 5.)

§ 50B-5. Emergency assistance.

(a)   A person who alleges that he or she or a minor child has been the victim of domestic violence may request the assistance of a local law enforcement agency. The local law enforcement agency shall respond to the request for assistance as soon as practicable. The local law enforcement officer responding to the request for assistance may take whatever steps are reasonably necessary to protect the complainant from harm and may advise the complainant of sources of shelter, medical care, counseling and other services. Upon request by the complainant and where feasible, the law enforcement officer may transport the complainant to appropriate facilities such as hospitals, magistrates' offices, or public or private facilities for shelter and accompany the complainant to his or her residence, within the jurisdiction in which the request for assistance was made, so that the complainant may remove food, clothing, medication and such other personal property as is reasonably necessary to enable the complainant and any minor children who are presently in the care of the complainant to remain elsewhere pending further proceedings.

(b)   In providing the assistance authorized by subsection (a), no officer may be held criminally or civilly liable on account of reasonable measures taken under authority of subsection (a). (1979, c. 561, s. 1; 1985, c. 113, s. 5; 1999-23, s. 6.)

§ 50B-5.5. Employment discrimination unlawful.

(a) No employer shall discharge, demote, deny a promotion, or discipline an employee because the employee took reasonable time off from work to obtain or attempt to obtain relief under this Chapter. An employee who is absent from the workplace shall follow the employer's usual time-off policy or procedure, including advance notice to the employer, when required by the employer's usual procedures, unless an emergency prevents the employee from doing so. An employer may require documentation of any emergency that prevented the employee from complying in advance with the employer's usual time-off policy or procedure, or any other information available to the employee which supports the employee's reason for being absent from the workplace.

(b) The Commissioner of Labor shall enforce the provisions of this section according to Article 21 of Chapter 95 of the General Statutes, including the rules and regulations issued pursuant to the Article. (2004-186, s. 18.1.)

§ 50B-6. Construction of Chapter.

This Chapter shall not be construed as granting a status to any person for any purpose other than those expressly stated herein. This Chapter shall not be construed as relieving any person or institution of the duty to report to the department of social services, as required by G.S. 7B-301, if the person or institution has cause to suspect that a juvenile is abused or neglected. (1979, c. 561, s. 1; 1985, c. 113, s. 6; 1998-202, s. 13(r).)

§ 50B-7. Remedies not exclusive.

The remedies provided by this Chapter are not exclusive but are additional to remedies provided under Chapter 50 and elsewhere in the General Statutes. (1979, c. 561, s. 1.)

§ 50B-8. Effect upon prosecution for violation of § 14-184 or other offense against public morals.

The granting of a protective order, prosecution for violation of this Chapter, or the granting of any other relief or the institution of any other enforcement proceedings under this Chapter shall not be construed to afford a defense to any person or persons charged with fornication and adultery under G.S. 14-184 or charged with any other offense against the public morals; and prosecution, conviction, or prosecution and conviction for violation of any provision of this Chapter shall not be a bar to prosecution for violation of G.S. 14-184 or of any other statute defining an offense or offenses against the public morals. (1979, c. 561, s. 1; 2003-107, s. 4.)

§ 50B-9. Domestic Violence Center Fund.

The Domestic Violence Center Fund is established within the State Treasury. The fund shall be administered by the Department of Administration, North Carolina Council for Women, and shall be used to make grants to centers for victims of domestic violence and to The North Carolina Coalition Against Domestic Violence, Inc. This fund shall be administered in accordance with the provisions of the Executive Budget Act. The Department of Administration shall make quarterly grants to each eligible domestic violence center and to The North Carolina Coalition Against Domestic Violence, Inc. Each grant recipient shall receive the same amount. To be eligible to receive funds under this section, a domestic violence center must meet the following requirements:

(1)   It shall have been in operation on the preceding July 1 and shall continue to be in operation.

(2)   It shall offer all of the following services: a hotline, transportation services, community education programs, daytime services, and call forwarding during the night and it shall fulfill other criteria established by the Department of Administration.

(3)   It shall be a nonprofit corporation or a local governmental entity. (1991, c. 693, s. 3; 1991 (Reg. Sess., 1992), c. 988, s. 1.)

Chapter 50C.

Civil No-Contact Orders.

§ 50C-1. Definitions.

The following definitions apply in this Chapter:

(1)   Abuse. - To physically or mentally harm, harass, intimidate, or interfere with the personal liberty of another.

(2)   Civil no-contact order. - An order granted under this Chapter, which includes a remedy authorized by G.S. 50C-5.

(3)   Nonconsensual. - A lack of freely given consent.

(4)   Sexual conduct. - Any intentional or knowing touching, fondling, or sexual penetration by a person, either directly or through clothing, of the sexual organs, anus, or breast of another, whether an adult or a minor, for the purpose of sexual gratification or arousal. For purposes of this subdivision, the term shall include the transfer or transmission of semen.

(5)   Repealed by Session Laws 2004-199, s. 50, effective August 17, 2004.

(6)   Stalking. - On more than one occasion, following or otherwise harassing, as defined in G.S. 14-277.3A(b)(2), another person without legal purpose with the intent to do any of the following:

a.   Place the person in reasonable fear either for the person's safety or the safety of the person's immediate family or close personal associates.

b.   Cause that person to suffer substantial emotional distress by placing that person in fear of death, bodily injury, or continued harassment and that in fact causes that person substantial emotional distress.

(7)   Unlawful conduct. - The commission of one or more of the following acts by a person 16 years of age or older upon a person, but does not include acts of self-defense or defense of others:

a.   Nonconsensual sexual conduct, including single incidences of nonconsensual sexual conduct.

b. Stalking.

(8) Victim. - A person against whom an act of unlawful conduct has been committed by another person not involved in a personal relationship with the person as defined in G.S. 50B-1(b). (2004-194, s. 1; 2004-199, s. 50; 2007-199, s. 1; 2009-58, s. 6.)

§ 50C-2. Commencement of action; filing fees not permitted; assistance.

(a) An action is commenced under this Chapter by filing a verified complaint for a civil no-contact order in district court or by filing a motion in any existing civil action, by any of the following:

(1) A person who is a victim of unlawful conduct that occurs in this State.

(2) A competent adult who resides in this State on behalf of a minor child or an incompetent adult who is a victim of unlawful conduct that occurs in this State.

(b) No court costs or attorneys' fees shall be assessed for the filing or service of the complaint, or the service of any orders, except as provided in G.S. 1A-1, Rule 11.

(c) An action commenced under this Chapter may be filed in any county permitted under G.S. 1-82 or where the unlawful conduct took place.

(d) If the victim states that disclosure of the victim's address would place the victim or any member of the victim's family or household at risk for further unlawful conduct, the victim's address may be omitted from all documents filed with the court. If the victim has not disclosed an address under this subsection, the victim shall designate an alternative address to receive notice of any motions or pleadings from the opposing party. (2004-194, s. 1; 2013-390, s. 2.)

§ 50C-3. Process for action for no-contact order.

(a) Any action for a civil no-contact order requires that a summons be issued and served. The summons issued pursuant to this Chapter shall require the respondent to answer within 10 days of the date of service. Attachments to the summons shall include the complaint for the civil no-contact order, and any temporary civil no-contact order that has been issued and the notice of hearing on the temporary civil no-contact order.

(b) Service of the summons and attachments shall be by the sheriff by personal delivery in accordance with Rule 4 of the Rules of Civil Procedure, and if the respondent cannot with due diligence be served by the sheriff by personal delivery, the respondent may be served by publication by the complainant in accordance with Rule 4(j1) of the Rules of Civil Procedure.

(c) The court may enter a civil no-contact order by default for the remedy sought in the complaint if the respondent has been served in accordance with this section and fails to answer as directed, or fails to appear on any subsequent appearance or hearing date agreed to by the parties or set by the court. (2004-194, s. 1; 2009-342, s. 3.)

§ 50C-4. Hearsay exception.

In proceedings for an order or prosecutions for violation of an order under this Chapter, the prior sexual activity or the reputation of the victim is inadmissible except when it would be admissible in a criminal prosecution under G.S. 8C, Rule 412. (2004-194, s. 1.)

§ 50C-5. Civil no-contact order; remedy.

(a) Upon a finding that the victim has suffered unlawful conduct committed by the respondent, the court may issue temporary or permanent civil no-contact orders as authorized in this Chapter. In determining whether or not to issue a civil no-contact order, the court shall not require physical injury to the victim.

(b) The court may grant one or more of the following forms of relief in its orders under this Chapter:

(1) Order the respondent not to visit, assault, molest, or otherwise interfere with the victim.

(2) Order the respondent to cease stalking the victim, including at the victim's workplace.

(3) Order the respondent to cease harassment of the victim.

(4)   Order the respondent not to abuse or injure the victim.

(5)   Order the respondent not to contact the victim by telephone, written communication, or electronic means.

(6)   Order the respondent to refrain from entering or remaining present at the victim's residence, school, place of employment, or other specified places at times when the victim is present.

(7)   Order other relief deemed necessary and appropriate by the court, including assessing attorneys' fees to either party.

(c)   A civil no-contact order shall include the following notice, printed in conspicuous type: "A knowing violation of a civil no-contact order shall be punishable as contempt of court which may result in a fine or imprisonment." (2004-194, s. 1; 2013-390, s. 5.)

§ 50C-6. Temporary civil no-contact order; court holidays and evenings.

(a)   A temporary civil no-contact order may be granted ex parte, without evidence of service of process or notice, only if both of the following are shown:

(1)   It clearly appears from specific facts shown by a verified complaint or affidavit that immediate injury, loss, or damage will result to the victim before the respondent can be heard in opposition.

(2)   Either one of the following:

a.   The complainant certifies to the court in writing the efforts, if any, that have been made to give the notice and the reasons supporting the claim that notice should not be required.

b.   The complainant certified to the court that there is good cause to grant the remedy because the harm that the remedy is intended to prevent would likely occur if the respondent were given any prior notice of the complainant's efforts to obtain judicial relief.

(b)   Every temporary civil no-contact order granted without notice shall:

(1)   Be endorsed with the date and hour of issuance.

(2) Be filed immediately in the clerk's office and entered of record.

(3) Define the injury, state why it is irreparable and why the order was granted without notice.

(4) Expire by its terms within such time after entry, not to exceed 10 days.

(5) Give notice of the date of hearing on the temporary order as provided in G.S. 50C-8(a).

(c) If the respondent appears in court for a hearing on a temporary order, the respondent may elect to file a general appearance and testify. Any resulting order may be a temporary order, governed by this section. Notwithstanding the requirements of this section, if all requirements of G.S. 50C-7 have been met, the court may issue a permanent order.

(d) When the court is not in session, the complainant may file for a temporary order before any judge or magistrate designated to grant relief under this Chapter. If the judge or magistrate finds that there is an immediate and present danger of harm to the victim and that the requirements of subsection (a) of this section have been met, the judge or magistrate may issue a temporary civil no-contact order. The chief district court judge may designate for each county at least one judge or magistrate to be reasonably available to issue temporary civil no-contact orders when the court is not in session. (2004-194, s. 1.)

§ 50C-7. Permanent civil no-contact order.

Upon a finding that the victim has suffered an act of unlawful conduct committed by the respondent, a permanent civil no-contact order may issue if the court additionally finds that process was properly served on the respondent, the respondent has answered the complaint and notice of hearing was given, or the respondent is in default. No permanent civil no-contact order shall be issued without notice to the respondent. (2004-194, s. 1; 2013-390, s. 3.)

§ 50C-8. Duration; extension of orders.

(a) A temporary civil no-contact order shall be effective for not more than 10 days as the court fixes, unless within the time so fixed the temporary civil no-contact order, for good cause shown, is extended for a like period or a longer period if the respondent consents. The reasons for the extension shall be stated in the temporary order. If a temporary ex parte civil no-contact order:

(1) Is granted without notice and a motion for a permanent civil no-contact order is made, it shall be set down for hearing within 10 days from the date of the motion.

(2) Is denied, the trial on the plaintiff's motion for a civil no-contact order shall be set for hearing within 30 days from the date of the denial.

When the motion for a permanent civil no-contact order comes on for hearing, the complainant may proceed with a motion for a permanent civil no-contact order, and, if the complainant fails to do so, the judge shall dissolve the temporary civil no-contact order. On two days' notice to the complainant or on such shorter notice to that party as the judge may prescribe, the respondent may appear and move its dissolution or modification. In that event the judge shall proceed to hear and determine such motion as expeditiously as the ends of justice require.

(b) A permanent civil no-contact order shall be effective for a fixed period of time not to exceed one year.

(c) Any order may be extended one or more times, as required, provided that the requirements of G.S. 50C-6 or G.S. 50C-7, as appropriate, are satisfied. The court may renew an order, including an order that previously has been renewed, upon a motion by the complainant filed before the expiration of the current order. The court may renew the order for good cause. The commission of an act of unlawful conduct by the respondent after entry of the current order is not required for an order to be renewed. If the motion for extension is uncontested and the complainant seeks no modification of the order, the order may be extended if the complainant's motion or affidavit states that there has been no material change in relevant circumstances since entry of the order and states the reason for the requested extension. Extensions may be granted only in open court and not under the provisions of G.S. 50C-6(d).

(d) Any civil no-contact order expiring on a day the court is not open for business shall expire at the close of the next court business day. (2004-194, s. 1; 2006-264, s. 41; 2013-390, s. 4.)

§ 50C-9. Notice of orders.

(a)   The clerk of court shall deliver on the same day that a civil no-contact order is issued, a certified copy of that order to the sheriff.

(b)   If the respondent was not present in court when the order was issued, the respondent may be served in the manner provided for service of process in civil proceedings in accordance with Rule 4(j) of the Rules of Civil Procedure. If the summons has not yet been served upon the respondent, it shall be served with the order.

(c)   A copy of the order shall be issued promptly to and retained by the police department of the municipality of the victim's residence. If the victim's residence is not located in a municipality or in a municipality with no police department, copies shall be issued promptly to and retained by the sheriff and the county police department, if any, of the county in which the victim's residence is located.

(d)   Any order extending, modifying, or revoking any civil no-contact order shall be promptly delivered to the sheriff by the clerk and served in a manner provided for service of process in accordance with the provisions of this section. (2004-194, s. 1; 2012-19, s. 1.)

§ 50C-10. Violation.

A knowing violation of an order entered pursuant to this Chapter is punishable as contempt of court. (2004-194, s. 1.)

§ 50C-11. Remedies not exclusive.

The remedies provided by this Chapter are not exclusive but are additional to other remedies provided under law. (2004-194, s. 1.)

Chapter 51.

Marriage.

Article 1.

General Provisions.

§ 51-1. Requisites of marriage; solemnization.

A valid and sufficient marriage is created by the consent of a male and female person who may lawfully marry, presently to take each other as husband and wife, freely, seriously and plainly expressed by each in the presence of the other, either:

(1)   a.   In the presence of an ordained minister of any religious denomination, a minister authorized by a church, or a magistrate; and

b.   With the consequent declaration by the minister or magistrate that the persons are husband and wife; or

(2)   In accordance with any mode of solemnization recognized by any religious denomination, or federally or State recognized Indian Nation or Tribe.

Marriages solemnized before March 9, 1909, by ministers of the gospel licensed, but not ordained, are validated from their consummation. (1871-2, c. 193, s. 3; Code, s. 1812; Rev., s. 2081; 1908, c. 47; 1909, c. 704, s. 2; c. 897; C.S., s. 2493; 1945, c. 839; 1965, c. 152; 1971, c. 1185, s. 26; 1977, c. 592, s. 1; 2000-58, ss. 1, 2; 2001-14, ss. 1, 2; 2001-62, ss. 1, 17; 2002-115, ss. 5, 6; 2002-159, s. 13(a); 2003-4, s. 1; 2005-56, s. 1; 2007-61, s. 1; 2009-13, s. 1; 2012-194, s. 65.4(a).)

§ 51-1.1. Certain marriages performed by ministers of Universal Life Church validated.

Any marriages performed by ministers of the Universal Life Church prior to July 3, 1981, are validated, unless they have been invalidated by a court of competent jurisdiction, provided that all other requirements of law have been met and the marriages would have been valid if performed by an official authorized by law to perform wedding ceremonies. (1981, c. 797.)

§ 51-1.2. Marriages between persons of the same gender not valid.

Marriages, whether created by common law, contracted, or performed outside of North Carolina, between individuals of the same gender are not valid in North Carolina. (1995 (Reg. Sess., 1996), c. 588, s. 1.)

§ 51-2. Capacity to marry.

(a) All unmarried persons of 18 years, or older, may lawfully marry, except as hereinafter forbidden.

(a1) Persons over 16 years of age and under 18 years of age may marry, and the register of deeds may issue a license for the marriage, only after there shall have been filed with the register of deeds a written consent to the marriage, said consent having been signed by the appropriate person as follows:

(1) By a parent having full or joint legal custody of the underage party; or

(2) By a person, agency, or institution having legal custody or serving as a guardian of the underage party.

Such written consent shall not be required for an emancipated minor if a certificate of emancipation issued pursuant to Article 35 of Chapter 7B of the General Statutes or a certified copy of a final decree or certificate of emancipation from this or any other jurisdiction is filed with the register of deeds.

(b) Persons over 14 years of age and under 16 years of age may marry as provided in G.S. 51-2.1.

(b1) It shall be unlawful for any person under 14 years of age to marry.

(c) When a license to marry is procured by any person under 18 years of age by fraud or misrepresentation, a parent of the underage party, a person, agency, or institution having legal custody or serving as a guardian of the underage party, or a guardian ad litem appointed to represent the underage party pursuant to G.S. 51-2.1(b) is a proper party to bring an action to annul the marriage. (R.C., c. 68, s. 14; 1871-2, c. 193; Code, s. 1809; Rev., s. 2082; C.S., s. 2494; 1923, c. 75; 1933, c. 269, s. 1; 1939, c. 375; 1947, c. 383, s. 2; 1961, c. 186; 1967, c. 957, s. 1; 1969, c. 982; 1985, c. 608; 1998-202, s. 13(s); 2001-62, s. 2; 2001-487, s. 60.)

§ 51-2.1. Marriage of certain underage parties.

(a) If an unmarried female who is more than 14 years of age, but less than 16 years of age, is pregnant or has given birth to a child and the unmarried female and the putative father of the child, either born or unborn, agree to marry, or if an unmarried male who is more than 14 years of age, but less than 16 years of age, is the putative father of a child, either born or unborn, and the unmarried male and the mother of the child agree to marry, the register of deeds is authorized to issue to the parties a license to marry; and it shall be lawful for them to marry in accordance with the provisions of this Chapter, only after a certified copy of an order issued by a district court authorizing the marriage is filed with the register of deeds. A district court judge may issue an order authorizing a marriage under this section only upon finding as fact and concluding as a matter of law that the underage party is capable of assuming the responsibilities of marriage and the marriage will serve the best interest of the underage party. In determining whether the marriage will serve the best interest of an underage party, the district court shall consider the following:

(1) The opinion of the parents of the underage party as to whether the marriage serves the best interest of the underage party.

(2) The opinion of any person, agency, or institution having legal custody or serving as a guardian of the underage party as to whether the marriage serves the best interest of the underage party.

(3) The opinion of the guardian ad litem appointed to represent the best interest of the underage party pursuant to G.S. 51-2.1(b) as to whether the marriage serves the best interest of the underage party.

(4) The relationship between the underage party and the parents of the underage party, as well as the relationship between the underage party and any person having legal custody or serving as a guardian of the underage party.

(5) Any evidence that it would find useful in making its determination.

There shall be a rebuttable presumption that the marriage will not serve the best interest of the underage party when all living parents of the underage party oppose the marriage. The fact that the female is pregnant, or has given birth to a child, alone does not establish that the best interest of the underage party will be served by the marriage.

(b) An underage party seeking an order granting judicial authorization to marry pursuant to this section shall file a civil action in the district court requesting judicial authorization to marry. The clerk shall collect court costs from the underage party in the amount set forth in G.S. 7A-305 for civil actions in district court. Upon the filing of the complaint, summons shall be issued in accordance with G.S. 1A-1, Rule 4, and the underage party shall be appointed a guardian ad litem in accordance with the provisions of G.S. 1A-1, Rule 17. The guardian ad litem appointed shall be an attorney and shall be governed by the provisions of subsection (d) of this section. The underage party shall serve a copy of the summons and complaint, in accordance with G.S. 1A-1, Rule 4, on the father of the underage party; the mother of the underage party; and any person, agency, or institution having legal custody or serving as a guardian of the underage party. The underage party also shall serve a copy of the complaint, either in accordance with G.S. 1A-1, Rule 4, or G.S. 1A-1, Rule 5, on the guardian ad litem appointed pursuant to this section. A party responding to the underage party's complaint shall serve his response within 30 days after service of the summons and complaint upon that person. The underage party may participate in the proceedings before the court on his or her own behalf. At the hearing conducted pursuant to this section, the court shall consider evidence, as provided in subsection (a) of this section, and shall make written findings of fact and conclusions of law.

(c) Any party to a proceeding under this section may be represented by counsel, but no party is entitled to appointed counsel, except as provided in this section.

(d) The guardian ad litem appointed pursuant to subsection (b) of this section shall represent the best interest of the underage party in all proceedings under this section and also has standing to institute an action under G.S. 51-2(c). The appointment shall terminate when the last judicial ruling rendering the authorization granted or denied is entered. Payment of the guardian ad litem shall be governed by G.S. 7A-451(f). The guardian ad litem shall make an investigation to determine the facts, the needs of the underage party, the available resources within the family and community to meet those needs, the impact of the marriage on the underage party, and the ability of the underage party to assume the responsibilities of marriage; facilitate, when appropriate, the settlement of disputed issues; offer evidence and examine witnesses at the hearing; and protect and promote the best interest of the underage party. In fulfilling the guardian ad litem's duties, the guardian ad litem shall assess and consider the emotional development, maturity, intellect, and understanding of the underage party. The guardian ad litem has the authority to obtain any information or reports, whether or not confidential, that the guardian ad litem deems relevant to the case. No privilege other than attorney-client privilege may be invoked to prevent the guardian ad litem and the court from obtaining such information. The confidentiality of the information or reports shall be respected by the guardian ad litem, and no disclosure of any information or reports shall be made to anyone except by order of the court or unless otherwise provided by law.

(e) If the last judicial ruling in this proceeding denies the underage party judicial authorization to marry, the underage party shall not seek the authorization of any court again under this section until after one year from the date of the entry of the last judicial ruling rendering the authorization denied.

(f) Except as otherwise provided in this section, the rules of evidence in civil cases shall apply to proceedings under this section. All hearings pursuant to this section shall be recorded by stenographic notes or by electronic or mechanical means. Notwithstanding any other provision of law, no appeal of right lies from an order or judgment entered pursuant to this section. (2001-62, s. 3.)

§ 51-2.2. Parent includes adoptive parent.

As used in this Article, the terms "parent", "father", or "mother" includes one who has become a parent, father, or mother, respectively, by adoption. (2001-62, s. 4.)

§ 51-3. Want of capacity; void and voidable marriages.

All marriages between any two persons nearer of kin than first cousins, or between double first cousins, or between a male person under 16 years of age and any female, or between a female person under 16 years of age and any male, or between persons either of whom has a husband or wife living at the time of such marriage, or between persons either of whom is at the time physically impotent, or between persons either of whom is at the time incapable of contracting from want of will or understanding, shall be void. No marriage followed by cohabitation and the birth of issue shall be declared void after the death of either of the parties for any of the causes stated in this section except for bigamy. No marriage by persons either of whom may be under 16 years of age, and otherwise competent to marry, shall be declared void when the girl shall be pregnant, or when a child shall have been born to the parties unless such child at the time of the action to annul shall be dead. A marriage contracted under a representation and belief that the female partner to the marriage is pregnant, followed by the separation of the parties within 45 days of the marriage which separation has been continuous for a period of one year, shall be voidable unless a child shall have been born to the parties within 10 lunar months of the date of separation. (R.C., c. 68, ss. 7, 8, 9; 1871-2, c. 193, s. 2; Code, s. 1810; 1887, c. 245; Rev., s. 2083; 1911, c. 215, s. 2; 1913, c. 123; 1917, c. 135; C.S., s. 2495; 1947, c. 383, s. 3; 1949, c. 1022; 1953, c. 1105; 1961, c. 367; 1977, c. 107, s. 1.)

§ 51-3.1. Interracial marriages validated.

All interracial marriages that were declared void by statute or a court of competent jurisdiction prior to March 24, 1977, are hereby validated. The parties to such interracial marriages are deemed to be lawfully married, provided that the provisions of this Chapter have been complied with. (1977, c. 107, s. 2.)

§ 51-3.2. Marriage licensed and solemnized by a federally recognized Indian Nation or Tribe.

(a) Subject to the restriction provided in subsection (b), a marriage between a man and a woman licensed and solemnized according to the law of a federally recognized Indian Nation or Tribe shall be valid and the parties to the marriage shall be lawfully married.

(b) When the law of a federally recognized Indian Nation or Tribe allows persons to obtain a marriage license from the register of deeds and the parties to a marriage do so, Chapter 51 of the General Statutes shall apply and the marriage shall be valid only if the issuance of the license and the solemnization of the marriage is conducted in compliance with this Chapter. (2001-62, s. 5.)

§ 51-4. Prohibited degrees of kinship.

When the degree of kinship is estimated with a view to ascertain the right of kinspeople to marry, the half-blood shall be counted as the whole-blood: Provided, that nothing herein contained shall be so construed as to invalidate any marriage heretofore contracted in case where by counting the half-blood as the whole-blood the persons contracting such marriage would be nearer of kin than first cousins; but in every such case the kinship shall be ascertained by counting relations of the half-blood as being only half so near kin as those of the same degree of the whole-blood (1879, c. 78; Code, s. 1811; Rev., s. 2084; C.S., s. 2496.)

§ 51-5. Marriages between slaves validated.

Persons, both or one of whom were formerly slaves, who have complied with the provisions of section five, Chapter 40, of the acts of the General Assembly, ratified March 10, 1866, shall be deemed to have been lawfully married. (1866, c. 40, s. 5; Code, s. 1842; Rev., s. 2085; C.S., s. 2497.)

Article 2.

Marriage Licenses.

§ 51-6. Solemnization without license unlawful.

No minister, officer, or any other person authorized to solemnize a marriage under the laws of this State shall perform a ceremony of marriage between a man and woman, or shall declare them to be husband and wife, until there is delivered to that person a license for the marriage of the said persons, signed by the register of deeds of the county in which the marriage license was issued or by a lawful deputy or assistant. There must be at least two witnesses to the marriage ceremony.

Whenever a man and woman have been lawfully married in accordance with the laws of the state in which the marriage ceremony took place, and said marriage was performed by a magistrate or some other civil official duly authorized to perform such ceremony, and the parties thereafter wish to confirm their marriage vows before an ordained minister or minister authorized by a church, or in a ceremony recognized by any religious denomination, federally or State recognized Indian Nation or Tribe, nothing herein shall be deemed to prohibit such confirmation ceremony; provided, however, that such confirmation ceremony shall not be deemed in law to be a marriage ceremony, such confirmation ceremony shall in no way affect the validity or invalidity of the prior marriage ceremony performed by a civil official, no license for such confirmation ceremony shall be issued by a register of deeds, and no record of such confirmation ceremony may be kept by a register of deeds. (1871-2, c. 193, s. 4;

Code, s. 1813; Rev., s. 2086; C.S., s. 2498; 1957, c. 1261; 1959, c. 338; 1967, c. 957, ss. 6, 9; 1977, c. 592, s. 2; 2001-62, s. 6.)

§ 51-7. Penalty for solemnizing without license.

Every minister, officer, or any other person authorized to solemnize a marriage under the laws of this State, who marries any couple without a license being first delivered to that person, as required by law, or after the expiration of such license, or who fails to return such license to the register of deeds within 10 days after any marriage celebrated by virtue thereof, with the certificate appended thereto duly filled up and signed, shall forfeit and pay two hundred dollars ($200.00) to any person who sues therefore, and shall also be guilty of a Class 1 misdemeanor. (R.C., c. 68, ss. 6, 13; 1871-2, c. 193, s. 8; Code, s. 1817; Rev., ss. 2087, 3372; C.S., s. 2499; 1953, c. 638, s. 1; 1967, c. 957, s. 5; 1993, c. 539, s. 415; 1994, Ex. Sess., c. 24, s. 14(c); 2001-62, s. 7.)

§ 51-8. License issued by register of deeds.

Every register of deeds shall, upon proper application, issue a license for the marriage of any two persons who are able to answer the questions regarding age, marital status, and intention to marry, and, based on the answers, the register of deeds determines the persons are authorized to be married in accordance with the laws of this State. In making a determination as to whether or not the parties are authorized to be married under the laws of this State, the register of deeds may require the applicants for the license to marry to present certified copies of birth certificates or such other evidence as the register of deeds deems necessary to the determination. The register of deeds may administer an oath to any person presenting evidence relating to whether or not parties applying for a marriage license are eligible to be married pursuant to the laws of this State. Each applicant for a marriage license shall provide on the application the applicant's social security number. If an applicant does not have a social security number and is ineligible to obtain one, the applicant shall present a statement to that effect, sworn to or affirmed before an officer authorized to administer oaths. Upon presentation of a sworn or affirmed statement, the register of deeds shall issue the license, provided all other requirements are met, and retain the statement with the register's copy of the license. The register of deeds shall not issue a marriage license unless all of the requirements of this section have been met. (1871-2, c. 193, s. 5; Code, s. 1814; 1887, c. 331; Rev., s. 2088; C.S., s. 2500; 1957, c. 506, s. 1; 1967, c.

957, s. 2; 1997-433, s. 4.5; 1998-17, s. 1; 1999-375, s. 1; 2001-62, s. 8; 2002-159, s. 14.)

§ 51-8.1. Repealed by Session Laws 1967, c. 53.

§ 51-8.2. Issuance of marriage license when applicant is unable to appear.

If an applicant for a marriage license is over 18 years of age and is unable to appear in person at the register of deeds' office, the other party to the planned marriage must appear in person on behalf of the applicant and submit a sworn and notarized affidavit in lieu of the absent applicant's personal appearance.

The affidavit shall be in the following or some equivalent form:

_____, [applicant] appearing before the undersigned notary and being duly sworn, says that:

1. I, _____, [applicant's name] am applying for a license in _____ County, North Carolina, to marry _____ [name of other applicant] in North Carolina within the next 60 days and I am authorized under G.S. 51-8.2 to complete this Affidavit in Lieu of Personal Appearance for Marriage License Application.

I attach: (1) documentation that I am over 18 years of age as required in county of issuance; and (2) documentation of divorce as required by county of issuance.

2. I submit the following information in applying for a marriage license:

Name:

_____

| First | Middle | Last |

Residence:

_____

| State | County | City or Town |

_____

Street and Number

Inside City Limits (Yes or No):
_____

Birthplace:
_____

County & State or Country

Birth Date: _____ Age: _____

Father: _____

Name   State of Birth

_____

Address (if living) or Deceased

Mother:
_____

Name   State of Birth

_____

Address (if living) or Deceased

Race (Optional):
_____

Number of this marriage: 1st, 2nd, etc.
_____

Last Marriage Ended by:
_____

Death, Divorce, Annulment

Date Marriage Ended: _____

Specify Highest Grade Completed in School (Optional):
_____

Social Security # _____ (If applicant does not have Social Security number, attach affidavit of ineligibility)

I hereby make application to the Register of Deeds for a Marriage License and solemnly swear that all of the statements contained in the above application are true and I further make oath that there is no legal impediment to such marriage.

_____

Signature of Applicant

Sworn to (or affirmed) and subscribed before me this _____ day of _____, _____.

_____

[Seal] Notary Public

My commission expires: _____

_____

[Notary's typed or printed name].

(2001-62, s. 9.)

§§ 51-9 through 51-11: Repealed by Session Laws 1994, c. 647, ss. 1-3.

§ 51-12: Repealed by Session Laws 1985, c. 589, s. 27.

§ 51-13: Repealed by Session Laws 1994, c. 647, s. 4.

§ 51-14. Repealed by Session Laws 1967, c. 957, s. 3.

§ 51-15. Obtaining license by false representation misdemeanor.

If any person shall obtain, or aid and abet in obtaining, a marriage license by misrepresentation or false pretenses, that person shall be guilty of a Class 1 misdemeanor. (1885, c. 346; Rev., s. 3371; C.S., s. 2501; 1967, c. 957, s. 4; 1993, c. 539, s. 417; 1994, Ex. Sess., c. 24, s. 14(c); 2001-62, s. 10.)

§ 51-16. Form of license.

License shall be in the following or some equivalent form:

To any ordained minister of any religious denomination, minister authorized by a church, any magistrate, or any other person authorized to solemnize a marriage under the laws of this State: A.B. having applied to me for a license for the marriage of C.D. (the name of the man to be written in full) of (here state his residence), aged ____ years (race, as the case may be), the son of (here state the father and mother, if known; state whether they are living or dead, and their residence, if known; if any of these facts are not known, so state), and E.F. (write the name of the woman in full) of (here state her residence), aged ____ years (race, as the case may be), the daughter of (here state names and residences of the parents, if known, as is required above with respect to the man). (If either of the parties is under 18 years of age, the license shall here contain the following:) And the written consent of G.H., father (or mother, etc., as the case may be) to the proposed marriage having been filed with me, and there being no legal impediment to such marriage known to me, you are hereby authorized, at any time within 60 days from the date hereof, to celebrate the proposed marriage at any place within the State. You are required within 10 days after you shall have celebrated such marriage, to return this license to me at my office with your signature subscribed to the certificate under this license, and with the blanks therein filled according to the facts, under penalty of forfeiting two hundred dollars ($200.00) to the use of any person who shall sue for the same.

Issued this ____ day of ____, ____

_____ L.M.

Register of Deeds of ____ County

Every register of deeds shall, at the request of an applicant, designate in a marriage license issued the race of the persons proposing to marry by inserting in the blank after the word "race" the words "white," "black," "African-American," "American Indian," "Alaska Native," "Asian Indian," "Chinese," "Filipino," "Japanese," "Korean," "Vietnamese," "Other Asian," "Native Hawaiian," "Guamarian," "Chamorro," "Samoan," "Other Pacific Islander," "Mexican," "Mexican-American," "Chicano," "Puerto Rican," "Cuban," "Other Spanish/Hispanic/Latino," or "other," as the case may be. The certificate shall be filled out and signed by the minister, officer, or other authorized individual celebrating the marriage, and also be signed by two witnesses present at the marriage, who shall add to their names their place of residence, as follows:

I, N.O., an ordained or authorized minister or other authorized individual of (here state to what religious denomination, or magistrate, as the case may be), united in matrimony (here name the parties), the parties licensed above, on the ___ day of _____, ___, at the house of P.R., in (here name the town, if any, the township and county), according to law.

_____ N.O.

Witness present at the marriage:

S.T., of (here give residence).

(1871-2, c. 193, s. 6; Code, s. 1815; 1899, c. 541, ss. 1, 2; Rev., s. 2089; 1909, c. 704, s. 3; 1917, c. 38; C.S., s. 2502; 1953, c. 638, s. 2; 1967, c. 957, s. 7; 1971, c. 1072; c. 1185, s. 27; 1999-456, s. 59; 2001-62, s. 11.)

§ 51-16.1. Form of license for Address Confidentiality Program participant.

If a person submits to the local register of deeds a current and valid Address Confidentiality Program authorization card issued pursuant to the provisions of Chapter 15C of the General Statutes, the local register of deeds shall use the substitute address designated by the Address Confidentiality Program when creating a new marriage license. (2002-171, s. 3.)

§ 51-17. Penalty for issuing license unlawfully.

Every register of deeds who knowingly or without reasonable inquiry, personally or by deputy, issues a license for the marriage of any two persons to which there is any lawful impediment, or where either of the persons is under the age of 18 years, without the consent required by law, shall forfeit and pay two hundred dollars ($200.00) to any parent, guardian, or other person standing in loco parentis, who sues for the same: Provided, that requiring a party to a proposed marriage to present a certified copy of his or her birth certificate, or a certified copy of his or her birth record in the form of a birth registration card as provided in G.S. 130-102, in accordance with the provisions of G.S. 51-8, shall be considered a reasonable inquiry into the matter of the age of such party. (R.C., c. 68, s. 13; 1871-2, c. 193, s. 7; Code, s. 1816; 1895, c. 387; 1901, c. 722; Rev., s. 2090; C.S., s. 2503; 1957, c. 506, s. 2.)

§ 51-18. Record of licenses and returns; originals filed.

The register of deeds shall maintain a separate index for marriage licenses and returns thereto. Each marriage license shall be indexed alphabetically according to the name of the proposed husband and proposed wife. Each index entry shall include, but not be limited to, the full name of the intended husband and wife, the date the marriage ceremony was performed, and the location of the original license and the return thereon. The original license and return shall be filed and preserved. (1871-2, c. 193, s. 9; Code, s. 1818; 1899, c. 541, s. 3; Rev., s. 2091; C.S., s. 2504; 1963, c. 429; 1967, c. 957, s. 8; 1979, c. 636, s. 1; 1983, c. 699, s. 2.)

§ 51-18.1. Correction of errors in application or license; amendment of names in application or license.

(a) When it shall appear to the register of deeds of any county in this State that information is incorrectly stated on an application for a marriage license, or upon a marriage license issued thereunder, or upon a return or certificate of an officiating officer, the register of deeds is authorized to correct such record or records upon being furnished with an affidavit signed by one or both of the applicants for the marriage license, accompanied by affidavits of at least two other persons who know the correct information.

(b) When the name of a party to a marriage has been changed by court order as a result of a legitimation action or other cause of action, and the party whose name is changed presents a signed affidavit to the register of deeds indicating the name change and requesting that the application for a marriage license, the marriage license, and the marriage certificate of the officiating officer be amended by substituting the changed name for the original name, the register of deeds may amend the records as requested by the party, provided the other party named in the records consents to the amendment. (1953, c. 797; 1959, c. 344; 1987, c. 576; 2001-62, s. 12.)

§ 51-19. Penalty for failure to record.

Any register of deeds who fails to record, in the manner above prescribed, the substance of any marriage license issued by him, or who fails to record, in the manner above prescribed, the substance of any return made thereon, within 10 days after such return made, shall forfeit and pay two hundred dollars ($200.00) to any person who sues for the same. (1871-2, c. 193, s. 10; Code, s. 1819; Rev., s. 2092; C.S., s. 2505.)

§ 51-20. Repealed by Session Laws 1969, c. 80, s. 6.

§ 51-21. Issuance of delayed marriage certificates.

In all those cases where a minister or other person authorized by law to perform marriage ceremonies has failed to file his return thereof in the office of the register of deeds who issued the license for such marriage, the register of deeds of such county is authorized to issue a delayed marriage certificate upon being furnished with one or more of the following:

(1)   The affidavit of at least two witnesses to the marriage ceremony;

(2)   The affidavit of one or both parties to the marriage, accompanied by the affidavit of at least one witness to the marriage ceremony;

(3)   The affidavit of the minister or other person authorized by law who performed the marriage ceremony, accompanied by the affidavit of one or more witnesses to the ceremony or one of the parties thereto.

(4)   When proof as required by the three methods set forth in subdivisions (1), (2), and (3) above is not available with respect to any marriage alleged to have been performed prior to January 1, 1935, the register of deeds is authorized to accept the affidavit of any one of the persons named in

subdivisions (1), (2), and (3) and in addition thereto such other proof in writing as he may deem sufficient to establish the marriage and any facts relating thereto; provided, however, that if the evidence offered under this paragraph is insufficient to convince the register of deeds that the marriage ceremony took place, or any of the pertinent facts relating thereto, the applicants may bring a special proceeding before the clerk of superior court of the county in which the purported marriage ceremony took place. The said clerk of the superior court is authorized to hear the evidence and make findings as to whether or not the purported ceremony took place and as to any pertinent facts relating thereto. If the clerk finds that the marriage did take place as alleged, he is to certify such findings to the register of deeds who is to then issue a delayed marriage certificate in accordance with the provisions of this section.

The certificate issued by the register of deeds under authority of this section shall contain the date of the delayed filing, the date the marriage ceremony was actually performed, and all such certificates issued pursuant to this section shall have the same evidentiary value as any other marriage certificates issued pursuant to law. (1951, c. 1224; 1955, c. 246; 1967, c. 957, s. 10; 1969, c. 80, s. 12.)

Vision Books Order Form

Fax Orders:	1-980-299-5965
Phone Orders:	1-704-898-0770
E-mail Orders:	www.visionbooks.org
Mail Orders:	Vision Books, LLC P.O. Box 42406 Charlotte, NC 28215

Shipp To:
Name_____
Address_____
City_____ State_____ Zip_____
Phone_____ Fax_____
Email_____ @_____

Bill To: We can bill a third party on your behalf.
Name_____
Address_____
City_____ State_____ Zip_____
Phone___(_____)_____ Fax_____
Email_____ @_____

Pamphlet Number ($15.00 Each)	Qty	Total Cost
_____	_____	_____
_____	_____	_____
_____	_____	_____
_____	_____	_____
_____	_____	_____
_____	_____	_____
_____	_____	_____
Full Volume Set 1-92	92 Pamphlets	1,380.00

Free Shipping Shipping & Handling on Full Volume Orders
Add $1.00 Shipping & Handling per pamphlet $_____

Total Cost $_____

Thank you for your support. Management!

DID YOU ENJOY THIS BOOK?

Vision Books, LLC would like to hear from you! If you or someone you know has been fasely imprisoned, we would like to hear your story. If the 'North Carolina Criminal Law and Procedure' has had an effect in your life or if you have suggestions, we would like to hear from you. Send your letters to:

Vision Books, LLC
Attn: Staff Writers
P.O. Box 42406
Charlotte, NC 28215
Email: staff@visionbooks.org

Order Additional Copies:

Fax Orders: 1-980-299-5965

Phone Orders: 1-704-898-0770

E-mail Orders: www.visionbooks.org

Mail Orders: Vision Books, LLC
                   P.O. Box 42406
                   Charlotte, NC 28215

www.ingramcontent.com/pod-product-compliance
Lightning Source LLC
Chambersburg PA
CBHW051627170526
45167CB00001B/93